Swords and Tequila: RIOT's Classic First Decade

Martin Popoff

 Swords and Tequila: RIOT's Classic First Decade

Martin Popoff

WYMER
PUBLISHING

Bedford, England

First published in Canada, 2015
Wymer Publishing
Bedford, England www.wymerpublishing.co.uk
Tel: 01234 326691
Wymer Publishing is a trading name of Wymer (UK) Ltd

ISBN: 978-1-912782-15-4

Printed and bound by
CMP, Dorset, England

A catalogue record for this book is available from the British Library.

Typesetting, layout and design by Eduardo Rodriguez.
Front cover photograph © Rich Galbraith.
Back cover photographs © Bill Baran.

TABLE OF CONTENTS

Introduction

As I get up in them years, I seem to be resigned to going down the rabbit-hole of projects that are squarely doomed to fall, ahem, into that "labour of love" category. Part of that, of course, is the fact that I do truly believe that if I don't write about some of these classic albeit slightly forgotten bands, heck, maybe no one ever will.

So it is that sense of purpose that has buoyed me forward to write a book on Riot, along with the fact that, as with all these books, the process allows me, guilt-free, to immerse myself in the catalogue at hand, revisit, reflect nostalgically, and in this case, think about the mounting deaths.

However, what I quickly found out is that I'd been regularly playing these damn Riot records all my life—and recently—so there was little sense of discovery as happy byproduct of the necessary studied listening. Riot's songs were so hook-laden and four-on-the-floor that each visit to these records was a filmy-eyed slump into the ol' familiar.

Now, what you've gathered by this point, is that what you hold in your hands here is a book not on the complete career and catalogue of Mark Reale's reality, but a tight and focused look at what I don't want to call the classic years, but instead a classic decade, operative there being the "the" verse the "a."

In other words, although I didn't want to write at this level of detail about the Riot albums after the first gradual, non-pinpointed break-up of the band in 1985-ish, I didn't want to consider any of them less classic. There's a ton of great material there, because, indeed, what you consider top-shelf depends upon what age you are all wrapped-up in your entry point to any given era of any band's catalogue. And, besides, there's a whole lot of argument to be made for *Thundersteel* and *The Privilege of Power* being part of the classic Riot catalogue, no?

But I think our current exercise is valid, for at this point in time, I think it's the majority view that *Fire Down Under* is Riot's stone-cold classic, and then perhaps that the Guy Speranza era is the classic era, and then, even more arguably, that the classic era includes the two Rhett Forrester albums. It's something I would argue, because I quite like *Restless Breed* and I really like *Born in America* and outside of opinion, Riot was still admirably making metal in America when it wasn't fashionable... yet. In other words, this was a band ahead of its time for that bloody complete ten year span.

This indeed is what this book proposes, first, again, 'cos I quite dig both those albums, second, because a lot of smart people consider them classics, and third, because other than a switch in singer, they are made by the same lineup that constructed *Fire Down Under*. Oh, and then the band broke up for three-ish years and Mark put together a band of all new members except him, and started making records that sound nothing like the classic era. Ergo, arguably, there goes a totally different band.

So yes, the construction of this book was a satisfying venture in that focusing on the first ten years allowed me to spend a lot of time and space and effort on the examination of the band's first five albums. And then satisfying my urge to be somewhat completist, I've used a lengthy epilogue to cover the many records Mark did as Riot utilizing later lineups and, as alluded to, utilizing considerably different writing and recording vibes. The "Dream Away" fan section was a last minute brainstorm, one that really drove home for me the similarity of experience—often amidst a dearth of information—that led many of us to Riot.

So in effect, one hopes that the reader will realize that it is all here, and rendered with much fresh interview footage. The looming presence of death is not ignored as well, for what makes this tale of rock 'n' roll hope (and hopes dashed) so compelling also includes the tragic fact that the three most high-profile members of our tale of ten years are all dead, two by disease, one by violent criminal act.

So there we go. Without further adieu, let's dive into our examination of Brooklyn's finest, Riot, and the bank of godly records that could have (and should have) made the band a bright hot spot on the American metal scene as brightly shined on as Van Halen, but for the grace of the music industry gods.

Martin Popoff
martinp@inforamp.net
martinpopoff.com

Rock City – "Montrose records and Derringer records"

First memory burned into my circuits—because forget any early press on the band—was flipping toward Riot's *Rock City* debut at Magic Mushrooms' second location in Spokane, WA on one of my trips to that gulden record Mecca of the mid '70s for a young teen formulating the prototype of the '80s headbanger. Of course the vinyl copy I was about to purchase, likely at four bucks and change, was a used but (S)ealed promo, a format of about half our purchases on them record-buying trips, a format that eased the pocket-book against the odd UK import at $8.99, once the NWOBHM arrived in the land of Doc Rockit and Rail.

On the cover was this rockin' New York band's Franken-seal (my term) mascot, later to be known as Mighty Tior (and sometimes as Johnny), which looked just as stupid at 13 as it does now at 52.

But yeah, the guys looked like long-haired rockers, some of the song titles rocked, and so it was acquired, gotten home up over the border to Trail, BC, and spun. Blown away? No. Even in 1976, my metal antennae was set to realize this was the work of a baby band disjointedly combining dated material with numbers that pointed to a future as fearless metal frontrunners. The walloping production was impressive, but a bit of a fluke, sounding way more expensive than it was, to be sure.

"There's millions of stories," laughs Riot guitarist and leader Mark Reale, who now, tragically isn't around to give any more of those to the world. "One of the earlier memories I have of the band is based around the first gig we ever did. After I had convinced Guy (Speranza, vocals) to give music a shot again, we did some demo recordings, and then he wanted to leave the band again (laughs). He decided that he didn't want to give it another shot. But I convinced him, look, we got this gig booked, and it was Max's Kansas City except it's our first gig—and on a Monday night. I said you gotta at least do the gig, because I thought this is the way I could convince him to stay anyways. After we did the gig, I was standing out in front of the club, and some girl approaches me and says that she works for Mick Ronson, the lead guitar player for David Bowie for many years, and he was doing his solo record. And she said he was looking for a second guitarist, and she gave me a place to go down and audition and stuff. And I thought, wait a second, my band, my first real band, I just had my first gig, I got Guy to agree to do this again, the whole thing, and Mick Ronson, what a break. I'm thinking, well, what am I going to do here? So I decided to... I showed up with the whole band (laughs). In the adolescent hopes that maybe he'll hire the whole band. Like maybe he'll join Riot, you know? That's where our minds were there. And I remember we got stuck on the Brooklyn Bridge in the van on the way to the audition. We had to push our van off the bridge. We finally made it, and he was in there playing a white Les Paul, and we jammed with him for three hours and left (laughs)."

Back to the beginning, this band of brothers we call Riot came by their '70s hard rocking honestly. "Well basically, we all grew up in Brooklyn in New York and it basically started in my basement," says Mark, offering a history of the band's origins. "One thing led to another. When I started to get serious about the guitar, I started putting bands together and we use to play local places and dances and stuff like that. We used to have block parties in the summer. And I guess the real turning point for Riot, was when I met Guy. He was also in a local Brooklyn band that used play the same circuits we played. And a lot of times on the weekends we didn't have a gig, we'd go walking around from block to block checking out the other bands."

Specifically, the band was mostly from the Flatbush area of the borough, smack in the middle, an area predominantly Jewish and Italian at that time, with Riot considerably Italian of heritage. They grew up together from school days, essentially, would go to the beach together, drive around together, and eventually, each fly on an airplane for the first time together. But as a bar band, Zappa's was the pinnacle for clubs in the area at that time, and so after conquering home turf, the band soon cast an eye askance across the East River to Max's, Great Gildersleeves and Club 82, where they were regulars and first discovered by the duo that would become their "backers," one night at the venue right after a stand at Max's.

"I came upon Guy's band one night and I thought he was really charismatic, a natural front man," continues Reale. "And basically me and the other guys, bass player Phil Fiet and drummer Pete Bitelli, who was on the first two records, I was doing the singing at the time and I knew I wasn't much of a singer, and I said to them, if we could get this guy I think we could really go places. So I approached Guy shortly thereafter, and he was actually planning to leave the business entirely, because he was preparing to go to college to be an architect. And as I said before, I pretty much talked him out of it and got him to do the music (laughs). That's officially I guess when you can say Riot began. As I said, we did our first gig at kind of an infamous place called Max's Kansas City, in New York City. It was on a Monday night, our first gig ever, which was probably 1976."

Before we get too far ahead of ourselves, there's the matter of coming up with the name Riot. That had originated with drummer Pete Bitelli. Pete and Mark, who was by Pete's estimation, an introverted, shy "only child," had learned music together ever since elementary school, beginning their journey in the late '60s together playing football together, playing records, with Mark also showing an interest in making movies. Both Pete and Mark were big into sports, beginning with touch football in the street and then graduating to a tackle league, where, unfortunately, they got stuck on different teams.

Along the way, serious or not, some of the names the two had for their solidifying rock act were Kontiki, The People and Green Tea. But both had been huge fan of *The Honeymooners*, and watched the show together religiously. Well, Ralph Kramden's signature line in the show was always some variation of, "You're a riot, Alice," and that is where Pete got the idea for the name, with the guys subsequently toying with the idea of spelling it Riet.

As Mark has alluded to, the first version of the band consisted of four members, deliberately so, says Pete Bitelli, given that they loved the idea of a power trio, but they also wanted a dedicated singer, a dedicated front man, fueled by the fact that none of the three other guys fancied themselves very good singers. First it had been Mark and Pete, expanding to include guys from around the neighbourhood, as well as Mark's Sinatra-singing uncle and Mark's bass-playing cousin. But then there was Phil Fiet answering an ad from the Mark and Pete looking for a bass player. And then, as Mark has described, it was simply a case of moving from block to block on Saturday nights, looking for a singer to poach, which was a tall order, because it was the hardest position to fill in a rock band back then. Pete says that Guy was spotted in a band called For Shake's Sake, and eventually, after a few hiccups, Speranza was in.

Which all eventually led to a deal to record a first album called *Rock City*... "What basically happened was that we started to play a lot in the city," continues Mark, "and we started to get a pretty big following. And we started dabbling in writing our own material. And what happened was Steve Loeb and his partner at that time were preparing to put together what they would call an anthology record, which a lot of people were doing then. Max's Kansas City did one, CBGBs did one; so these guys wanted to put together an anthology of New York-based bands, and this guy, Ritchie, who worked at one of the clubs we used to play at all the time suggested us to Steve as one of the acts on the record. I think each band was supposed to do two songs. So we didn't even know at the time what was happening. We just got a call to come down to the studio, to see if we wanted a chance to record two tracks for this record."

"So we went down and recorded two songs, which, by the way, actually appear on the first Riot record. But we never heard from them for four or five or six months. We finally heard from them. But apparently what had happened was that they took this project over to that big convention in France called Midem, and they took this thing over to sell this anthology project. And what basically happened was Steve said, 'Hey man, we went over there to do this thing, and like everybody is really responding to your two tracks.' So they trashed the idea of the collaboration record and said, 'Look, we'll do a six-month deal with you; we want to record tracks with you guys.' Basically, they abandoned the idea of the anthology record, and when they got back to New York they called us down to the studio and approached us with the idea of doing a whole record. And that's what became *Rock City*. But they recorded it before we had any deals or anything, and pretty much just put it on Fire Sign, which was their own production company. And through that they made some licensing deals overseas. I know we had a deal in Canada on Attic, and they made some licensing deals in Europe. In fact, when we first started to play in the States, a lot of people thought we were from Canada, because all these import Attic records were coming down into the States. And a lot of people, I remember when we first played in Texas, they thought we were a Canadian band."

"So lets start by setting out the landscape of things that were simultaneously occurring," begins band manager Steve Loeb, who together with Billy Arnell guided Riot's career, from producing the records at their upstairs haunt in Soho to dealing with labels. "Because they play an important role explaining the 'how' and especially the 'whys.' The studio, Greene Street Recording, which I think was still called Big Apple, was not yet entirely ours, so we had to keep to a tight budget. We were still organizing things and were not so clear on the engineers yet. I believe we were then the studio managers and still working out the buy-out from the original owner."

"There were a few tracks on *Rock City* that were recorded as part of a larger compilation of NYC bands at the time," continues Steve, who proceeds to assign credit with respect to the band getting such a hi-fidelity sound on the debut record. "'Angel,' I know was one and 'Desperation' and 'Warrior' were worked up. These tracks were produced by Richie Alexander and he chose the engineer and okay'd the set-up which, once we decided to expand the initial tracks into an album, for the purposes of continuity, we continued to employ. Tom Duffy continued as the engineer and the set-up remained relatively the same. And Duffy loved those UREI 1176 limiter compressors—and that's the secret of Mark's guitar sound and would continue throughout, although that would be augmented when money was available for additional gear. Sometimes we used earlier compressors like the LA 2s and 3s and Pultecs—good old-fashioned analogue crunchers."

"We needed to maximize whatever time we could get in the studio and sometimes when you are severely limited by budget and must make decisions, you get interesting results, which I think we did to a great degree. Lots of spontaneity, but there was also lots of sloppiness which I suppose made it very accessible and so it was— but fans everywhere loved it. The crudeness of it, the genuine end product—and it was very genuine—worked, and we tried whenever we could to keep that flavour. But that's easier said than done, as I will explain as we proceed."

As discussed, *Rock City* would be issued on Fire Sign Records in the US, late 1977, following recording sessions at Big Apple that took place on and off from November of 1976 to June of the following year.

Opening the album is "Desperation," a tight modern metal rocker on which previous bassist—and big Kiss fan—Phil Fiet receives a songwriting credit, along with Mark and Guy (Phil would go on to play with Joan Jett and Billy Idol). It's an action-packed opener, with punchy stops and start typical of the day. Lyrically, Guy tells the tale of a trucker on the road fulminating over his love/hate relationship with his lady at the end of the line.

Next up is "Warrior," which explodes out of the gate all proto-speed metal and dramatic. Credited on the track along with Guy and Mark is ex-keyboardist for the band, Steve Costello. An early rehearsal version from 1975 recorded in Mark's 20' x 25' basement reveals a long keyboard intro from Costello that renders Riot much more Deep Purple-like—or Legs Diamond-like—than the band

would soon become (even if Steve is in fact utilized on the album as a guest, but is essentially buried in the mix). On the record, Guy

Speranza turns in a power metal or gothic metal lyric and vocal melody, which gets melancholic and memorable come chorus time. But musically, the song is in fact quite remarkable for its housing between "Fireball" and "Exciter" as pioneering the idea of speed metal, further made modern by a memorable twin lead. Also memorable is the melodic chorus, which gives the band its anthemic "shine on" slogan, used later for the name of a Riot live album.

"I liked Mark's solos in 'Warrior,'" reflects Steve. "But I was not thrilled with *Rock City* as a whole. I loved 'Overdrive,' 'Angel' and the title track was a glimpse of what might be achievable; so I liked aspects. I liked 'Tokyo Rose' as well. But the band were far from what I wanted to do with any band I worked with and I wasn't sure the raw material was there to do it—at least not yet. Mark was a natural who spoke in musical paragraphs, not sentences as most solo players do. I knew he had massive potential and was completely dedicated and was something very special. After a decade working with him, I can confidently say I was 101% accurate in that assessment. Mark remains one of the most under-rated out there. I may have had disagreements along the way, but his skills were seriously under-rated."

It's curious that Steve plumps for the title track, because as an up-tempo boogie number, "Rock City" is the most dated construct on the record. One suspects, as manager, what he meant is that the song had the potential to be a hit single for the band, which indeed it does. The performances are frenzied, the production sparkling, and the chorus simple yet hooky. "Rock City" is indeed party metal in full flight, buoyed as well by its raving break late in the sequence, its invitation to handclaps, and its police siren straight outta Kiss and that band's "Firehouse" shtick. As Pete explains, the song existed long before anybody thought to call the album *Rock City*, but that given its party rock accessibility, it seemed like a good idea to name the album after this old school number.

Closing side two is "Overdrive," which adds to the sense of hard rock variety on the album, the track lumbering like "Rock Candy," with a riff that wouldn't be out of place on Montrose's top-shelf debut. Twin leads, slide, a punishing fast section... this one's killer modern metal distinguished by pounding, grooving drums. it is the perfect bedding for a lyric that equates driving a hot rod with getting it on.

"The drummer Peter Bitelli, I was of two minds about," says Steve. "I was concerned he would limit the band as a time-keeper providing a solid back beat, but on the other hand his fills were extremely creative and when he was on, he really brought something special to the table. 'Overdrive' I love because of Mark; I love his solo and vamp solo—he rocked it. I still wasn't sure about Guy. He wasn't my favourite sort of voice and he kind of had a 'one note' thing happening and that often means he lacks the confidence to sing notes. I knew I could work with him, but walked away from that *Rock City* album not sure. The bass player Jimmy Iommi and whatever the other guitar player on that project was as well as the keyboard player I knew were probably one-time players and if we went further, they would probably go."

The "other guitar player" Steve doesn't name was, in fact, Lou "L.A." Kouvaris, who wasn't from Los Angeles, but Queens, far enough away to be a foreigner.

"We were very compatible at the time," begins Lou, asked about his fit within Riot, especially next to the leader of the band, who also happened to be his co-guitarist. "Later Mark went off into a whole different direction, but then we were just real hard and heavy; wouldn't say metal, because we weren't metal. We were a very hard rock band, in the vein of Montrose and Derringer. And we were very compatible as far as we had the same kind of style and liked the same type of riffs. We both came up with a lot of good stuff. I remember sitting in Mark's room and we would listen to Montrose records and Derringer records and say how cool that was. And we would play back and forth and get ideas; that's how a lot of things started."

"I was in a band called Harlequin, the New York Harlequin," says Lou, providing a bit of extra background. "There were a couple of bands called Harlequin. But this was a band called Harlequin with a guy named Mike Raffinello, who was the original guitar player on *The Good Rats*. He was a really strange dude, but if you saw him play, he was a remarkable player. And he took me a bit under his wing, and I kind of learned from him how to play scales and stuff—he really made my playing so much better."

"But as far as Riot is concerned, when I first met the band, I went down for an audition some time in May 1975," continues Lou. "They had called me from this musician's referral service, which was in Manhattan. All it was, was a room in the city. A musician back then would pay $25 and he'd get three months to sit in this file and get looked at by any musician or singer, and if they picked you, fine, you got lucky, you got into a band. It wasn't like today. You have the Internet and so many ways of getting into a band. Anyway, my name was in a file with all these guitar players, and I guess because Mark and I had the same interests— we both liked Montrose and Johnny Winter and Rick Derringer—I guess that evolved into what we started playing down in Mark's basement, when I came down to audition."

Then it was down to business—enter Steve Loeb and Billy Arnell. "Yes, well, we found ourselves in the recording studio even before we had a production deal," explains Kouvaris. "So we were in the studio recording the record, and we were really excited about everything. And Steve and Bill, they said, 'You guys need an attorney,' and, 'We want you to take this contract

                    Martin Popoff

and look it over' and blah blah blah. So we did. And so we went to our attorney, and they turned and said, 'This contract is pretty lopsided' and, "You guys, this is not a very fair deal. You might want to ask for this, this and this.'"

"And so we went back to Billy and Steve, we sat at the table, and said, you know, this is what we thought. And we gave them back the contract with the revisions, and Billy and Steve said, 'Okay guys, wait outside.' So we went out, and we're all sitting outside in the room. And they called us back in, and they said, 'Guys, do you guys really want to get a record deal?' We said, 'Yeah, of course we do.' And he goes, 'Well, sign the contract just the way it is, or you don't have a deal.' And my thought... my jaw went onto the floor. And a lot of the guys will tell you, I was a little bit more in tune with what was going on than the rest of the band. I think Mark was clueless. He was just very enamoured with the whole music thing. He just wanted to play music."

"And you've got to remember, we were 22, 23-year-old kids then. I call us kids—young adults. But we looked at each other, and after we went out of the room, I said, 'Guys, we can't sign this contract like that. We're getting like no money. We're like locked in for the next five or six albums. You know, we get no money for this, we get no money for that.' And we're all looking at each other. And Guy Speranza turns around and says, 'Lou's right, we can't sign this thing.' And then Mark turned around and said, you know, 'Well, what are we going to do?' So Mark and Guy went back into the office and signed the contract."

Which sounds like a rare case of divide and conquer—two guys are easier to strong-arm that five. "Yeah, and you know, we all signed it—including my dopey self. But at this time, I was a team player, so we went and did our thing. And if you know anything about the later things that happened with Mark and the rest of the band, he really got taken over the coals."

With respect to what Mark and Guy had said as they emerged from the room, Lou explains that, "They said, you know, we really had nowhere else to go—what were we going to do? And they were ready to put an album out and things would get better. And I turned around and said, 'Mark, Guy...' I said, 'Guys, I'm not an expert, but I know when an attorney tells you that you're getting fucked, you really should kind of listen to them.' But, you know, I think it was just being naïve and we all were."

"And listen, how do you think they felt about me after I made that kind of comment? If I said absolutely nothing, don't you think I would probably have been on the *Narita* album and the *Fire Down Under* album? Of course. Of course. I was the troublemaker. And I wasn't even a troublemaker. I'm just being... again, politically, I didn't know what was right, but I had some sense. And Peter will tell you and Jimmy will tell you, that, hey, Lou had it down. He knew what was going on. Ask any of those guys. Years later, my meeting with Gina, Guy's wife and Jimmy, they were really unhappy with the way they were getting treated. I mean, they were making all the money and not sharing it with anybody. That's no way to run a band."

And so Riot found themselves signed with Fire Sign... legitimate label? "Yeah, well, define label," laughs Lou. "They had signed some production deals. I don't think it was a label. I think they created the label to put something on the vinyl they put out. But did they have any credibility at the time? No. I don't think they had any credibility. I think they had six or seven artists, and if you want one day, I'll show you the albums that they had. I mean, it was a sax guy and singer, and a couple of other albums that they made with some different artists. But never a Riot-type thing, never rock."

As we get back to *Rock City*, we were about to transition to side two of the original vinyl, which finds "Angel" opening the half, party-rocking hard, the band throwing in a bit of boogie rock. All told, the construct of the song anchors it to the hard rock rule book of the '70s, but it also presages the rise of hair metal in the '80s. Riot, like Montrose and Y&T, would peak too early to participate. Y&T tried, but as history would have it, Riot would sit out the golden years, and then return with a big enough deal at the close of the decade. Unfortunately for the commercial prospects of the band, however, Mark had by 1988 moved on to a speedy and technical form of "power metal," that was neither pop enough for hair, or aggressive enough to fit with thrash, which was also enjoying some success in the late '80s. These circumstances throw into high relief that Riot would prove to be ahead of the music industry curve at various points in their career, and that being ahead of the curve doesn't always pay dividends.

"Angel" is the third and final track on the debut Riot album to feature a Phil Fiet credit, and this one's a considerably fast, energetic-of-cymbals party rocker with a hint of boogie, some circuitous Aerosmith-via-Zeppelin riffing, and a curious lyric where the verses and chorus barely match. And if "Angel" wasn't enough melody for you, "Tokyo Rose" lightens things up further. Riot's trademark explosive and expressive performance and sound picture is robustly represented by this song, although given its '60s pop chord progression, this is a confusing track mixed in with the others. Face is saved come chorus time, however, where the band rocks hard this cautionary tale against the wiles of an Oriental lady of the night who will leave you both spent and broke.

It's back to well-crafted proto-metal come "Heart of Fire," which rocks madly with riff and twin lick, all atop a muscular shuffle beat from Pete. Guy Speranza is particularly of thespian mood, as he aggressively demands passion in matters of love.

Notes Steve, "I used a talkbox in 'Heart of Fire' in the intro and I used backwards echo in the chorus of 'This is What I Get' because I thought those two songs just weren't strong and couldn't stand up on their own, much less stripped-down. I was always looking for a song with room where I could show Mark's soloing skills, something like the solo and vamp out of 'Warrior' or his fiery solo and vamp out of 'Overdrive.' When I had that in the song structure, I never felt I needed to obfuscate. So aside from using certain effects on Guy's voice to enhance his performance, that was it. We kept it very simple."

"So yes, I opted for these things when I thought the song was weak and needed something to make it at least a little interesting. Riot were neighborhood kids from Flatbush, Brooklyn who all grew up together and made a band. In my opinion why some thought they had potential was because Mark from the very beginning was obviously something very special, and Guy was a good-looking front man, and they had a few good songs with real song structure people noticed and remembered. There were other bands that were doing heavy metal but nothing as young and energetic as Riot—and no one had a virtuoso guitarist like Mark. So the other bands never really made it out of the outer boroughs or out of New Jersey. But Riot seemed to transcend that limitation. Part of my job was to figure out why."

"I had a few parts in 'Heart of Fire' that I wrote with Mark," explains an Lou Kouvaris, uncredited on the song. "Mark and I really worked well together. We used to sit in his room and work at guitar parts, and as young as we were, we were very, very compatible. For example in 'Warrior,' Mark and I sat down, and I said Mark, why don't we do this and extend the solo a little bit more? And we wrote kind of an extended part of that middle solo, which was kind of neat and I was very happy about, because Mark was really receptive to that."

The lack of songwriting credits are a bit of a thorn in Lou's side, although, by his tone, not a considerably painful one.

"No, well, in terms of contribution, when I got into the band, there were two songs that were written, maybe three, including 'Desperation' and 'Warrior,' I believe. They were already written, and they had gotten a production deal on those particular songs.

So when I got into the band, there weren't really any other songs written, except for maybe 'Rock City,' which was on the verge of being written. And I wrote some parts in that song. But I had a lot to do with other songs I never got credit for. That was one of the things. I mean, I never made a stink about it and went on Facebook and said, 'Oh, you know, these pricks; you never put my name on anything.' I kind of kept it quiet and left that in my own world. I'm not the kind of guy to spew any kind of venom towards anybody—I never was like that, never will be. So I kind of let it lie. But I was very surprised that I never got credit for the things I contributed, including 'Overdrive' and 'Gypsy Queen.' I had nothing to do with 'This Is What I Get.'"

And no lyrics either. "No, Guy was a great lyric writer. I think 'Warrior' is fantastic. I never was a lyric guy. I was more of a... I used to come up with choruses. My thing was choruses, hooks, melodies, and I left the verses and stuff like that up to the lead singer. I would never really contribute to any of the lyrical stuff, or naming any of the tunes. Guy was a great dude. He was such a mild guy, a sensitive guy. I got along really well with him. We had a lot of talks about family and just music in general. He was a real nice, nice man. And he's a style singer. I mean, he wasn't what you would call, for the sake of argument, like a Celine Dion-type singer where every note is perfect. Guy was a nice, raw, style singer. But it was very precise and fantastic for our music. He was just right there. Different from anybody else—if you listen to any other singer, you can't compare him with anybody."

Perhaps given that after his time with Riot Lou transitioned into a life of production and engineering work, one might consider him overly critical in his assessment that *Rock City* lacks in production quality...

"I mean, as far as I'm concerned, from today's standards, even back then, I didn't know much," reflects Kouvaris. "I had taken a course in recording back in the old days in the same building, which was really ironic. It was the same building as Steve Loeb. I was in a studio called Generation Sound Studios, where I took a course there, and little did I know that upstairs I'd be hanging with these people a couple of years later. But when we recorded the album, I had gone into Greene Street Studios with the rest of the band, and they had some great stuff in there. They had an

SSL board, a small one, but a good one. And I didn't know shit from Shinola as far as what sonically things should sound like in the studio. I know what they would sound like, you know, me playing out of my amp, but I didn't know what it was going to sound like. My reference was the other bands I listened to on vinyl. So when the album came out, I was really excited, I guess, like everybody was. But I thought the production was not as good as it could've been. After a while, yeah, the albums got better and better, and I said, well, what could this band have sounded like if we would've recorded ten years later? So I think the album could've been recorded much better. But still, it came out pretty good for a band of that caliber, at that time, in that studio."

I thought so. The songwriting is another question, as we will see as we continue through side two of the original vinyl. But I thought the clarity was there, the guitars sounded molten, the drums had snap, and everything was the right volume. If anything, perhaps there wasn't quite as much bottom end as there could have been.

"You're exactly right. That's the thing—the bottom end. Remember, we went in there and did that album in, I don't know, maybe four or five sessions. You know, getting all the tunes down, and then the production and mix took however long the production took. So that album was recorded in '76 and '77, but yeah, it was quite an event when it did come out."

With "Gypsy Queen," sporting a typical hard rock lyric celebrating the idea of the wayward seductress, we are back to a sort of middle-of-the-road melodic hard rock, which continues to be the theme for album closer "This Is What I Get," which is practically a Chinn-Chapman type of pop that Sweet might have considered pre-*Sweet Fanny Adams*, or, conversely, a rootsy, casual inclusion on one of the first three Kiss albums.

And with that, *Rock City* was over and done. Comprising nine tracks, indeed, three of the four heaviest rockers were on side one, causing a sense of droop as the record got flipped. Nonetheless, in 1977, the album stood out as the work of one of the few new bands willing to propose a new place for heavy metal smack in the age of punk. Which, to reiterate, Riot very deliberately did not want to sound or look like a punk band. Fully aware of CBGBs and The Ramones, as Pete explains, they wanted to be a "clean and pressed" high energy rock band—in tennis shoes and coloured shirts! The image is one of boys from a working class neighbourhood, mostly Italian, fairly quiet of disposition, and then, yes, sort of "turned out good." It is a sense of fashion and chemistry that Def Leppard (from sleepy Sheffield) would utilize in high relief against the rest of the NWOBHM, and pretty much at the exact same time Riot might have been able to do the same, if only...

Wrote David Fricke, Riot, "recalled the better moments of Aerosmith, Nugent, Zeppelin… with a surprising amount of hooks, riffs, dashing about and a rhythmic overdrive that grabbed you on first listening." Apt comparatives, because indeed, in 1977, American rock was riding high, led by the aforementioned Aerosmith and Ted Nugent but also Kiss and Blue Öyster Cult. Riot, Angel, Yesterday & Today, Legs Diamond and New York compatriots Starz—and perhaps Canadians Moxy, Triumph and Teaze—would represent the tight bank of baby bands chomping at the heels. But then again, to close out the decade, most US hard rock bands would go light, battered by the market forces promoting new wave, punk's palatable younger sister. Of the above bands, truth be told, Riot seemed most like Starz and Legs Diamond, American hopefuls not quite there in the songwriting department, not exactly brimming with larger than life personalities, and then perhaps doomed to failure by label forces not attuned to the potential positives of heavy metal music.

As far as live work goes, Lou recalls that during his tenure, Riot "opened up for Rick Derringer, Southside Johnny, Journey, Tom Petty and the Heartbreakers, The Outlaws, Mark Farner and more. But those are the major dates, and I say major, you know, we were just starting out. We went from a basement band to playing clubs, all in the city, and then opening up for major rock bands, because we got interest from Japan and some of the other places. And then, you know, Steve Loeb and Billy Arnell got us deals all around the world with different labels. Attic Records in Canada, Ariola in Germany, which, if you see the German copy, I believe I have

credit there on 'Gypsy Queen.' It was good. We got a lot of press from Japan. I have a list of these radio stations in Japan that put Mark and I as the twin killer guitar players, you know, just as good as the guys from Kiss. And this is all documented. I have the sheets from it. And our live shows were just so energetic and people would just love coming to the shows."

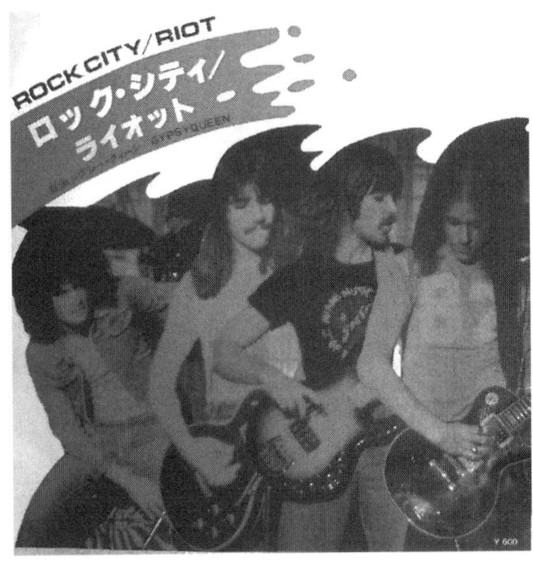

But it's the club days that are remembered fondly by the guys. Everybody was living at home still, but Mark's parents had provided them with a practice space as well as an old mail truck for their gear. The pay was bad or nonexistent, but the circuit was extensive and the chemistry in the band was good. Pete says that the band played so hard, he would get off the stage and wring the sweat out of his clothes into a bucket—one that had a line on it from the night before, just to see if he'd managed to sweat more after this show than the previous one.

As a result of the band's hot shows, and their ability early on to get on some tours, *Rock City* soon became the #1 rock album in San Antonio, forever to be the band's hottest hot spot, with Riot also establishing strong bases in Dallas and Cleveland. And later on, Riot would cultivate that relationship the band had established with Texas, through Mark moving there on and off but also through playing there very early on and regularly. Specifically, San Antonio dates would include September 22, 1979 second on the bill to AC/DC with Molly Hatchet supporting (the famous bill switch that was a surprise, given Molly Hatchet's gold record status), a club show at Cardi's on September 28, 1981, an arena show supporting Saxon and headliner Rainbow on August 18, 1982 and on January 14, 1984, a support slot to Vandenberg and then Kiss.

Charting the rise, Lou says that, "Before I got into the band, with Phil Fiet and Steve Costello, they were playing block parties and stuff like that. I came to it a bit after that phase, when they got production deal; they did a two-song demo with a guy named Ron Alexander, and that's where they were starting with me. And when they called and I went down, they already had some interest with Billy and Steve. I don't think it was formally Fire Sign Records at the time, but Anacrusis Music, which I think was their publishing company or something. But I did Club 82, Max's Kansas City, Gildersleeves, Rock Palace, Private Eyes, CBGB, and then after we did those, we started getting some nice gigs. We did a tour down in Florida which got a lot of exposure. That's where The Outlaws recorded their live album, on that same stage. We backed that tour up. Like I said, we were just starting to get big stuff, because now we had the agents, we had the management, we had the producers, we had everything that a band was supposed to have."

"After the recording of any album," explains Steve, "the issue always becomes how or how much do we translate to the live environment that will follow if the band needs to get on the road to promote. Fortunately we did make the cut and little did I know *Rock City* was the first of a dozen albums that would follow and become part of my own career as a producer."

A business-oriented piece in *Billboard*, August 19, 1978, provided all the details with regard to what Riot's management team were attempting to do with Rock City and their hot young band. Reported Adam White, "Fire Sign Records, one-year independent label headquartered here, is utilizing international interest in its first rock act to generate domestic acceptance. The combo is Riot, heavy metal rockers in the Deep Purple/Uriah Heep mold. Mapping the strategy are Billy Arnell and Steve Loeb, whose fledging label is part of a publishing/studio/production complex. Working with them is Riot's management, helmed by Art Santucci. Fire Sign has licensed Riot to Ariola for Britain and Western Europe, Victor in Japan, EMI in Australia, Attic in Canada and Teal in South Africa. Product has been released in territories ahead of US availability, with good initial results. In Japan, for example, Arnell claims album sales of some 50,000 units to date."

"The Fire Sign ploy to break an act at home by emphasizing its overseas credentials stems from what Arnell admits are the label's limited resources," continues White. "He feels that strong competition from the major companies in the US market works against small independent units with new acts. Hence the unusual strategy for Riot. 'We've held back here until the foreign deals begin to yield results.' He adds, 'Now we've got something to talk about.' The plan also boasts the added advantage of bringing in royalty advances from foreign licenses in readiness for the American thrust."

"Now Fire Sign is looking to Riot's dates with Journey, Mahogany Rush, Tom Petty and the Heartbreakers and others to establish their quintet domestically. Arnell holds that its major asset is on-stage excitement. Riot's first Fire Sign album is *Rock City*. Executives from Ariola will be flying in to witness the act's August 24 date at Great Gildersleeves in New York, along with a party of overseas journalists."

"Riot is the Fire Sign unit's first rock act. Its main emphasis previously has been in jazz and R&B. The label sprang from Arnell and Loeb's seven-year business partnership in production, publishing and management. The pair own the Big Apple recording studio, which has handled sessions by Gloria Gaynor, Andrea True Connection and others. Its policy now is to recruit, record and build artists, while being prepared at some point to pass them on to major labels, either via direct signing, production deal or custom label."

"I confess that *Rock City*'s 'success' took me completely by surprise," continues Steve. "I measured what was a success by whether they got noticed enough to get us all to the next stage, i.e. another record. We had no money and whatever came in was immediately plowed back into the band. That worked for a few years until it didn't. *Rock City* was completely self-financed. Just like Mark says, we took the compilation of NYC bands to France, played it for A&R people and publishers at the Midem music convention in Cannes and listened to their feedback. Some liked this band or that, but *all* liked Riot. It was because of that, that we decided to do a complete Riot album. And as explained, we came back to NYC and began to work on the extra tracks we needed."

"At this point I think for anyone wondering about the thousands of dollars it was obviously costing us and the fact there was no money we were making from the band... there had to be some money, right? Were we wealthy? No. We were pretty broke and just barely getting by. Billy and myself wrote and arranged commercials and did make decent money—and that too *all* went into Riot. It paid for an office, an office assistant, office supplies, telephone, a telex—which I bet no one's ever heard of—and kept us in Popeye's chicken and Big Macs. Plus it bought back lines and strings, and mics but not much else."

Indeed, controversy over the band's finances would become a theme all through Riot's run (and we will hear more about that), but closing on a lighter note, we return to Mighty Tior, Riot's abomination of a seal-headed monster, rendered on the cover of *Rock City* arguably as skillfully and narratively rich as he ever would be, given that successive covers got simpler until he was gone completely. Still, as much as we make fun of the seal, given its toughness below the neck, Riot's genetic disaster deserves some of the recognition and praise that goes to Derek Riggs and his invention of Eddie. Iron Maiden's green ghoul is generally cited as the first name in heavy metal mascots, but all evidence points to Mighty Tior as a clear predecessor, especially given his appearance on two Riot sleeves before Iron Maiden's 1980 debut.

"Everybody asks about that," laughs Lou. "There really was no rhyme or reason to it but it stuck. On *Rock City* you have in the background the city of New York on fire. The mascot is holding an axe and some humans or aliens are lying on the ground. Supposedly it was the baby seals getting back at man for going for their furs."

"The album covers were a mixed blessing," adds Steve. "That was done by my sister Marcia who really just did what I asked her with slight modifications here and there because what I wanted wasn't feasible for one reason or another. The paintings themselves were done by her late husband Steven Weiss. Why did we choose the harp seal? For no other reason than to attract attention. I suppose that critter was always getting his head bashed in so it did work into the heavy metal theme. I don't know who started it but the other NWOBHM bands would all be using mascots so why not continue it? There was Maiden's Eddie, which I liked a lot. These were very useful—until they weren't. We could put it into different environments. As you see on the next album, *Narita*, it's in Japan mode as a Sumo and all the imagery there was speaking directly to the Japanese kids who completely understood the messaging and loved it."

"But it created a demographic ceiling I couldn't figure a way out of," continues Steve, in closing. "No older buyer would buy the record because they were too embarrassed to walk up to the counter with an album with that image. I know I needed one more record to figure a way out where I wouldn't alienate the loyal early fans for the more fickle older fans who I needed to grow this thing. And I didn't have the money to do what Iron Maiden did, which was create a story of the mascot getting killed by saving the band. Anyway, my sister is still active in San Francisco as a graphic artist and my late brother-in-law did photo-realism paintings until he died a few years ago—and his theme was disasters."

Narita – "If it's not really going the way he wants it to go, you might be dismissed."

The story of the fine second album from Brooklyn baby band Riot needs a bit of a preface, as Mark Reale's co-guitarist Lou Kouvaris gets the boot.

"I was in the band until August '78," begins Lou. "We had started what would become *Narita,* and then I was fired, or whatever you want to call it, I think six or seven months after that. Mark and I were writing tunes. We had stuff in the can, and we were trying more; plus we did a lot of practicing. There were so many ideas but you can't get to everything. We didn't have recorders; we had little cassette players that we would put things on, and then our memories were what was keeping it together. But I was actually the main writer on '49er,' which most people don't know—I wrote the main riff and the majority of the song. And also a song called 'White Rock,' which I'm also not credited on."

But Lou's tenure was about to end. "Yes, well, what happened was, we had been on tour and we were opening up for Journey one night, at Triple City Stadium in Binghamton, New York, upstate. That Journey gig was a really, really nice gig. As a matter fact, Neal Schon, when we were at the hotel, I had met him and we talked a little bit. We had gone to the show, we opened up, and after we played, I was going down the stairs, because it was a very, very tall stage, and as we were coming off the stage, Neal Schon stopped and grabbed me by the shoulder and said, 'Hey, dude, man, you're great guitar player.' And I'm looking at him, like this guy thinks I'm good?! I'm floored. You gotta remember, I'm a 23-year-old kid. And I turned around, and as all the rest of the guys walked down the stairs, I said to Neal, 'Would you mind very much if I came up and watched you play?' He said, 'Yeah, man, come up.' He was very gracious. So I went up and I sat on stage and watched him for the whole set."

"Anyway, so the other part of this, we were in our little trailer, so to speak, and Mark and I had a little bit of an argument. Most people would say it was a fight but it wasn't. There were no fists flying or anything. It was an argument. And most people who work together know it's like a marriage. So we had an argument over using a piece of equipment. I wanted to use my echoplex, which I used on everything that we've ever done. And he said, no, man, I don't want you using this. And I said, you've got to be kidding. We're playing outside. I said, you know, I want to use it, and this is what it's going to be. And he said to me, no, you can't use it. And as we are fighting, Steve, the producers and the managers, they all walked in to the actual trailer, and they caught us arguing, and I guess that was kind of like a big 'no no' on my part. And they looked at me as causing trouble. Which I wasn't. We were just having an argument."

"To be quite honest with you, a lot of that stuff is like any other business in the world: there are a lot of people that control your day and what you're going to do. Steve Loeb... I don't know if you have any connections with any of those guys, but they were really responsible for the demise of the band in various areas. And I was talking to Pete Bitelli years later about that gig we had in upstate New York, and telling him that fight that Mark and I had was just a regular argument. And when they walked in, I don't know what they felt or what they thought, but it might've left a bad taste in their mouth, because that was to be my last gig. I woke up the next morning and everybody was gone."

"I woke up in the morning... where is everybody?" continues Lou. "And the photographer, who was a good friend of Steve or Billy, we had breakfast together, and he was asking me all these questions. I was a young kid, I wasn't politically correct, and I didn't know much about life in general much less the business world, and I'm spilling my guts out to this guy. How I felt and how I wished we would go in more of a, how would you say, commercial way, like Boston or Van Halen, so we could get our music out there and get played. And concentrate on maybe getting some real exposure and getting a hit song, you know? So I voiced a couple of things and then went home that night. We actually drove in our car, because we didn't have a bus or anything. We drove in our cars at that time. I went home, and the next day I got a call from the manager saying that they no longer needed my services. And I never got a reason. And I was heartbroken because nobody called me, nobody said anything to me. And that was the end of my journey with Riot."

"Here's Jimmy... Jimmy was a monster bass player. I mean, if you never saw him play, he is like one of the most energetic bass players, and perfect for Riot. Peter Bitelli was a decent drummer. He played the parts; he was a good drummer. But they were nice guys. They were very quiet. Peter was very, very quiet, very good friends with Mark. And I got along with everybody. But I was very shocked that nobody called me back and said, 'Lou, this is what happened; this is the way it went down.' I had a talk with Peter about a year ago, and he told me the same thing. He said, 'Lou, after I did my last record, nobody called me, the band broke up, nobody said anything to me. I had no clue, just like you.' I thought, that's very odd, because Mark was the leader of the band, and as the leader, you reach out. You keep in touch and maybe say, 'Hey, listen, man, sorry what happened; this is what happened.' I never got an explanation. Pete never got an explanation. And it's kind of a sad turn. But emotionally we weren't at our peak at that point. We were still growing as people."

"But it's a shame because the band was really starting to evolve; it was starting to go places. There was label talk and there was quite a bit of buzz happening. We were growing and doing a sequel to *Rock City*. If you notice, a lot of the tunes on *Narita* are kind of in the same vein, except I think the production got a little better on that album."

"And listen, Mark was living with his father for how many years, until the band broke up, and then he moved to Texas," continues Lou. "And I don't know exactly what year that was, but that's when all these problems started happening with his stomach. That's when I started hearing about it anyway. But it was a very, very sad situation. I felt bad for him. And again, I never talked to Mark after that. Not one word."

Mark Reale would die from complications related to a stomach affliction called Crohn's disease, January 25, 2012, after slipping into a coma on January 11th. I asked Lou if there was much evidence of a stomach aliment when he was Mark's co-axeman back in the late '70s.

"Mark never really felt well. I mean, even as we were young—and I had stomach problems myself—I think he internalized everything. Contrary to what people believe, Mark and I were friends. You don't just come out with music like that. I mean, we used to hang out in Mark's bedroom, hang out with his mother, hang out with his father. We did a lot of things together. We never really went out and went to places together. We played music. We were just musical buddies. And we talked about life, and he never had a girlfriend at the time. That was something that was missing out of his life. So he didn't really have an emotional connection to people in that way; he was very emotionally stifled. And he internalized a lot of things. I used to say Mark, you really should do certain things and go out and have some fun. And he would just sit in his house and play. And when I would come over, that's what we did—that was our fun."

Lou says Mark paid attention to what he ate. "He did. Believe it or not, Mark... I don't know how into it he was, but he had a cousin who was really into running and so was he. And they would try to be health-conscious together. We weren't. We had to go to Roll-n--Roaster in Brooklyn and eat our brains out on the roast beef sandwiches, right? (laughs). With the rest of the band. We would go and eat that great Brooklyn food. But I think he had a lot of internal problems, and his stomach got worse as time went on. Because I heard through the grapevine that he wasn't feeling well and he was having some problems. But no, Crohn's disease was not diagnosed then, with me being in the band."

Enter Lou's replacement, one Rick Ventura, who charts his entry into the ranks of Riot, for which he'd help craft the next four records.

"Mark started the band, and I was a buddy of his. We grew up together and we had similar influences. I always thought that we came out a few years too early, because we basically started out as hard rock. I mean, toward the end of the lineup I was in, through to *Born in America*, we started turning into more of a metal band. But basically Mark and I grew up listening to Ronnie Montrose, Jeff Beck, Eric Clapton, Johnny Winter, Edgar Winter, Jimmy Page, Deep Purple, the high energy American and British hard rock, while Guy was more into the English boogie bands like Foghat. That really shapes the early Riot. So it's a very interesting mix of people and influence. And the sound just developed. Guy had a unique vocal style, and it was basically pretty much straight-ahead rock 'n' roll."

"I think there was an issue between Mark and Lou," figures Rick, on the switch. "I think it had to do with songwriting credit, if I'm not mistaken. There also might've been more competition between Lou and Mark as guitar players. There might've been a touch of that. I was around them from the beginning, so I witnessed a lot of it. On Mark's part, it might have been more of a style issue. But I've spoken to Lou numerous times regarding songwriting credits, and he wrote riffs and he wasn't credited for them. '49er' might have been one he wrote on; it reminds me of his style. So a lot of the bitterness was due to songwriting credits. And Mark had a tendency to say, okay, if it's not really going the way he wants it to go, you might be dismissed (laughs)."

Pete Bitelli, although he was perfectly fine with Rick, says that Rick was "from the neighbourhood," fitting Mark's modus operandi of hiring guys out of convenience (as with Jimmy Iommi), rather than perhaps placing an ad and auditioning guys from other boroughs or states. In essence, Riot was an insular band in this way from the start and remains so in its ex-state, with both Lou and Pete and even original bassist Phil Fiet still living in Long Island, and indeed their longtime soundman Mike Castellani, now 57, still keeping in touch, and still doing sound, only now for the New York Mets at Citi Field since 1994.

As Pete frames it, there are positives to being a "band from the neighbourhood," as well, most notably a special bond (since childhood in the case of himself and Mark), that creates a chemistry that cannot be replaced. Indeed, palpably, this sentiment would ring true in reverse with Riot when they looked afield; it would take a band member from much further away—a singer from Georgia—to create a situation where a perceptive enough music fan might notice a pronounced lack of chemistry, especially set against the earlier records.

Back to the task at hand, however, the author's personal copy of the record Rick was about to make with the band was picked up somewhere in Canada (Canadian Capitol copy), possibly on a cross-nation family trip, and the sizzling promise of the *Rock City* debut was indeed to cash dividends. Riot were now one of the best young metal bands me and the buds knew and dug and freaked o'er, and it wouldn't be long until our garage bands and then for one summer, our (technically) professional bar band, Torque, would be grinding through *Narita*'s "Road Racin'" and *Fire Down Under*'s "Outlaw" to blank stares from the crowd putting up with us over watery pints at lacquered wooden tables across the West and East Kootenays.

The Riot of the classic two-fisted punch of *Narita* and *Fire Down Under*... it was fast but it was also accessibly stadium-rocking. This was not roughshod Motörhead and Saxon NWOBHM grimness, although the UK was fast to be digging the riffing of Mark Reale and the sweet vocal prowess of Guy Speranza but quick, quicker that folks from the US would catch on, to be sure.

As discussed previously, Mark Reale is not with us any more, having succumbed to the painful and debilitating effects of Crohn's Disease, with the after-story adding to the many reasons why the band never achieved the fame so due to them, namely that its leader was often incapacitated by pain. I had the pleasure of speaking with Mark a number of times over the years and always found him to be thoughtful, courteous, self-effacing, and endearingly in love with being a metalhead.

Still, it was Mark's versatility and love of all forms of music that helped infuse Riot with a magic touch that left so many of us scratching our heads as to why upon the release of *Narita*, Riot weren't out there axe-battling it out with Van Halen for US rock supremacy through the heady heavy metal daze of the '80s.

Says Mark, articulating the alloy of silk and steel that was Riot, "The thing is, I don't want to say it's like ego or whatever, but I got involved with musicians that were incredible, so I knew that we could play fast; that's always been the Riot thing from the beginning. But at the same time, I like pop music, man. The melodic aspect... it was the combination of those two things that I think created that whole vibe. Because you've got bands that can play their asses off, and play 100 miles an hour and it's pretty much all it is, or you have bands that basically do pop-oriented stuff. The thing with Riot was, I combined the two elements of that. And I think that was the appeal to it. I like both aspects of it. I like the testosterone-driven guitar stuff, but at the same time, I'm very emotional, and I like to feel, I like melody, I want to feel melody. So I think it's those two things that pretty much formulated the whole Riot thing."

"The first three Riot records, you had *Rock City*, *Narita* and *Fire Down Under*, we were still searching on *Narita*," continues Mark, quite accurately, given the now only slight throwback to the '70s on this very heavy record for the '70s. "It's like the third is the charm. The first record was like a bunch of kids from my basement in Brooklyn, New York, just doing whatever we did, and *Narita* was a little bit more formulated. It was kind of getting there, and I think I finally hit on it with *Fire Down Under*. *Fire Down Under* is more focused than the first two records, and I think we finally hit on it there. And then of course Guy Speranza left the band and the whole thing went into disarray (laughs), and I had to rediscover myself."

"So yeah, *Narita* is our second attempt. By the time we reached *Fire Down Under*, we had basically found our niche, so *Narita* was our next step in our development. Because the first record, *Rock City*, we were really green at that point. With *Narita* I think our songwriting just chilled a little bit more, and by the time we hit *Fire Down Under*, we pretty much had the concept down. So that was a big point of development."

"We never spent as much time in those days as we do now, that's for sure," answers Mark, asked how long it took to make those early records. "The process was, we basically played as a band in the studio. We were all in the room at the same time,. In most cases, Guy would even sing. And we would do overdubs, vocal overdubs, solos and stuff. As far as the recording process itself, it didn't really take that long. It's probably, the producers took time doing their thing, but for us to play, we did this stuff off-the-cuff, or not off-the-cuff, but live; there wasn't a lot of overdubs like there is now. I think that *Narita* probably went quicker than *Rock City*, because *Rock City* was kind of like, that was like the first one. But some of the songs on *Rock City* were even on the original demos, so it was done over a long period of time. *Narita* was more concise, done over a shorter period of time. At that time, an average time of actual recording might've been between a month and two months, but it's not like we would be in there everyday. Maybe we would put in like two or three days a week. We didn't go into the studio and do it all in one shot."

As discussed, concerning the transition between *Rock City* and *Narita*, perhaps some of the shift lies in the fact that Mark's co-guitarist on the debut is gone, replaced by Rick Ventura.

"Okay, L.A. was on the first record, *Rock City*, great guitar player, okay? Great guitar player. What basically happened was the first record we did, like me and Guy were like 18 years old and we signed contracts with these two crazy dudes, that basically produced those first three records. But to give them credit, they knew about marketing and focusing, and with L.A. it was like he was writing songs like Steve Miller. He was writing songs that were on a very straight rock/pop-oriented situation. Because I don't know if you know, we had a keyboard player at that point. I was stumbling around. I didn't know what was going on. The thing with L.A. was, he was a great guitar player, he was writing stuff, good songs, really good songs, but like I said, they were akin to something like Steve Miller or whatever. And the producers were like, 'Look, this is what you need to do. You need to cut the keyboard player, you need to do guitar music, and this is the direction you should go in.' And basically he kind of got cut out of it, because the stuff he was writing wasn't... because we were moving more in a heavy direction. And to be honest about it, it was like our producers were controlling the situation at the time, and they were basically cutting him out. It's like those songs may be okay, but that's not the direction we're going in. You've got to remember, around that time you had this whole thing going on with the New Wave of British Heavy Metal, to coin a phrase, and that's where they saw us going, and so he just kind of got bumped out of it."

Narita, issued October 5, 1979 (and actually five months earlier in Japan) opens with a perfect example of hooky yet brisk modern metal called "Waiting for the Taking." Instantly, one is swept up into a froth of enthusiasm that this band could go places, much as one felt back at Montrose's debut, this track definitely evocative of that band's first record and, with its ascending strummed chord structure, specifically "I Got the Fire" from the second album. Speranza is singing with authority, the band chemistry behind him is palpable, and it's all captured in warm yet forward-thinking heavy metal high fidelity, the hope in the sound underscored by Guy's lyric about fighting hard for ones goals.

"Basically the whole style just came from the fact that there was just this amalgam of influences we had," says Mark in agreement with that assessment. "I was heavily influenced by Ronnie Montrose and that first Montrose record. I was heavily influenced by that whole high energy kind of approach. We used to go see them in concert. And that was the model I had in my head. I was also into the European bands like Deep Purple and Rainbow, so from my end, it was the heavy guitar thing. Guy Speranza was more into bands like Thin Lizzy, more of a pop thing. And when it came together, Riot is pretty much what came out. You had this very guitar-driven music with this melodic vocal on top. So we were pretty much just feeling our way through on those first two records. I don't think it was until *Fire Down Under* that we pretty much nailed our sound."

And yet there seemed to be no problem capturing a huge stadium rock sound production-wise, right there on *Narita*, and even, arguably, on the *Rock City* debut.

"It was all pretty much experimental," says Mark on the fortuitous and even lucky knob-jobbing on those early Riot records. "Steve had his own ideas about what the deal would be. As far as production goes, we were pretty much just following. We really didn't have a lot of control at that time other than writing material. We'd go write the songs and we played them. But as far as the studio went, we were pretty naive. When we did *Rock City*, and even on into *Narita*, we had no idea what we were doing in a sense. We had no idea of a concept. To Steve's credit, because we were really young, we were coming in there with heavy metal songs, we had pop songs, rock songs, we were coming in with all sorts of things. And you can hear it on *Rock City*. There was no real solid definitive direction at that point, and I think during those first two records, we were trying to feel our way through what we were doing. And I think *Narita* was just the second step in that. It was a little more solidified in terms of concept than *Rock City*."

"I guess we pretty much built it," laughs Reale, with regard to where *Narita* was recorded, as it is stated in the credits, "The Big Apple Recording Studios, Ltd., Greene Street, New York City." "Basically, it was these two dudes that owned it, and during the course of our progression there, I mean, when we first went there, it was a 16-track analog studio, a little studio, and then by the time we got to *Fire Down Under*, it was like a 24-track analog studio, and by the time we got to *Thundersteel* it was like digital. The whole thing progressed. But at the same time, that studio was doing a lot of hip-hop and rap stuff. A lot of people don't know that I played... I did a lot of session work at one point. The early '80s, I played on a lot of hip-hop stuff, with friggin' Flavor Flav, because at that point, ever since the Michael Jackson/Eddie Van Halen thing, a lot of hip-hop stuff at that point wanted rock guitar players on their records. Run-D.M.C., they were out of there, and I forget the guitar player's name who played on those records, but that became the thing there, and nobody knows that. You know, like I was on motion pictures, like *Breakin'* and stuff, because a lot of those artists wanted rock guitar players, and there was a little stretch of period where I did a lot of session work that nobody knows about. But I remember that studio. Run-D.M.C. was a big thing out of there, and as for where that came from, man, with the heavy guitar over the rap stuff, they did a lot of that stuff there, including Public Enemy."

As for working with Steve in the early days, "The only argument there ever were were more so not arguments, but frustrations between me and Steve in a sense. We were young and inexperienced and we had our own ideas, whereas Steve was more of the mature brain of the operation. And to his credit, he knew he had to package us a certain way. We pretty much had no idea of a concept, and those records were pretty raw. *Rock City* was done quite live. We just went in there and played, with minimal overdubs. Like I say, I think *Rock City* was actually 16 tracks, as was *Narita*. It was 16 tracks, which by today's standards would be considered primitive."

Riot's newfound heaviness continues unabated into *Narita*'s second track, "49er," which tells the tale—appropriately with a heavy metal gallop—of those making the western migration. Sure, it's an artful, oblique and deftly generalized history tale of the wild West, but it's also prescient of the great hair metal migration so many bands would be making not four and five years later, to create gleaming metal communities that Riot should have been in the thick of, rewarded for what they helped spark through *Narita*. Lyrically, there's an essence of both UFO and Thin Lizzy, and with that gallop, a link from "Doctor, Doctor" to Iron Maiden, if not also countless obscure NWOBHM anthems, including Dark Star's "Lady of Mars," to name but one.

"Kick Down the Wall" finds the band turning in a chunkier rocker, evoking buffalo burger power-chording like Kiss circa *Hotter than Hell* and BTO at their heaviest. The delivery is massive, but the construct is definitely of a '70s ilk, building the argument that *Narita* was the record on the way to full-blown classic *Fire Down Under*. Fitting is Guy's lyric, which paints the picture of a typically raucous night down at the local bar, again, evoking the memory of both Phil Mogg and Phil Lynott.

"Mark did most of the solos," notes Rick, "but 'Kick Down the Wall,' okay, that's me on that. And 'Waiting for the Taking,' I co-wrote that, but Mark is on that. So we did split the solos. We share solos on 'Hot for Love.' If you're a guitar player, even if you're a listener and you're into the styles, you can tell us apart. My style is more bluesy and melodic while he touches more on the speed. Mark was a great guitar player. It was a lot of fun playing because it made both of us better guitar players. We fed off each other, and you could really see how it developed from *Narita* through *Fire Down Under* to *Restless Breed*. On the songs I wrote, that's my guitar playing. And on some songs, Mark did all the guitar playing while on some we split it. And then the harmonies, we did that together."

Riot's was a blue collar rock formula that, as mentioned earlier, would work for the band in that classic rock stronghold of the day, San Antonio, Texas. Which, combined with the band's strong presence in Canada through Attic Records, sets a confusing and interesting tie-in with the Canadian bands who found a cult following there as well, namely April Wine, Triumph and Moxy. Pete Bitelli unequivocally calls San Antonio his favourite place to play, going so far as to say that the town was instrumental in breaking the likes of both AC/DC and Rush—long after his run with Riot, he would vacation there regularly.

"Like I say, it went on from there and it turned into *Rock City* and one thing led to another," continues Mark. "But the big problem with the whole thing was, was that these two guys were crazy. They were like coked-out crazy dudes, okay? And they were very obsessive about the whole thing with us, okay? It got to the point... by the time we did *Fire Down Under*, it was like, we had big industry people that wanted to handle us. We went on the *Black and Blue* tour with Black Sabbath in 1980, and I remember being at Boston Gardens, man, and Black Sabbath's manager coming up to

                    Martin Popoff

me and saying, 'Hey man, it's like, you're on this tour, we think you guys are cool, we want to manage you, but I can't deal with these two like crazy dudes calling me up at four o'clock in the morning.' And then there was Cliff Burnstein from Q Prime, who signed Metallica; twice he came, twice he met with them to try and handle us. And they basically scared everybody away, and it completely hurt the band. The only thing that saved anything was the fact that whatever records we made, we developed this really loyal fan base, that would still support us."

And how does Billy Arnell fit into the picture?

"That was his partner, okay? Steve superseded like... they broke up around the time when we were doing *Born in America*. They had a falling-out, but they were partners, and they were both crazy (laughs)."

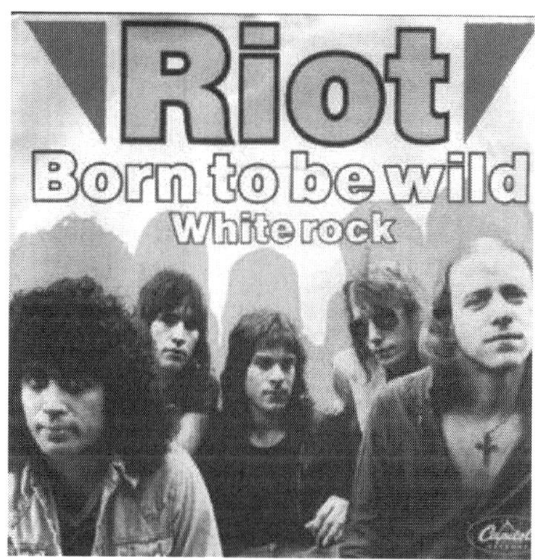

Back to the record, next we get the band's searing, heavy metal version of Steppenwolf's "Born to Be Wild," which stomps dead the version done by Long Islanders Blue Öyster Cult seemingly a rock 'n' roll generation earlier. Says Mark, "I don't remember how that happened. It's just something I wanted to cover, I suppose. I like covering other stuff. I guess just at that point of time it was like, 'Hey, man, let's do "Born to Be Wild."' It was probably just an idea."

Adds Steve, "Being on Canadian Attic Records, they asked if we could do something that was Canadian-written because it would give them an edge with the Canadian content rules. And anyway, the band had a pretty decent arrangement that worked in context, so we did it and it worked well." Pete figured it was a good fit because it was fast and easy and a regular song for the band, but also because Riot always did tons of covers, by anyone from Humble Pie to Peter Frampton to Kiss to much of the first album by Montrose. As well, it was perfect for Guy's range so he enjoyed singing it.

Further concerning "Born to Be Wild," Riot exhibit what equates to a demonstration of impatience with this proto-metal classic, guitars speaking out of turn, the band tormenting the original melody with heavy metal impertinence.

Closing side two of the original vinyl is a ripping instrumental that full-on finds these Americans in New Wave of British Heavy Metal mode, unwittingly helping to invent speed metal, even adding the twin riffing found with Priest and soon-to-be NWOBHM flagship band Iron Maiden. Pete Bitelli is aggressive and frantic with his drum part and chucks in extra cymbal work lest any spaces be left for anything approaching quiet, and the overall vibe is one of Ritchie Blackmore kicking classical up the backside. As soaring leads take us to conclusion, one can't help but think that "Narita" is the blueprint for some of those instrumental wind-ups and axe-dueling passages Iron Maiden would soon make famous, including their own full instrumental compositions such as "The Ides of March."

Asked why the band did an instrumental, Rick figures, "Mark was always into instrumental guitar players—he liked Jeff Beck, he liked Ronnie Montrose. And that melody line just worked as an instrumental."

The tie-in with Japan, from the title *Narita* through to the sumo stance of the seal mascot and the Japanese script on the cover, would prove beneficial for the band, as Mark quickly found himself set up with relationships with Japanese labels that would persist nicely through all the years we had Riot with us.

"Actually, our producers had something to do with that," says Mark, concerning the use of the name *Narita*, taken from the city that contains the airport of the same name, the main air hub for the city of Tokyo. "If you look at the album cover… Narita's the Japanese airport. And supposedly the story is that it was built on sacred ground, and there were protests going on at one point, because they built it on some kind of sacred ground and people were buried there and stuff. So it was our producer that came up with the idea. They didn't write the song, but at the time, we were also starting to get rumblings that we had some kind of popularity in Japan. So it was kind of like a nod towards Japan, basically. Although at the time we made *Narita*, we hadn't been to Japan yet. But we were getting rumblings from the magazines and the press and stuff, because there was a song we had called 'Warrior,' okay? And there was a female Japanese artist who covered it. I forget what it's called (laughs). In English it was different words, and it was 'Warrior'—that was the name of the song—but I think it was 'Bye Bye Boy' or something (confirmed as Yuki Igarashi's 'Bye Bye Boy,' and there is also Misako Hinjoh's 'Warrior' cover from 1982's *Messiah's Blessing*). And she covered it, and we were starting to get the impression that we had some degree of popularity there, at that point."

"I asked Mark to write the title track as an instrumental Japanese fans could read into and relate to," explains Steve. "As I said, Narita means good luck on the road, and of course there was a great deal of controversy about Narita airport, which was built on an ancient burial ground. If you listen to the track, at the very end you hear as I faded it, a steady crash crash crash with air raid sirens and what is actually a native American reciting a prayer. I thought Mark delivered the assignment perfectly. And when the band years later finally went to Japan, I saw how clearly he had. But I love that record. I enjoyed making it and I still enjoy listening to it. Some tracks more than others, but over all I really like it. I like especially 'White Rock,' '49er' and 'Road Racin'.' 'White Rock'... I love Guy's performance; I could tell he was opening up and there was way more just waiting to be mined. With the addition of Rick Ventura, there was new colour with his guitar approach and his writing. And Guy began to stretch out vocally. I changed engineer to Jim Jordan and although Jim's wasn't the most contemporary sound, it was more Midwestern, thicker. It would also be the final record for bassist Iommi and drummer Bitelli who would be replaced by Kip Leming and Sandy Slavin for *Fire Down Under*."

And what are we to make of the band's strange seal mascot this time? "That's just simply an idea that Steve had," says Mark. "When we first did *Rock City*, he wanted to have a cover created that was completely going to stay in someone's memory. Something that was going to catch your eye, be a bit outlandish. So we got an artist,

I think from San Francisco; I forget the guy's name. But he pretty much came up with this concept out of the clear blue sky. What had basically happened was that people started to associate this thing with us, so it kind of became this trademark."

Pete Bitelli adds a little colour to the story, which ties in the first two album covers. In essence, on the debut, the foremost idea was the fact that at the time, it was big news in the states that there were these Canadian hunters clubbing baby seals for their pelts. So the debut was a simple turning of the tables on mankind, a revenge scene. On the second one, as Pete explains it, our superhero now has a new political cause, protecting the ancient dead from the Japanese government, who had brought sacrilege upon the deceased by building this airport and not moving the dead to new ground.

Onto *Narita*'s action-packed side two and "Here We Come Again" is another less celebrated deep album track with a '70s vibe, even, arguably, a Canadian vibe, which might have helped cause the confusion in Texas, at least subconsciously, given how perceptive to cultural differences in their metal those fans were and still are. Lyrically, Guy writes an artfully vague tale that seems to equate an aerial dogfight with Riot hitting the stage.

But with "Do It Up" we're back into the raging Riot metal that was fully cutting edge for 1979, the type of swaggering back-switching construct that had UK tastemakers taking notice, none bigger than the legendary Neal Kay, DJ of the overseas heavy revolution (to quote Budgie).

"Now there's a personal story with Riot," regales Kay. "We considered the NWOBHM—well from my point of view, probably from Malcolm Dome's, too—we would say there was one exception to the word British. We include Riot as our family. Now there's a really good reason for that. I got a phone call one day after all this publicity had been floating around for a while. I was accepted and recognized by most of the major record labels and I could walk into most MDs offices unannounced. Never had a problem. I had an ear at eye-level. I got a phone call one day from a dude called Billy Arnell. He told me that he lived on a houseboat somewhere in New York, probably up the Hudson I would think, and he managed a band called Riot and they had self-financed an album which was *Rock City*."

"And their record label in America put it out. But over in Europe and in Britain, Capitol Records who had it—I think it was Capitol—refused to put it out because they said no one had heard of it. But actually what happened was at the same time as Geoff Barton started all this publicity with me and the drive was on, he suggested that I put a weekly chart in *Sounds* made up of punters' requests, and he'd print it, which he did. And the chart went worldwide in *Sounds*. It was like a Top 20 of heavy metal things in the Soundhouse requests. And Billy Arnell saw that, and oddly enough I had an import sent to me, a Riot album, and one of their tracks was riding real high in the charts, probably 'Warrior' I would think. Then 'Rock City' went in as well, and they had seen the chart, and they couldn't understand how the record company wouldn't release it. And yet it was in my chart."

As the story goes, it was indeed "Rock City" showing up in the chart, and then Billy Arnell's secretary showing Billy the copy of *Sounds* containing the chart, which she had received from the UK. "I couldn't believe it!" said Billy at the time, interviewed by Geoff Barton. "It was like a bolt out of the blue." Added Mark, "We were astounded. We didn't realize we were so popular in Britain. We didn't realize we were popular at all. Seeing that chart gave us the strength to carry on," to which Guy simply said, "God bless the UK."

"No one wants to know us here," continued Guy, in the *Sounds* piece with Barton, referring to the band's lack of traction on home soil. "The people are so blasé. They've seen it all. At concerts, they just sit with their arms folded, waiting to be impressed, for something to happen. We used to wonder how it was that new bands got signed over here. Ariola had us for England, Germany and stuff; we knew we were good, we knew we had something, but people kept passing on us in the states. We used to get real disheartened. Not with our music, because we believed in it, but with the business and the way it worked. Yeah, things were really getting on top of us. Billy was having terrible trouble promoting the band; he was like banging his head against a brick wall."

"It was a constant dilemma," says Billy. "We'd be getting the crowd reaction but no company was interested. It was a completely schizophrenic experience." Added Mark, "When we first started, we'd play a local club and the reception would be like nothing. Not because we were bad players or anything, but because of our material. Of course, that was when punk was really happening. But even so, the situation's much the same today. I think it's better it's happened this way, though. I don't think we'd have been ready if we'd secured an American contract a couple of years ago. Back then, we were very naïve and extremely impressionable. We're more together now."

Continues Neal, "So Billy phoned me up and said, 'Look, we're having this problem here; can you help?' And a lot of my followers and kids, they wanted the album and they couldn't get it. And it was obvious that it was going to sell. It was just a matter of getting it done. And so I walked into the MD's office unannounced as usual, slammed my fist on the desk and basically told him to release the bloody album, quickly! (laughs). And before he had me arrested, he calmed down (laughs) and over a cup of coffee I kind of explained the thing and said, 'Look, it'll sell as well as any other classic rock album does and there's a huge amount of fan base out there waiting for it.' And after a few minutes he looked at me and said, 'I hope to God you're right—okay.' And within two weeks it was in the shops. And they came over… I think they came over with Sammy Hagar. I've got a feeling. But what happened was we invited Sammy Hagar to do a personal appearance at the Soundhouse. He did it, and a few days later Riot, we invited Riot to come in. I got on real good with those guys. They were terrific guys. They were just like street blokes from New York. They were like us. They weren't high-faluting, rootin' tootin', son-of-a-guns from the big stage. They came over as really easy-going, street Americans."

So *Rock City* came out on Capitol?

"Yeah, over here it did. Basically what happened was we invited them to do a personal appearance at the Bandwagon at the Soundhouse, and they came down, the whole band, and Billy Arnell and I think it's Ezra Cook came with him. That's Billy's partner. And we had an incredible time. They went out on the floor and headbanged and air-guitared with all the kids and stuff, even to their own track. That was so damn funny. And they made a lasting impression with the Soundhouse because they were so down to earth and so like us, and they kind of got accepted into the family as long lost cousins from over the water. And they were always welcome there, and the Soundhouse nation loved them."

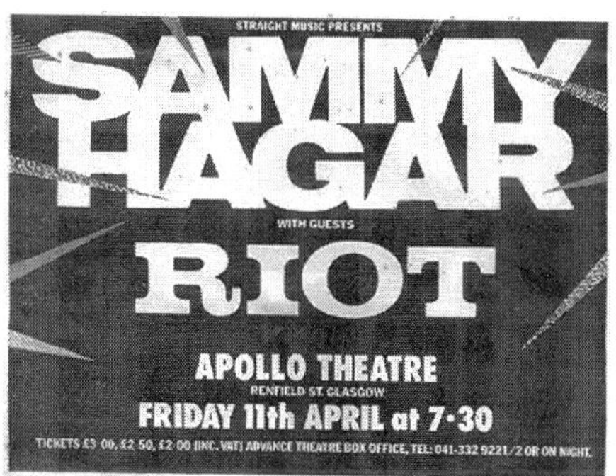

"I love the story about the band and the UK," recalls Steve. "It was one of those quirky things. Just when you're about to fold up… After a year, we just couldn't do it financially anymore. Not unless we had a US label and we didn't, so one night after talking about it for hours, we all decided to call it a day on the project. We decided to let the band know the following day they were free of any further obligation—and so were we. Maybe an hour later, our office assistant Rhonda called me at home—no cell phones. She had just gotten a letter—there was also no email or internet back in 1977—from a pen pal in England who, like Rhonda, was a music/record fanatic, who enclosed a record chart from a newspaper called *Sounds*. And there in black and white was 'Warrior' at #1 and it indicated it had been #1 for three weeks already. There was a note to Ron from her friend asking her if this wasn't the band Ron was working with."

"So because of that, Riot got a stay of execution until I could get my hands on this *Sounds* and see what it all meant. I did speak to Neal Kay who compiled this chart, and discovered Riot was already a pretty popular band in this new movement, something everyone was calling the NWOBHM. Riot's heightened profile in the UK caused many thing to happen next. Japan took much more notice and Germany began to as well. I began to learn that success in certain markets caused specific things to happen in others. And then something began to happen in the US too. It was a classic example of demographics playing out, cause and effect, and how and why things were spreading. I did my best to decipher and use each success as a step to the next step."

When *Narita* hit the street, both band and new label, Capitol, were hopeful. "We put out *Rock City* on an independent label in the US and signed to major labels overseas," said Guy, quoted in *Narita*'s press materials. "We got great reviews, began gigging all over the US, going on tour with Sammy Hagar, AC/DC and Molly Hatchet, playing 15,000-20,000 seaters. It blew our minds when audiences thousands of miles from Brooklyn shouted out the names of our songs." Added Mark, gamely,

"We are loud, we're powerful, a lot of running around, visual, but without too much smoke-bombings and things."

Explained guitarist Rick Ventura (described as the third Brooklynite in the band), also in the bio, "I used to watch Riot playing at block parties and Mark and I would talk guitars, but we never played together. I started traveling with Riot's road crew, helping out on a Midwest tour of one-nighters. At one point, they began to audition scores of guitarists. They didn't know I could play—I knew all the songs by then—but I didn't want to audition. If they'd had to say 'no' to me, it might've been weird and I didn't want to spoil our friendship. On the third day of auditions, I got in early to set up and was playing this great Les Paul Sunburst. Guy and Mark walked in and they just couldn't believe it! An hour later, we were jamming and it all just clicked."

The Capitol bio closes with the following: "Completing Riot's lineup are bassist Clifford 'Kip' Leming, and drummer Sandy Slavin. Leming claims roots in heavy metal, as do the rest of the group, while Slavin has studied with Dave Brubeck's drummer Joe Morello. Both were members of the East Coast group Mistress before joining Riot and both came to the group after the completion of *Narita*. *Narita*, the group's first Capitol release, is ten tracks of high-energy hard rock, all written within the group with the exception of Mars Bonfire's classic 'Born to Be Wild.' Previously available on the small Canadian Attic Records, *Narita* caused such excitement that the stores in Texas and the Pacific Northwest couldn't meet the demand for the import. This enthusiasm was repeated with a #1 selling import in England (according to *Record Business*), and smash success in Canada and Japan. The album, in fact, takes its name from an airport outside of Tokyo which caused considerable controversy and student riots when it was built a few years ago. This time out, *Narita* will be getting headlines of another sort because with Riot, the message comes across loud and clear."

It is of note that the bio is dated May of 1980, while the author's personal Canadian copy of *Narita* is in fact dated 1979. As well, in terms of personnel, on the back cover, the bassist is listed as Jimmy Iommi and the drummer, Pete Bitelli, which of course is the actual rhythm section on the record.

And what does Mark remember about the New Wave of British Heavy Metal, in which Riot had been inserted by the fans?

"Well, as far as American bands (laughs), I remember the first time we went to England was 1980, and I remember the Capitol guys telling us—we were all jetlagged and shit—and they were like, 'Hey man, you guys wanna go out? We just signed this new band called Iron Maiden.' And I didn't go, because I was burnt. But the other guys went. And it was like right on the crux of that whole scene. The thing was, we were in the right place at the right time, doing the right thing, but we had two sticks in the mud that were blowing up the works for us. That's basically the story."

Back to *Narita*, next up is "Hot for Love," which hides behind its (typical for the band) innocuous title, another rip-roarin' rocker that surreptitiously adds to the argument that *Narita* is as heavy an album as *Fire Down Under*, cheesy chorus notwithstanding. In fact, listen to the clang of this one and then that chorus and it reminds one of the conflicted transition Savatage found themselves making from *Sirens* through *Power of the Night* through *Fight for the Rock*, from "Twisted Little Sister" to "Hard for Love" to "Crying for Love." The song ends in a proto-hair metal sex session before giving way to "White Rock," a tidy melodic rocker more indicative of the material on the first album. Lyrically, the focus is shifted from the likely unintended suggestion that heavy metal is for white guys, through references to white fury, the suggestion of a Riot show being white hot, and the fact that on the drive to the show, it's snowing!

And then it's raucous closer "Road Racin'" a classic speed metal maven of gigantic proportions. "I remember 'Road Racin'' was a milestone," says Mark. "I came up with that song, and when we first went into the studio with it, it totally clicked. And it was like, we've got to do more of that. There wasn't a whole lot of pretense there with what I did. A lot of the stuff that I did was just like knee-jerk reaction, whatever came out of me. But 'Road Racin',' I can definitely remember bringing that into the studio and recording that, and everybody going, 'Yeah, this is good, this is cool.' And at that point, you're still finding yourself. And that's why, like I said, at the point we did *Fire Down Under*, we finally hit the niche in terms of focus. If you listen to the first two records, you can hear, especially the first one, there's a little bit here and there, but when you get to *Fire Down Under*, it's focused. That's where the band was coming from."

As for Steve's assessment of this lethal spot of speed? "Here's where I heard the whole band's potential and what was awaiting me; all of them rocked on this track. Mark, Guy... it told me they could click and listeners would all get it."

"'Road Racin'' was a great live song; there's so much energy in that," says Rick, who offers a summation of *Narita*, now at its end. "There's a lot of melodic songs on that record. I like it better than *Rock City*; it's a nice progression and it sounds better. I like 'Waiting for the Taking,' which is basically a melodic song. 'Hot For Love''s got some really good guitar playing, and overall, Guy really came into his own writing-wise. From those to 'White Rock,' there's a lot of variety, even if overall it's just very straight-ahead, hardcore hard rock."

"Road Racin'" is a blazing rock finale to an album that somewhat unjustly lives in the shadow of *Fire Down Under*. The track is exquisitely dialed in, produced, mixed, and there are sophisticated twists including the break and the shifting of the melodic sands for the closing section. As well, Pete Bitelli keeps the track disciplined and resolute through his use of mostly snare for any of his fills.

All told, in some respects, *Narita* is additionally remarkable over and above its illustrious follow-up, given its crafting and execution a year before a newly modern metal became a norm. Sure, credit must go to Van Halen as perhaps the first band to wake hard rock up after a long and slow decline into the recline of a cozy nap, but Riot has to be your first asterix band when viewing the trajectory toward the heavy '80s.

Even hip Detroit rock mag *Creem* was somewhat on board with Riot, Rick Johnson including the band in its survey of the metal scene, writing, "I've had a weakness for East Coast heavy metal ever since the glory days of Dust, Boomerang and the truly insane Sir Lord Baltimore, and Riot follow in that fine tradition of barely restrained excess. Their *Narita* disc, although available only as a Canadian import (that's okay, guys, it's not *your* fault) passed up Roger Whittaker, pineapples, and Lucky Strikes on the prestigious U.K. import chart. Now available here on Capitol, they're faster than the speed of science, but not too heavy to get off the ground."

"Project #2 was about Riot on the road," reflects Steve, summing up. "We now knew for certain we had something and needed to do at least one more record to know just how much we had. On *Narita* we needed to project Riot playing live and show listeners what they would be seeing if they bought tickets. 'Narita' actually means 'Good luck on the road' or at least that's what the Japanese kids were telling me. The Japanese label was not very happy about any of this. They thought it was all too Japanese for their market. They wanted an American band. They even removed the Japanese lettering from the cover. I was concerned I was making a serious mistake but I just didn't agree with them. But in the end, the Japanese version of *Narita* deliberately marketed the record without the lettering. They did in fact remove it, and years later I would see how right I really was."

"We had two goals for that project," continues Loeb. "Make the band look viable live and use certain tracks on the record to speak directly to fans in specific markets. I love retail politics, so this was really up my alley. I read every fan letter, I knew where we had pockets of support, I knew every sign that something was happening and I always, always had the band reach out personally. Later when they traveled on tour buses I would find letters from all the cities we would visit and call a fan or two from whatever city, invite them with a friend—for a witness—and have a band member hang with them and speak to them about something personal they said in their letter, like a name of a girlfriend, a pet, something that was personal. On the earlier records I just put their names on the covers. I thought how cool that would have been when I was fan."

"There were lots of things we did but one really stands out," says Steve, still on the fan end of things. "I got a fan latter from Brandon, Florida. The fan explained how he loved the band, and that he had started a band in Brandon that played locally and was a Riot cover band. It was obvious he had a single mom who was struggling; he must have been about 13 or 14 and was very serious. But his drum kit was sub-par and he was saving up to get something better. By that time, Peter Bitelli was leaving the band and I had his drum kit which he was no longer interested in, so I packed up his drums in their travel cases and shipped everything—drums, stands, logo and all—to this kid. Just did it—never even told the kid they were on the way."

"A few days later his mother called my office. She told me she didn't really know what to say, didn't know how to thank me etc. All he did was practice with the band and she was thrilled because it kept him off the street. They came up to New York to visit me some time later. Brandon, Florida and the surrounding area became one of Riot's strongest sales and radio markets. I attribute that fact to that drum kit. I'm so sure that one fan told another and another and it was like a prairie fire. I'll bet everyone in Brandon knew that story."

Fire Down Under – "Not even greed could convince Capitol to believe in us."

We begin our examination of *Fire Down Under* with a fascinating expansion of the story behind the band's often contentious relationship with their previous label Capitol and Riot's assault on the UK, which, complicated as it is, really hinges on this third all-important record for the band and its temporal placement right when the NWOBHM was at its peak. Adding intrigue to the tale is how another "honourable NWOBHM band," namely Sammy Hagar, also on Capitol, dovetails into the tale of Riot.

"Well, yes, so by this point," begins Steve, "Riot had now licensed their first record *Rock City* everywhere except in the US where they lived, which made matters very difficult because of the financial pressures it all created. But the band had caught the attention of fans and followers of the NWOBHM and bands of that new genre were making headway and money for several labels and that was the opening opportunity for Riot. We had done a few mini tours in Texas and so we were now approached by a few bands trying to crack that market to help them fill venues with our fans. We were also a badge of credibility for those who were suspect—like Sammy Hagar—and needed to touch base with the heavy metal street."

"With a new Capitol record, Sammy went off to the UK to tour, only to discover his new record was sadly way out of step and he desperately needed street credibility. And who you gonna call for US/UK credibility in the UK back then?—not Ghostbusters but Riot. We had done some touring with Sammy Hagar through Texas earlier and Ed Leffler knew what we could deliver. And all we wanted was a US label, and so Capitol Records stepped in to save Sammy who had made himself into a Peter Frampton, gone to England only to discover it was Iron Maiden and Riot that fans were clamouring for and certainly *not* Frampton."

Indeed Steve is of the opinion that it was his and Ed's little secret that Riot was responsible for virtually half the ticket sales when his charges supported Hagar in front of a crowd of 12,000 at the

Convention Centre in San Antonio. Loeb was also of the opinion that what Sammy needed at this time was more Montrose and less sort of singer-songwritery pop, and that Riot, by support proxy, could swing the pendulum at least in a live environment. Surely, it's a weird concept, but let's re-state it this way: the band one chooses as support is supposed to represent a tacit admiration for that act, and, again, by proxy, perhaps an indication that the headline act might lean that way stylistically next time around—in this case, Sammy might be viewed as making a heavy metal pledge of sorts.

As much as the UK was digging Riot, however, the more discerning and demanding of the UK press, i.e. Geoff, wasn't ready to give the band full marks. Perceptively conjuring a past legendary mismatch, of Riot supporting Hagar, Barton wrote:

"A possible Black Sabbath/Van Halen situation, did I say? In retrospect, maybe that was rather a rash statement. For while Riot were *good* Saturday night at the Odeon, they were far from *great*, and in the end, pose no serious threat to headliner Hagar. Arriving at 7:45 I found the New Yorkers about midway through 'Tokyo Rose,' third number in on their support set. It was an accurate honest-to-the-album rendition, and as such was entertaining enough. But the lack of deadly live distinction meant that the hold of the band's hands on my jugular was so slight, I'd have been in more of a stranglehold if I'd been wearing a polo neck sweater. Which was generally, the performance pattern throughout. Like, 'Overdrive,' 'Road Racin',' and 'White Rock' came across faithful to the last speck of dust in the grooves of 'Rock City'/'Narita,' but the Riot representation of the songs left something to be desired in the stage spectacle department."

"'Course, the group were nervous, the sound was shrill and a troupe of roadies holding cigarette lighters aloft would've probably made for a more effective light show. But Riot should really have overcome all that and projected beyond Halfin-domain. Vocalist Guy Speranza rarely capitalized on his electric blue stretch pant potential; gawky axeman Mark Reale had it in him to be a manic Pete Way-style figure, but tonight he appeared subdued and withdrawn; even drummer Sandy Slavin, usually the most crazed-looking of the bunch, seemed to have suffered a sudden attack of sanity."

"Mr. Speranza shouted, 'Let's make some noise, London,' asked, 'How are you muthas tonight?' (twice), and said, 'It's been too fucking long, man,' but it wasn't until the encore that things really started to move. An extended version of 'Warrior' it was, Riot shone on in all of their glory, for the first time in the show, and sword and sorcery sucker that I am, I loved every minute of it. Disappointing or not, I look forward to Riot's return when they'll be less awed by the event and considerably more impressive, I'm sure."

Ian Ravedale, also writing for *Sounds*, was even less impressed. "Support combo Riot typify your average everyday American boogie band. Very tight, super proficient, 'good' musicianship, and not an ounce of originality between the five of them. At times, I wonder what the saturation level for heavy bands is, as every passing week seems to bring yet another set of riff regurgitators louder, faster, and more tiresome than the one before. Still, judging by the exceptionally enthusiastic reaction from the Hagar fans, there's room aboard the Titanic for Riot. They'll be back too, unfortunately."

"Suddenly there was an offer on the table for a US deal," continues Steve Loeb. "Now, I've really never told the story, but here we are decades later and why not? We had been used a few times before for this same purpose. Capitol did it for Billy Squier, for example, who needed some 'cred' and used a Riot track on one side of a promotional 12 inch. Okay, I got what they were doing but never understood to what extent they would go to make a priority act happen while losing some other act that they were only exploiting. I always believed that greed would speak louder."

"But I was about to learn a very harsh lesson," continues Steve. "Sammy Hagar needed credibility and he knew it. He went off to the UK to promote his new record and discovered he was being seen as dated and soft. He quickly looked to record some harder music back in the States and return to the UK as if he'd never just been there. He wanted Riot as his support act. Capitol would sign Riot and so two Capitol acts would tour England. But Leffler, Sammy's manager, wanted a 'buy-on' from us, so Capitol would advance us X dollars and we would turn around and pay Leffler Y dollars to 'buy on' to the Hagar tour. What choice did we have? So we agreed. The balance of the money went to the Riot back line, our tour expenses and fortunately, since I smelled a rat, a reserve we might need for something. And off we went to England, never dreaming the reserve would save us."

"After a few gigs, it became obvious Capitol was really uninterested in Riot—but the fans certainly weren't. They loved us and we loved them back. We made lots of new friends in the music press and fans who would soon be crucial to our survival. When we finished the tour, Capitol 'released' *Narita*, which looked as though they wanted to lose... but remember that money we kept in reserve? We could be called many things but stupid wasn't one of them. Capitol was deliberately losing us at the radio level. So, we bought a dozen independent radio promo guys who didn't rely on Capitol. Some of them were the best in the game, and soon enough, to Capitol's absolute horror, we had Riot rocking all over radio and Capitol horrified that we dared to challenge them."

To recap, as Steve saw it, the signing of Riot was essentially a ruse to keep Ed Leffler and Sammy Hagar happy, and happening. Most of the advance paid to the band for tour support filtered straight through to Leffler for the buy-on. Out of the tour support and the signing advances, Loeb soon found himself with under $20,000 left, which he then spent on the aforementioned promotion of the ignored and buried *Narita* album, in an attempt to create enough buzz around the band so that Capitol would commit to the band or failing that, that a new label might be interested in this "up and coming" act.

"As I saw it, we had no choice," continues Steve, "and had to force Capitol to renew the contract option and call for another record. I thought then we'd finally get enough respect where they'd at least promote us like any other band. But I would soon discover I was dead wrong, and it would be the fans in the US and the UK and key music journalists that would save us. Not even greed could convince Capitol to believe in us. They hated the band earlier on, and I suppose their egos never let that go despite all the evidence that proved we were more than viable."

"So I embarrassed Capitol into picking up the option. How could they drop a band that was being played by more than half of US radio? They couldn't and I knew it. So they picked up the option and advised us that they wanted a record they could market—well, so did we."

"We were all very excited by what we were making in the studio for the follow-up to *Narita*. We had some of our new friends come over from London to listen and tell us what they thought. Geoff Barton and Ross Halfin from *Sounds*, who were our new best-est friends, came by and they loved what they heard. The Capitol guys kept showing up and they seemed to like it and so we laboured and sweated over this project like no other and finally we came to an end—at least enough to present to the label."

"Capitol had given us half the money of what the contract called for, with the other half payable upon this new record being 'accepted.' Oops, I forgot that in the legal world, every word has its own meaning and 'accepted' was a word I came to understand in a much deeper way. They just wanted to be rid of us and so they waited as long as they legally could and then would advise us that the record was 'commercially unacceptable' and given we no longer had the resources to survive, that would be the end of it as far as they were concerned. Their position was they wouldn't let us go. They wouldn't tell us how to make it 'commercially acceptable' which was what they said it didn't have, and of course there was the legal wording on the contract that gave them an out. So we found ourselves in no man's land. The only way to move things along was create terrible PR for them which I was seriously contemplating."

"Okay, so fair enough, so what's it going to take to get the record back, I wondered? Capitol's response: 'Sue us.' And to me that was a declaration of war. But this was my very favourite area of expertise. I fancied myself a 'political organizer' of sorts and loved being the underdog. It was way more powerful if you could just harness all the power that was there. So the game was on, and although they didn't know it, we did have money. We

                    Martin Popoff

had Madison Ave. money and we were willing to spend it. We contacted our friends in the UK press and flew them over to tell them the story first-hand and play them the record. Like I say, the UK journalist we flew over to do the story about 'the album Capitol wouldn't release,' *Fire Down Under*, was Geoff Barton, along with photographer Ross Halfin. I organized fans in the US and the UK, although on the English side I had help from very loyal and committed people who organized fellow heavy metal bands, some who told EMI (a Capitol label) that they refused to consider signing with them unless the Riot issue was sorted out."

"Can you imagine that? Fans of NWOBHM bands gathered in London at gigs and organized for us, and fans in LA actually spray-painted Capitol executive cars. It was something I will never forget and I am forever grateful for. EMI and Capitol were beside themselves and wanted out of the situation. They continued to ask Riot's manager Fred Heller, where we were getting all the money from to do all of this? Well, we were getting it from Miller Beer, Ponderosa steaks, Sony and Hanes etc., and we were not about to let them take us down because they thought we didn't have the resources."

"It was EMI in England that was not amused the most, I suspect, because as long as this thing was out there, they couldn't dive into the NWOBHM with as much gusto as they wanted to. Remember, they had invested in Iron Maiden and they had a good start in it, so suddenly being tagged with some horrible PR that was all over the front pages of *Sounds* week after week, thanks to Geoff Barton, was making a difference."

"But Capitol in Los Angeles dug in their heels—but the pressure was on them. It seemed like they needed a face-saver and an exit ramp so they could get off this road that went nowhere for anyone. We had an excellent lawyer and a very close friend of the executive VP of Capitol managing the band and meanwhile I could feel we were building a movement based on the fan mail which had grown exponentially. Fans loved a good fight, especially if you could make it as much theirs as it was ours—and I could. I got them all involved. In New York we became the 'war room' for the political fight I would wage to get them free of these guys. And I knew if I could position Riot in a way that everyone identified with it—the underdog and victim—everyone would feel they had a stake and would want to right the wrong. Fans loved it, it grew, and as it grew, within the scene it became a cause célèbre."

We're now at the pivotal point, explains Steve, where Riot transitions form one major label to another...

"Yes. Enter Tom Zutaut from Elektra who Cliff Burnstein called on our behalf. And there was Mike Bone at Arista who was another in our corner. Bone was a radio promo guy, as I remember, who just really appreciated what we were making happen on what was essentially running on fumes. Why did I need to buy ads in major mags when for a fraction of the cost I could buy multiple full pages in pre-Metal Blade Brian Slagel's fanzine? That was where my head was at, and I think the younger A&R and promo guys at labels appreciated this 'new way' I was using of how clearly it would benefit a young heavy metal band like Riot or any of the bands that were now emerging. The less slick the approach the better, at least in the earlier stages."

"We set up a small show in Flatbush, Brooklyn for Tom and Cliff and I think Peter Mensch came along as well," continues Steve. "Tom was willing to sign the band to Elektra and Capitol agreed to work out the particulars, i.e. Elektra's repayment to them for the first half of the advance I forced out of them earlier that year. And with that, finally, after almost a year in limbo, we were free. Free with a really good completed record and thousands of new fans that were hungry to celebrate *their* victory."

"And things began to fall into place. A US tour was set with Sabbath and Blue Öyster Cult, and Billy agreed to let go enough to let Sandy Pearlman co-manage Riot for the length of the tour. Riot would do a few festival dates in the UK, including Port Vale, as well. Promotions were being done to prep Europe for an upcoming tour. But bad things with Billy and myself were growing with the band being in the middle. And there was something else that was about to happen but I never saw any signs of it coming although I should have and it would change everything."

"My pre-signing signing to Elektra was a band called Riot," recalls Tom Zutaut, of those days, "and they had a record called *Fire Down Under* and the song 'Swords and Tequila.' They were very early, and so close to breaking and making it on radio, and they paved the way for Dokken and Mötley Crüe. But for me, reaching back, those first couple of Judas Priest records, *Sad Wings of Destiny* and *Rocka Rolla*... to me, those were seminal records. Those were records that inspired me as a teenager to get out of LA and find great metal bands. If I hadn't listened to Budgie and those early Priest and Sabbath records, I never would have even paid attention to bands like Riot. *Fire Down Under* is a masterpiece, and the album before that, *Narita*, is highly regarded too, but 'Swords and Tequila,' that's the song that should've broke big. But it ended up that the Dokken record was really the first metal record to break big. Riot was really pre-Mötley Crüe's explosion and pre-Quiet Riot's explosion."

As for Mark Reale's summation of the situation, he says, "Actually, what happened was, I guess after we did *Narita* we were on tour with Black Sabbath, and we were on Capitol Records, and I remember going out to lunch. We were on tour; we toured all over the country, and we were with a Capitol representative, and because me and Guy had written a few songs that were very commercial-sounding—very commercial-sounding—these Capital dudes really liked the songs. And they were telling us, 'Would you be into wearing makeup?' This is sort of like the '80s, okay? 'Would you guys be into wearing makeup?' And doing this and that and the other thing. And it's like, we were still floundering about at that point."

"But sure, we had experienced the New Wave of British Heavy Metal," continues Mark. "We went to England in 1980 with Sammy Hagar, on Reading, so we had experienced it. And when we came back from England... as I say, we had signed with Capitol Records at that time, worldwide, and we went from England, we went on the *Black and Blue* tour with Sabbath and Blue Öyster Cult, and it was right in that period that I remember having meetings with the Capitol Records guys. They had these big plans with us, and they had these ideas they wanted us to do stuff that was a little more commercial, and would you guys be okay with wearing some makeup, and that kind of thing. After the tour was when we actually went into rehearsals for what would become *Fire Down Under*, and we had written those commercial songs; we made an attempt."

"So, yes, what wound up happening—to give Steve Loeb credit, okay? Because he was a talented musician and he knew what was going on—what happened was, we came back to New York, and we had some journalists coming over from England, like *Sounds* magazine, people from England, and he was like, 'Look, there's this whole thing that is bubbling under here, this New Wave of British Heavy Metal business,' and he says, 'Look, when these dudes come to the studio, play "Swords and Tequila,"' all these heavy songs. He said don't play that stuff that you were doing for Capitol. He was very aware of what was coming in Europe, and he said listen, don't play any of that commercial junk; play the heavy stuff. So we played 'Swords and Tequila,' and they were very, very impressed. After they left, Steve said to me, you know, to hell with this. To hell with this commercial stuff. Let's just go for it. So we wrote all the stuff on *Fire Down Under*, which just came out of us naturally. So yeah, these guys dug it, and Steve was like, 'Look, man, this is what you've got to record. You know, just be yourselves. Do the heavy stuff.' And so when we did the new record, the Capitol people were expecting these other songs, this commercial stuff, and they get this record with 'Outlaw' and 'Swords and Tequila' and those heavier songs."

"And they said to us," continues Mark, "'We'll release it, but we're not going to promote it.' Flat out, okay? And that's when Steve started this whole thing to get off of Capitol. Now, they had put up the money to make the record. They paid us the money to make the record, so we've got to work this out. So like I say, they said, well, we're not going to really promote this, because we feel it's commercially unacceptable. We were technically still on the label. So it was a whole six-month ordeal of trying to get away from them, because they had paid for the making of the record. So what ended up happening, was like he started this petition thing to get us off the label, which ultimately we did. And we reimbursed them, and we wound up on Elektra. So *Fire Down Under* was actually made when we were on Capitol, but Elektra Records wound up releasing it, and then the rest is history (laughs). It was like, they expected one thing, okay? They expected one thing; you know, they had meetings with us and expected one thing, and they wound up getting something else. So they were like... they were disappointed."

Into the '90s, there would be a CD reissue on which we could hear the poppy direction that the band attempted as an appeasement to Capitol. Explains Mark, "Right, that actually already came out in Europe on this small German label. I don't know what the status of *Fire Down Under* is. The whole rap with that is that Elektra had lost the original masters, and what wound up happening is that Steve remixed it and a lot of people are complaining that the remix doesn't sound as good as the original. And on that version there would be out-takes, and what they basically were was that basically we were on Capitol at the time, and they wanted us to go in a very commercial direction, and we'd made a feeble attempt at that in rehearsals. And we began to record some tracks that Capitol wanted us to do that were pretty much horrendous. And of course midway through the recording we decided, the hell with this.

And we knew what was happening at the time in Europe with the New Wave of British Heavy Metal, and we just said the hell with this, and we went on to record what became *Fire Down Under*. Of course, when Capitol got it, they were really pissed. And that's why we left them. But these out-takes that are on that release are these unfinished songs or whatever you want to call them that were the songs we started to do for Capitol. Supposedly, when we were over for the Wacken festival in August, Brian Slagel from Metal Blade was over there, and I was talking to him about it, and he had said something to me about that they had found the original masters. So they'll use those. But it's probably the same bonus tracks I would imagine."

Further on the momentous *Black and Blue* tour (which the author documents at length in his book *Black Sabbath FAQ*), Mark recalls, "I do remember I was told that because Tony Iommi used to do this guitar solo... so we used to have this thing where Riot did a little guitar solo, which recently I still do, playing Gibson Les Paul mostly, but at the time I had a guitar that had a whammy bar on it, so I used to do this thing in there on the guitar solo. And I was accused of... I think somebody said they saw me on the side of the stage taking notes while Iommi was doing his guitar solo. So there was a little bit of crankiness there. Because you know what it was? I'm like an introvert; I wouldn't go out and party that much, but the other guys and the crew stuff told me, would you like to go up... and I got to go with Dio and be seen with him at the time, and hang with him and stuff. But they were still pretty good about it. And I remember I was in San Antonio... I saw the last tour with Ozzy when Van Halen opened up for them, and they got destroyed. But the gig I saw, they had so much technical trouble with Sabbath on stage. I mean, the PA went off on them, and Van Halen were like primed and ready to kill, definitely. And I think they never got over that, or at least not by this point. Like, there were these younger new bands coming up and kind of doing them in. So this was right on the heels of that. And there was actually another time too—yeah, but that was with Rhett; we played with Kiss on *Lick It Up*, and we were restricted to a certain portion of the stage."

"But yes, with *Black and Blue* there were some weird politics going on in that situation," continues Reale. "Because, when you get out there... I can understand it. I mean, the headliner, it's live or die

                    Martin Popoff

for them, you know what I mean? That's why there was always common practices of cutting the PA system for the opening act. It was always an understood thing. And a lot of times, it's not just the band, it's the management. Because everybody's got their stake—the management, the record company—so there's no way they're going let the opening act sound as good as the headliner."

"There were actually some festivals on that tour," recalls Mark. "I remember there was Seattle, where they had Molly Hatchet on the bill. And I know in Houston it was blistering hot. I remember, because we had just come back from England, and we were all white and pale and sickly (laughs). We were over there for a month, and we wound up right down in Houston, Texas, and it must've been by this time in June or something, and it was 100°, outdoors and just brutally hot. And I remember later on, Molly Hatchet was on one of the shows as well as Alice Cooper—they added other bands. And I remember sitting backstage and the guys in Molly Hatchet, one of the guitar players, telling me that he didn't think they could… because they had a record of kind of looking pretty good. They really deserved to be there, but he was really down on himself. And the one final story I have about them is, '79, we did a brief part of the *Highway to Hell* tour with AC/DC—it was Molly Hatchet, us and AC/DC. Of course we were third on the bill, except when we got to San Antonio, where for some reason we had cult status in San Antonio, and they switched the bill around, and they were really pissed about that. Because they had a gold record at the time. So to make amends, Angus let Dave Hlubek carry him around the crowd on his shoulders."

Continues Steve, citing how all this strife was causing stress on management and general direction as well, "My partnership with Billy was coming to an end and not on amicable terms. I had put almost everything I had financially into Riot, but Billy was from a different world. He liked the touring and the girls and the glitz and even the shmooze. But he spent all his money. I liked making the records and keeping a low profile and having a life. I still do. Like I say, Cliff Burnstein from Q Prime and his partner Peter Mensch came by to talk to us about managing Riot. I was all for it. Billy was not, but that was only the tip of the iceberg. Billy just didn't get it. I always knew we could and should take things just so far, but then like a relay race, hand off the baton. But Billy was not interested whatsoever in ever letting go. I knew we were headed for a bad confrontation. I just didn't know when. It was coming sooner than I thought."

"But back to the music, we arrived at project #3 with a substantial advance," says Steve, meaning from new backers Elektra. "Our goal for this project was with a new promise of label support to finally break internationally. We would try and take the band to six figure sales and at least a 1000 to 1500 seat headline level. The band's configuration was Speranza and Reale, Ventura, Lemming and Slavin. It was as solid as it gets and we had money and time for pre-production. I could review material. We could rehearse it and fine-tune before recording. We had dreamed of this for years."

"And so we began. This was the era when everyone was on the same page. Billy and I now owned the studio so the time constraints were gone. Guy was confident after having performed in England and the *Monsters of Rock* festival where the band played for 50,000 fans. It was a heady time and we all thought the struggle was behind us. We were so wrong."

"We changed engineers again now using a young guy who had been the protégé of our one-time chief engineer, who had now moved on to head up the prestigious tone-meister program at McGill University in Montreal, Prof. Wieslaw Woszczyk. Our new engineer was Rod Hui, who Wieslaw had mentored and nurtured, and it would be Riot amongst a few others who would be the beneficiary of Rod's incredible skills."

"So slowly but surely we began. Some things became immediately obvious. Ricky Ventura's playing and writing approach became a wonderful counterpoint to Mark. And Mark, having not an iota of insecurity, was all for it. Guy was all for experimenting, and with various approaches to recording vocals, he made the vocal sessions a joy and far from the chore they had been. And Kip and Sandy were the solid back beat we hadn't had; they gave us something solid we could finally lean on. We were finally a band in every way, five guys who were a single unit, thinking in a focused way all after the same goal."

"This was a dream album to record," continues Steve. "As I previously said, we finally had money, the entire band was all on the same page, almost all the material was a perfect fit for what was needed, and the overall sound was terrific. Ricky added enormously. He had a whole different approach than Mark. Mark was a technical monster while Ricky was all about just feel. If it felt good and sounded good I don't think Ricky cared about the rest. Mark on the other hand needed to know every little thing about it. They were a perfect pair to play off of each other and thankfully Mark was fine with it. Rick was a bit intimidated by Mark but he was able to deal with his insecurities. Meanwhile for me the combination worked great."

"Sandy and Kip were a dream," adds Steve, moving on to the rhythm section. "Not a single issue. Listen to the track 'Fire Down Under' because that says it all. They were like a machine. And Guy was finally open to the sort of expression it was going to take to get him fully recognized. I recorded Guy laying on his back in the dark, running around with a cordless mic and trying every which way to simulate whatever it was we needed to simulate. Bad guys on the streets or having sex—Guy finally understood what it was all about and was able to do it. Even now, when I hear it, there's things I'd like to do over, but so much of it I love and am really proud and surprised it holds up after all this time."

As far as the guts of the production job, Loeb figures, "Pre-production and having a complete story to tell with song selection is crucial. Making sure your singer can get the story across even if the listener doesn't understand the language. You need to have your singer tell you exactly what the lyric is about. And finally, breaths. Do *not* ever edit out the breaths. Make it all sound close. You *want* it to sound close and intimate."

Riot band and management were as serious about the actual production as they were about pre-production. For this record, they bought a new drum kit, new mics, and installed in the studio a new Trident TSM mixing board. Recorded November and December of 1980 and issued February 9, 1981, *Fire Down Under* proved to be an instant underground classic. Not so much, really, when it came to the album cover, which pictures Mighty Tior in a simple head-and-shoulders shot, albeit with lightning strikes in his eyes. For those who want a clearer picture of what might have been, survey the jacket of April Wine's *The Nature of the Beast*. "Okay, the thing was," says Mark, in conversation with Cliff Dunn, "we had the *Fire Down Under* cover of a beast-like animal playing on stage, and when the record was rejected (by Capitol, also April Wine's US label), we found later that April Wine's cover looked almost exactly like it, only toned down a bit. Probably (April Wine drummer) Jerry Mercer was asked not to reveal too much about the issue. It doesn't matter now. It's all in the past, and we really like the current cover of *Fire Down Under*. It's not really anything but a symbol people could identify with Riot. He's mainly a modified baby seal, but has variations. He's the only true heavy metal beast."

Opening the proceedings—as well as the recording sessions—was "Swords and Tequila," a meat and potatoes mid-metal rocker during the verse, and a soaring metal monster for the new decade come chorus time. "Guy Guy Guy Guy came alive on this," laughs Steve. "I believed every word he said. But of course I had him running with a cordless and laying on the floor with the lights out and being as alive as it gets—and it sounds it." Steve also says that it was his idea to add in the obtuse chord pattern just before the guitar solo, after which Mark does his thing with a Jackson and a whammy bar. As well, the band had decided to take the song right through to completion, through to mix, to provide a guidepost for what they wanted to achieve with the final completed album.

"Well, Guy wrote almost all those lyrics," explains Mark. "'Swords and Tequila,' he was really into that whole Thin Lizzy/Phil Lynott 'band as a gang' routine, the street gang thing, the urban scene. So 'Swords and Tequila' is like that."

Indeed it is, but let us ponder that phrase "swords and tequila" for a moment. Memorable as it is, in the context of the song, it's also somewhat humourous—picture Riot, the band as gang, occasionally making their marauding forays over the bridge into Manhattan. Or, picture the protagonists of the song, who seem to be your basic street gang from New York, a big deal at the time of Riot's big fish in a small pond reign. In either case, the tequila would indeed make it easier to cope with any shyness or insular reticence, but a sword is of an entirely different era—in New York, a sword would only get you laughed at, and arrested. On an additional note, the great Phil Lynott is in fact approximately quoted, when Guy warns of "killers without a cause."

An opener with heft (and no, not a pirate metal song either), "Swords and Tequila" nonetheless holds back, allowing for the speed metal majesty of the album's title track to take centre stage. "Fire Down Under" is this record's "Road Racin'" and Riot is now exploding onto what will be their penultimate record.

"To tell you the truth, this was a learning experience for them," laughs guitarist Rick Ventura, asked how Steve and Billy got such a bright, stadium-rocking sound on the record, as evidenced by an extreme rocker like 'Fire Down Under' drinking down so smooth. "They had no experience with hard rock at all. If you listen to the progression from *Rock City* to *Narita* to *Fire Down Under*, all done in the same studio, it's a band really trying to get a better sound out of each record. We knew what we wanted to sound like, the guitar sounds we wanted. So it was a learning experience for the engineer and them, because they'd never ever recorded a hard rock band. Really no experience in it. If Mark was around, he would tell you the hell we used to go through trying to get a great drum sound, trying to get good guitar sounds. And I thought Mark and I had some excellent guitar sounds. There's that classic Les Paul through Marshall amplifier sound. But the band had a lot to do with the sounds, developing and spending countless hours. We'd actually bring in records and say, "Okay, we have to get a sound like this,' and then work with the engineer and experiment on different mic techniques. We brought in Led Zeppelin records, because they just sounded amazing. I remember saying, 'Listen to the drum sound on this; just listen to the sound of the room.' That was really critical. And so if you listen to each record, they sounded successively better."

Lyrically, "Fire Down Under" echoes the album opener in celebrating the allure of the big city at night, only this time, the mission is essentially street racing. Steve, writing about "Fire Down Under" for the High Vaultage reissue, explains that it was, "called 'the cramper' by the band since it was so fast and so tricky to play. It was also the new bassist Kip Leming's first opportunity to try his hand at writing, which he did so well, it became the title track. When the record finally came out on Elektra, they screwed up the title on the spine of the album cover and printed *Fire Down Below* instead of the real title. I guess they thought it was the Bob Seger song… who knows what they thought!"

Next up was "Feel the Same," which finds the band sticking faithful to the metal direction of the album, but with a subdued and almost doomy feel. Nonetheless, the clouds part for a chorus that is interestingly commercial, making for a cool pastiche of a track.

"I wrote that one, as well as 'No Lies,'" says Rick, who gets sole credit on these two, plus a co-credit on "Don't Bring Me Down" and "Flashbacks. "Mark and Guy were a writing team. It was almost like John Lennon/Paul McCartney and George Harrison threw songs in. I basically wrote my own songs and I would present them to the band, and we would try them out and whatever worked, worked. Writing style, maybe a touch different; I guess that makes it have a unique sound, when each person has his personality in it together as a band, and it works as a band. So we had a lot of diverse songs on that album, from 'Fire Down Under' to 'No Lies'—very, very different. My style is more on the melodic side, influenced by the English bands."

All told, "Feel the Same" is quite the sophisticated track, with Rick's textured music supporting a mysterious, oblique lyric about taking chances through a couple of inscrutable verses, before the song decides to sit on that comfortable chorus through to the end, with Guy throwing in a reference to "Tokyo Rose," just to keep us guessing further.

Asked about the lineup changes for *Fire Down Under*—with drummer Pete Bitelli replaced by Sandy Slavin and bassist Jimmy Iommi replaced by Clifford "Kip" Leming, who joins March of 1980—Rick figures, "Peter was in the band from the very beginning, but there might've been a falling out between Mark and Peter. Mark pretty much had a vision of how he wanted the band to sound and the kind of players he wanted. If you look at the history, Phil Fiet, the original bass player, was replaced by Jimmy Iommi because he had a falling out with Phil too (laughs). Yeah, Phil did a lot of work in the early days and was pretty instrumental in getting them involved with bringing tapes around in the whole Billy and Steve era. But they had a falling out too and Jimmy wound up getting into the band. And when Lou Kouvaris was gone, Jimmy said, 'Oh, you've got to get Rick in the band. He's perfect for the band.' And that's how I fell into it."

Peter says that Phil was in fact fired from the band right in the middle of recording the first album, literally at a recording session. Falling out or not, the official reason given was that he was not a good enough bass player. Peter to this day still seems genuinely baffled by his own ousting, wondering whether it was the influence of Billy and Steve on Mark, or whether fame and recognition had changed Mark for the worse. After all, these guys were friends since grade four. No real explanation was given, with the face-saving party line being that, well, the band has actually broken up, i.e. it's not just you.

In fact, the last time Pete ever saw Guy Speranza was after a concert date they had just played together in Texas, after which the guys were told that the band was going to take a rest. Oddly, the next time Pete ever saw Mark, the second to last time, was also in Texas—San Antonio to be exact—only it was an REO Speedwagon that he and his girlfriend went to, knowing that Mark was attending as well. Mark, after emerging from backstage had told Pete he was trying to put something together, but if it doesn't work out, maybe he and Pete could join forces again. The very last time Pete had seen Mark was also in Texas, where Bitelli had been playing in a band called Stryker. The two spoke before Pete's band went on, but somewhere along the way Mark had left and that was it.

"Sandy Slavin was just an amazing drummer, and I think Mark just liked his style," continues Rick, concerning Pete's replacement. "And then, yes, Kip replaced Jimmy (laughs). Jimmy was frustrated. You've got to realize, a lot of it has to do with frustration with management. I should say that from the very beginning. Everybody was frustrated, and Jimmy was too—he didn't trust them, Billy and Steve. There was always the issue of the band getting paid. They basically controlled the band, and we really felt… I think Mark and Guy had signed everything to them. Publishing… everything was pretty much turned over. And it always seemed that Mark and Guy were obligated to Billy and Steve. And band members, at times, felt, okay, it's Mark and Guy and Billy and Steve, and the rest, you know, we weren't really the band."

Sandy had been a drummer since his teen years, becoming an instant convert to rock 'n' roll when at age ten, he saw the Beatles. Picking up the sticks at age 15, Ringo was his first hero and then local legend Carmine Appice as well as Ian Paice and John Bonham. A breakthrough came when he got to study with Dave Brubeck drummer Joe Morello at age 18, an apprenticeship that affects his style to this day. His initiation into Riot would have him drumming the support slot to a red-hot AC/DC out promoting *Highway to Hell*. Notes Steve, "Sandy was a serious musician; a very serious guy. Yeah, he was the odd exception to the usual drummer rule in that he was stable, conventional and serious with a very healthy attitude. I've nothing but good things to say about Sandy."

"Things really started to change during *Fire Down Under*," continues Rick. "where the band really came into its own. Where that lineup became the classics Riot lineup. That's where the band really started to break and did extensive touring. Jimmy… great bass player, so there really wasn't an issue with that. But he was getting frustrated at not getting paid and not being able to survive, and he didn't see any change coming. And when Sandy came in, Sandy played with Kip, and Kip was brought in. I mean, it just fell into place. Everybody just had great attitude and were great players—it just felt right. That particular lineup… it was a period there where we were doing a lot of touring with top acts. We toured with AC/DC, Black Sabbath, Rainbow, Sammy Hagar, Judas Priest. That lineup, with the change in players, was prepared for that transition to breaking big."

Back to *Fire Down Under*, by track four we are onto yet another metal style represented with arena-aspiring bravado. Mark cites "Outlaw" as his favourite track of the entire Guy Speranza era. "Outlaw" is also a Riot fan favourite, and indeed, the author's band Torque, circa 1984, played the song in our set, along with *Narita*'s

                                    Martin Popoff

"Road Racin'." "'Outlaw' was a Mark tune," says Rick. "He was fascinated with the wild West. The first time we went to Texas, he was just so in love with it. You can tell in the songs that he wanted to be there, and he just loved the whole vibe so much, he eventually moved there."

"I came up with 'Outlaw' when we were in England on tour with Sammy Hagar," recalls Mark, "and I had a Pignose amp in the hotel somewhere, and I remember coming up with that riff at the beginning, at that point in time. And I was always into western movies a lot—that whole scene—although Guy did write the lyrics. That was my influence; I was always into the old West. And that Mexican chatter in there...

that was actually Steve Loeb's idea. He felt that, what they did was, there was this guy that Steve knows, he was a Puerto Rican percussion player, and he threw him in there, just talking Spanish in the fade, in the vamp-out. I don't know what he's talking about (laughs). Actually, our new bass player, he's from Texas—maybe he can translate it for me."

Back in '81, Reale understandably had a clearer recollection of what went down, telling Cliff Dunn, "Some of the things on *Fire Down Under* were the producers' ideas. Take for instance Antonio, talking at the end of 'Outlaw.' After recording the song, we got him drunk, told him what to say and recorded it, later mixing it in over the guitar solo. He's mainly talking about getting wasted, losing a bunch of gold and not caring about it."

Indeed that's a taste of what the English lyric is about as well, Guy relating the tale of a bank robber "crazed on tequila," on the run, and then somehow wrapped up with a woman who's going to do him wrong, o'er which our hunted outlaw muses about life through the analogy of roulette.

Elektra issued "Outlaw" as an edited single (both in the US and the UK but with different picture sleeves), backed with a live version of "Rock City," captured at the Hammersmith Odeon in London. Was the single instrumental in sending the album to a #99 placement on the *Billboard* charts? Probably a little but not much—Riot was proving itself very much a band to experience through the majesty of the full album. And like the first Montrose record, any accolade that *Fire Down Under* received was purely on hard-fought merit.

Closing side one is a track credited to the whole band, "Don't Bring Me Down" being an energetic and melodic number along the lines of top shelf Saxon. Notes Rick, asked if any of these songs were holdovers from the *Narita* days, "Not with *Fire Down Under*, no. Sometimes songs are left over that are never done, but on that album, it was just fresh, because it was a new lineup. I started contributing and co-writing on *Narita*, but as I say, here I had songs that I wrote by myself. And there is some co-writing there too. 'Don't Bring Me Down'—that's my riff; I basically wrote the music and everybody then contributed lyrically."

Recalls Mark, "'Don't Bring Me Down' is the one with the crazy lyrics. I don't know, we were cracking up. Rick wrote the music, but I don't know who's responsible for the lyrics. I think Sandy Slavin might've had a little bit of thought in that; he was a real cut-up. I remember we were cracking up coming up with these lyrics because it didn't make any sense. I don't know if they're listed on the CD, but yeah, it was just like ridiculous. I just remember gorilla dump or whatever they are in there. Yeah, that one I remember in particular."

Indeed, if the outlaw from the previous tale has trouble, this guy's dealing with a complete psycho, a gal who steals his cigarettes and money, kills the dog and cat, and even manages to somehow borrow the car, bend the tailpipe and lose the engine, but leave a Springsteen 8-track playing while he figures out what hit him.

Side two of the original *Fire Down Under* vinyl opens with what is perhaps the strongest track on an American metal classic. "Don't Hold Back" once again demonstrates this band's heroic and accessible stadium metal sound, of which Steve Loeb vehemently agrees: "Suffice to say, if I had to choose a single track that represented what I thought was the epitome of the band at that point in time, 1981, it would be 'Don't Hold Back.' The band on this was the band in every way. This is what I saw Riot as being. There isn't a weak link in the track. It was so hopeful sounding and that was the vibe on the project—confident and hopeful. This was recorded early on in the project and set the tone. It was full of energy, very, very expressive vocals by Guy, and Mark and Rick were complimenting each other perfectly. And it's this track that I can listen to over and over and never tire of. It certainly holds up and had things gone seamlessly, the band should have built from right here, from this foundation. This was a classic Riot track that I'd point at to describe them for that era and what I'd hope would have continued."

Guy has to spit out a lot of lyrics in this one and he executes with passion, promising the ocean, the sun, a rainbow, a crystal ship as well as a "diamond sky of love" to the woman he wants to whisk away from the soul-crushing city.

Notes Steve in the High Vaultage reissue, "I also remember the worst sore throat I ever had from singing in the group chorus. I'm the one singing with the very hoarse voice. I love the feel on this song, its hopefulness, boldness and strength. I love the lyric, and when Guy says, 'Let it shine, don't you remember,' he's referring to Riot's 'Warrior' chorus. I still get a chill up my spine whenever I hear that part."

"Altar of the King" is another strapping heavy metal number, its mellow intro and gothic, epic tones creating a mood that fit well with the band's hard rock brethren toiling away as part of the NWOBHM. "For some reason this brought me be back to 'Overdrive,' but not really," reflects Steve. "Guy was really into his own thing here and his references to past songs, like 'Tokyo Rose' on 'Feel the Same' was wonderful, with Mark just getting better. I still get chills listening to this track."

"'Altar of the King,' bears a fair bit of Rainbow influence," figures Rick. "I know Mark was into Ritchie Blackmore and so was I. At the same time, bands you tour with are an influence— you listen to them every night—and we toured with Rainbow. Great Guy lyric. His method, he would write by himself, yeah. I remember there were times that we got together and tried to get some ideas happening but it was strange. It was Mark and him that had the writing partnership. He would write lyrics on his own, but he played some guitar too, so he would have some riffs and chord structure along with his lyrics, and then bring that to Mark, and Mark would then refine it or come up with his own riffs to the song."

Says Mark, "'Altar of the King'... I mean, I would usually come up with the music and he would write the lyrics for what I had. We always thought in terms of live, because I always thought we were best live. So I was thinking of grooves and patterns that would work best in a live situation, and 'Altar of the King' had that good shuffle thing going. But in general, I don't think any of those songs had been around much previously. A lot of them were written while we were on tour, or even after we came back. It was done pretty much around the time. Because like I said, we were developing. Those first three albums, you know, you'll notice, especially on the first one, sometimes it sounds like it's power pop, sometime it sounds like it's heavy rock. We were all over the place. But *Fire Down Under* was where we real did it 'all in;' so most of the material was written around the time. There was a lot more thought behind that one. It was when we started to become a lot more aware of what was going on, a little bit more structured."

Most definitely Guy's lyric reads like Rainbow 101, but it's also amusing to see tequila used again in "Outlaw," and then a sword reappearing here, one that emits lightning, a tie-in to the front cover art of the album, with Mighty Tior in essence reflecting the scene of this song in his eyes.

Rick's own "No Lies" is next, and as promised, it's in quite a bit of a different style than the core Riot identity, being very melodic, tribal of beat, and almost new wave of verse, even if the chorus points to a Bad Company or southern rock vibe. Notes Steve, "Rick was writing primarily these very dreamy songs that with the right vocal felt like they were floating. He also had difficulty explaining what he was hearing so things I suspect often took on their own life and Rick just went with it. As for Kip, I don't actually remember what Kip wrote but I can't imagine it was something beyond bass riffing. He didn't play anything except bass."

"He was a talented songwriter, really," reflects Mark, asked about his partner-in-Gibson-crime Rick Ventura. "The unfortunate thing was for him though at the time, was that we had... we used to play a lot then. I mean, we'd go on tour and our whole thing was the high energy thing on stage. That was the thing that really put us over. We were a band that had the energy of a punk band. Although we had melody and had a guy who could sing. So it was like, we really needed to have that energy, and Rick was more like into the... not the laid-back, but more... he was really into Zeppelin. He was into lighter stuff and more medium tempo, groove-orientated stuff. But he wrote some great songs. Unfortunately, we never played that many of them live, because we wanted to keep the pacing up in the live show."

"It's like he had his own little thing going," continues Mark, "and he would come in with songs. He still actually... we almost got together. I hadn't seen him in years, but this mutual friend, a guy I hadn't run into for 20 years, turned out living near me, by accident, and they had a little reunion, while we were rehearsing. Rick, I'm probably going to meet up with one of these days..."

Rick's "No Lies" lyric is as emotionally tense but also as opaque as his previous missive on the album, here a range of motivations colliding with each other until the listener—or reader—needs to accept the ambiguity of it all.

As for the splitting of the guitar duties with Rick, Mark says, "I tried to give him a solo; like I didn't want to make him a rhythm guitarist. Even though in those days, we didn't do the guitar army or anything much, but we switched back and forth and tried to split it up so he was getting a good share of the solos on stage. He'd obviously do the ones that he wrote. On the record, 'Swords and Tequila' was me, pretty much all me. 'Fire Down Under''s me, 'Feel the Same,' I think it's Rick for the first solo, and I think there's a later solo the might be him, in 'Feel the Same.' 'Outlaw''s me. 'Don't Bring Me Down,' that's a Rick tune, so that's probably Rick. 'Don't Hold Back' is me, 'Altar of the King' is me, 'No Lies' is Rick. 'Run for Your Life' is probably me and the last track is a collage."

"In those days we didn't plan anything," laughs Mark, on the scheduling of the solos. "In those days, I mean, we'd write the song and we'd go in there, but most of the solos, 95% were just like roll the tape and we played—it was no plan. Which I think worked. I've always been a fan of that, because I think the things you do off-the-cuff, you never do—there's a certain magic to it that you capture.

If you're having an off day, it's not too cool, but no, I don't think we planned that much. It was like, here's a solo, play, and there's no need to do it again. I'd start to get a little theme in my head. But in the late '80s, a lot of that was written out, because me and Mike, the then guitar player, we had a lot of the harmonies going on. But then I tried to move back towards the improv thing more."

Back to the black wax, after "No Lies," a stylistic correction is in order, and so the band goes for a razor-sharp proto-thrasher called "Run for Your Life," guitar tone for miles, Speranza shouting out his threatening exhortations at the far reach of his range. Nonetheless, Steve considers this track as well as "Don't Bring Me Down" essentially as filler, although, really, "Run for Your Life" sports quite an impressive and voluminous lyric, with Guy warning about the dangers of drug addiction and its toxic effect on honesty in relationships.

"This was a free-for-all track," recalls Steve. "I think we were just about finished with the album when we cut this one. There's a feeling here like it's finally over and everything turned out great, and here you go, here's one for nothing. Lots of great guitar playing from both Reale and Ventura."

One would think that leaning more toward filler is a spot of sound collage called "Flashbacks," which closes the record. "'Flashbacks' wasn't really a song," notes Rick, "but just something pieced together in the studio. It was a fun, creative period. Everybody was writing, there were a lot of ideas and riffs, and the band had the right energy and the right attitude."

Explains Steve, "I wanted to have that on the record to benchmark some of what we'd been through to get where we finally arrived. On that one track I put the introduction of Riot on the stage in Painesville, Ohio, a date that would catch the attention of Cleveland's WMMS radio which in turn caught the attention of San Antonio's Joe Anthony at KISS Radio and the beginning of the band's Texas success that led to so much more. Then I put the intro of the band by UK *Sounds* and the Heavy Metal Soundhouse head honcho and one of those at the forefront of the NWOBHM movement, Neal Kay, who introduces the band to the audience at London's Hammersmith Odeon. And finally there's the Riot chant coming from 50,000 fans at the *Monsters of Rock* festival.

We'd come a long way and we were now making the record we all knew would take us the rest of the way. Or so we hoped."

"That was Steve's idea," says Mark, asked about the back cover dedication of "Flashbacks" to Neil (sic) Kay. "It was dedicated because Neal was the major, major supporter, not only of us, but of that whole New Wave of British Heavy Metal scene that was happening. We went over there and Neal was always around, and he was actually at the shows and he was DJing. You know, they had the air guitar thing that was big there. You could go to these clubs, and they had this massive PA system and he would blast the music and these kids would do air guitar. In fact, one memory just came to mind again: they took us out to one of these clubs, and we had to judge an air guitar contest while we were there. I remember Guy got right down there with them, and I give him credit for that. So Neal was one of the main protagonists of that whole thing; he was very instrumental in it."

"Flashbacks" didn't go down too good with one member of the Canadian press, Chris Churchill, who supported his 6/10 review by writing, "Their bio calls *Fire Down Under* 'an uncompromising expression of loud, fast and lusty heavy metal,' which is a pretty accurate assessment of this, Riot's third album. This New York quintet churns out electrifying mind blasters like, 'No Lies,' 'Feel the Same' and 'Run for Your Life,' but also intersperse enough tempo changes so that the band isn't going flat-out all of the time. Perhaps that is why *Fire Down Under* isn't as tedious as most music to bang heads by. I might have even awarded it a 7 except the last cut, 'Flashbacks,' is one of the most pretentious exhibitions of self-indulgence recently put on wax."

No surprise that Brian Slagel, writing in his legendary 'zine, *The New Heavy Metal Revue*, adeptly understood the magic of Riot—years later, nearing the end of the second decade of his venerable label Metal Blade, he would become a substantial issuer of Riot product.

"After what Riot went through to put out this album, you might figure that it was worth the struggle," wrote the aspiring metal journalist. "Well, Riot should be very proud of themselves; they have put out an album of awesome magnitude. For sheer power, this album rates 100% rock. Crisp production and extremely tight playing by the band shine through. The album's ferocious content is hard to be equaled. After one listening, you will be impressed, continued listenings will cause you to become a fan, and intense listening may cause your stereo to blow a fuse. Be sure to pick this one up!"

Summed up Mark, speaking with Patrick Prince of *Powerline*, "*Fire Down Under*, because it basically put us on the map, was so influential on a lot of musicians, and 'Swords and Tequila' was such a big song which is still played on radio and we continue to play it live. We actually didn't know that *Fire Down Under* would become so iconic and influential at the time. We just gathered some great ideas and put them together like we did with *Rock City* and *Narita*. We added a new rhythm section in Kip Leming and Sandy Slavin and the record ended up coming out heavy for that time period standard. The production of that record was very good for that time as well. It was one of those magical moments where everything was clicking musically. The songs, the sound... it definitely put us on the map, just as the *Thundersteel* response was later on in our career."

As mentioned, the German High Vaultage reissue of *Fire Down Under* include five tracks on which Riot was scratching its collective head trying to sound a little more commercial. "Misty Morning Rain," is a melodic, slightly boogie-rocking number with sweet backing vocals, on which Guy pines in the rain for a lost lover. "You're All I Needed Tonight" is a punchy party rocker celebrating a rote bar room seduction, and come chorus time, it's hard not to be reminded of the similarly titled smash hit by The Cars. "One Step Closer" is a quality number, combining melodic hard rock with southern rock picking—spirited Blackfoot, essentially—but awkwardly brief at 2:13. "Hot Life" is nothing more than a short riff idea, and then finally, "Struck By Lightning" is a substandard and thumpy throwback to the type of song the band might have written in the mid-'70s and then discarded. Still, one can hear an appreciable amount of work and talent poured into this full side of music, and discussed against the list of bands going shockingly commercial at the time—Starz, Moxy, Derringer, Blue Öyster Cult, Teaze, Rainbow—Riot barely capitulates.

Back in the world of working it, Riot's stand at *Monsters of Rock* was a definite trip, a career highlight, says Rick. "That was mind-boggling, because that was playing for a sea of people. It was just the ultimate experience. Probably one of the highlights of playing with Riot, actually, was doing that festival because the fans were just so enthusiastic. I don't think anything topped that. But it was a lot of political maneuvering and negotiating by managers just to get us in there. I grew up on and was fascinated by British bands, so for me it was like going to heaven. Unbelievable experience. The fans just absolutely loved the band. That's all I can say. They were so into it and they just lived it."

"It was definitely an honour to be asked to be a part of history, being one of the very first metal festivals!" mused Mark, speaking with Patrick Prince. "Along with hard rockin' bands like Rainbow, Scorpions, Priest, April Wine and thousands strong, we were paving the way for bigger things to come in the metal community. We found that Europe really embraced the band and our sound and also keep in mind we were the only American band on this bill (ed. correction: bottom undercard band, Touch, significantly managed by Rainbow's management, Bill Payne, was from New York). The soundtrack is legendary as well and our song 'Road Racin'' appearing on it was an honour. A lot of bands were up-and-coming at the time. I think Riot was one of the handful of bands that were the USA's answer to the NWOBHM at that time period. We basically helped create the US version. I think we helped pave the way and acceptance for this type of music."

This was in fact the inaugural of many *Monsters of Rock*, taking place August 16th, 1980 (making it essentially a *Narita*-era gig), with Riot and Touch playing baby band roles in support of Rainbow, Judas Priest, Scorpions, April Wine and Saxon, the latter of which stole the show—and then later hired Riot on as a support act. Riot in fact had been in the midst of the monolithic *Black and Blue* tour with Black Sabbath and Blue Öyster Cult, and flew to England for the weekend and then back again to the states to resume their support duty to the sparring rock giants. Riot was considered good but not great at Donington, but to be fair, the guys were somewhat harried and spooked by arguments between management and the label, arguments which nearly got them scotched from the gig. Still, UK fans were surprised at how the possessor of that legendary power metal voice could be somewhat reticent in his role as front man.

Back in '81, Cliff Dunn had asked Kip Leming about the experience, and why UK punters seemed to dig Riot. "I think Riot has always had that little bit of English influence in the sense that we play a style very similar," answered Leming. "Our style is a lot like the feeling of British metal in the way that it is not prepared, but rather spontaneous when we are in concert. The English like their metal hard and heavy without the feeling that they're being put on. Some bands put on a show with all the lights, explosions and choreographed movements, and that really turns the British off because they feel they're being dazzled by the show rather than the music."

"Well, it was my first festival, and it was the first *Monsters of Rock* festival, yes," affirms Mark. "That was a trip. I met Bobby Rondinelli for the first time, backstage, because Richie was grooming him to replace Cozy, who was leaving after that. For some reason, I remember playing *Fire Down Under* songs on stage. I know it was in the summertime, so I don't know if the record was out. But then again, we did Port Vale the next year (ed. August 1, 1981, with Motörhead, Ozzy Osbourne, Mahogany Rush, Triumph and Vardis), and maybe I'm confusing them. I just remember a huge festival in England playing those songs."

At scorching hot Port Vale Football Stadium, Stoke-on-Trent (for this event known as *Heavy Metal Holocaust*), Riot's set list consisted of "Swords and Tequila," "Fire Down Under," "Overdrive," "Altar of the King," "Hot for Love," "Outlaw" and "Rock City." Riot played after an unknown Vardis and before an underwhelming Triumph (by most accounts, Frank Marino stole the show). Port Vale is remembered as the festival for which Sabbath had canceled, making way for a ready an' willing Ozzy and his fledging band, who took the occasion to one-up Tony's new collaboration with Ronnie James Dio.

"I would have to say everybody was great," continues Rick, asked about the long list of big bands Riot supported during their run. "It was a great period. We played with Rush and I actually remember Sandy filling in for Neil Peart during a sound check (laughs), because Neil wasn't there yet. And I remember Geddy checking us out when we opened for them at the Nassau Coliseum. A few times, actually, he would listen to us at sound check, and I'd think, wow, that's Geddy out there listening to us—interesting. Got to hang out with the guys in Black Sabbath. We played with Ozzy. I mean, it was almost like a big family, very good memories. I can't say anybody really treated us bad. Maybe some managers of other bands had felt threatened (laughs). There's always that. Yeah, there were some stuff with some of the managers of some of bands, political stuff."

Adds Steve on the subject of the road, "Scorps were cool, AC/DC were drinking already at breakfast, and Blackmore made everyone clear the corridors when he was on the way to the stage. The coolest band was by far Rush—not a single issue. You want full sound and lights? You got it. That did not go down with anyone else. Sammy Hagar's guy Ed Leffler—but I'm not sure it was Ed or Capitol who was behind that—shit went down in England that was pretty lame with sound and lights, which was always a sign that the band or manager was suffering from insecurity. Triumph had that issue as well. But we never had any money to do much in the way of staging anyway. Sandy Pearlman tried and failed to steal the band from us. But there again it may not have been Sandy but his tour manager who went for it."

"Oh, Sandy Pearlman, there you go!" laughs Mark. "Yeah, Boston Gardens; like I said before, I'm backstage at Boston Gardens, and he's like, 'I think you guys are cool; I would like to handle you guys, but I can't deal with these two crazy dudes calling me at four o'clock in the morning.' That's what I remember about him. And Cliff Burnstein, twice... I mean, all these people, once we'd gotten to that point, we were going to England, we had been to England twice by 1981—first time with Sammy Hagar, second time with Saxon—and then we were fixing to go back there to do a headlining tour, and then Guy quit the band. But we had all that vibe going on, and that was it, and these dudes squelched everything. Whenever anybody would think of Riot, they wouldn't think of us, they would think of these two crazy guys, Steve and Billy (laughs). And they were obsessed with the band, because they were worried about the fact that the more popular we got, if we let anybody get in there, if we let anybody else get in there, they would get bumped out of the picture as producers. Somebody would get like Tom Allom to produce us or something. But they were worried about that whole thing, so what wound up happening, being obsessive like that, you got this whole situation. But in spite of that situation, any of the music we made that got out, we managed to acquire, if you want to call it, a cult following or whatever, but a really strong fan base that is with us to this day."

"Our business arrangements were very dodgy at best," sighs Mark, remembering the chaos that was Riot at its frenzied peak. "I mean Steve... he's a very talented guy, producer and musician, and apparently his heart might've been in the right place. But like I say there was always this fit of paranoia that the band's going to get stolen from them. And as a result, we never brought the right people in that we needed to bring in, especially, when we came back from England. I remember the *Fire Down Under* period... we were peaking, and all these heavyweight people were approaching us. Burnstein, Q Prime management, had said they wanted Riot. But it was never to be, because of the contracts we had, and how we were kind of under wraps, so to speak. So as far as what is sold to this day, to be honest with you, I'm only realizing now and over the last ten years, because we've actually done quite a bit of touring, from like '96 up until about 2000, we've gone to Europe, Japan and stuff, that I realized... I mean, I remember getting on stage in '96 and playing songs from *Fire Down Under* and playing outdoor things and things and hearing just this thunderous applause. It was only then that I started to realize how popular that record was. So God only knows how much it sold (laughs)."

As for touring the record, Mark says, "I think we went out in the states with Frank Marino and Mahogany Rush and Triumph. We went to England with Saxon, who were great, great guys, and then we were supposed to go into Europe on that tour and hook up with Saxon and Ozzy Osbourne. And what happened was, we had been hooked up with this booking agency, saying could you book us, because in this case we were always the third band on a bill. And we said, we gotta get the second spot. And they can tell you that to break into the Top 100 charts, you have to get in the album charts. So Steve hired some independent promo people and we actually did break the Top 100. So while we were on tour with Saxon, they offered us the Rush *Moving Pictures* tour in the states, and it was like a dream come true. So we came back from the English tour, and we hooked up... I think we did two quick weeks with the reunited Grand Funk Railroad, and then we hooked up with Rush which was amazing, the best. It was just us and Rush, and every night, I think we played for almost an hour in sold-out arenas. Ironically, that was the tour that Guy told me he was leaving, at the height of... in spite of all the bad business arrangements that we had, things that were holding us down, even though we were at the pinnacle."

"And I loved that lineup, " reflects Mark. "It was a real shot of enthusiasm and energy. Sandy was great. I mean, aside from being a really great drummer, he really had a passion for it. He was also the comic relief. And I just got off the phone with a guy by the name of Larry who'd been with Sandy before Sandy joined Riot, and these two guys, it was like Abbott and Costello. I remember one of the first times we were with them, you were dying laughing for a half hour straight. So they were great. Kip was great; he was like a real down-to-earth guy, no ego, really easy to get along with, and as a band at that time, it was unlike most, where there is always strife and fighting. It was a pretty cool period."

Rick Ventura remembers the UK as fertile territory for Riot, with the band selling out 16 of their 18 shows there, and *Sounds'* Phillip Bell turning in an expectedly rave review, writing, Riot "blasts the majority of the current British competition to the grave like six slugs from a magnum 44." But the aforementioned political mess with Capitol seemed to follow the band overseas where it intensified. Concerning the campaign to get the band properly represented in the shops over there, Ventura says, "Iron Maiden was part of that. You know, a lot of the early heavy metal bands in England, they heard of us, and they just liked the band. Even Metallica—I remember Lars was a big Riot fan."

Indeed the guys in Maiden were supportive, but also championing the band were Praying Mantis, Motörhead and Krokus, with Ronnie Montrose's name on the petition getting played up at the time as well. As for Pete Bitelli, his fondest memory of someone who was a fan of the band is none other than fellow Brooklynite Peter Criss, who at the peak of Kiss mania, still made time to come see Riot practice and disseminate career advice and generally socialize with the boys.

"Basically, what it was down to, Steve and Billy were very demanding," sighs Rick, in closing. "And they wouldn't let go. Riot was their baby, and they would not let go. So we were on Capitol, and then Capitol didn't want anything to do with the band due to Billy and Steve. They basically turned off many record companies, because they were very demanding, and they basically had the rights to everything. And I remember speaking with some big name people at the time of *Fire Down Under*, right at the time we were hoping to really break big. I remember talking to Cliff Burnstein about the band, and I remember he was saying just to get away from those guys (laughs). And when we were on Elektra for a while, I had a friend who knew the head of Elektra, and I remember meeting with him once. And it was the same story, talking about how Billy and Steve were controlling. It came to a point where I don't think anybody wants to touch us anymore."

Restless Breed – "Guy really did become an exterminator."

"Let's go back and finish up what happened with *Fire Down Under*," regales Steve, "which was the benchmark where everything fell into—and then out of—place..."

"As I was saying, it was all going great guns," explains Loeb. "We had now done the *Black and Blue* tour, and earlier on we did the Texas leg of AC/DC's *Highway to Hell* tour, where I was able to watch Bon Scott close up every night, who I personally loved. I had been a fan of that band and Scott long before that record. We did touring with Kiss and Sammy Hagar etc. Elektra released "Outlaw" and the album entered the *Billboard* charts and we scored with the support slot on the US Rush tour. And where we could,

we'd do a local club gig *after* we opened for Rush earlier in the
evening. I don't think you could do that with an older band, but
the Riot guys were okay with it. As long as they had the tour bus
to crash in, they did as many of these local gigs as they could. It
was retail politics at the grass roots, which I love. We were really
making progress…"

"And then the shit hit the fan. I got a call from the road from a
few of the guys. Apparently Guy wanted to quit. I was stunned.
Everything was happening and he wanted to quit now?! Yes, he
wanted to get married and quit. Now I had no problem with any
it, but why couldn't he do both? Because he also found God and
he didn't think God would think very much about the heavy
metal lifestyle."

"They had a date coming in New Jersey and I figured I'd go
speak to Guy and see what if anything could change his mind. At
the Brendon Byrne arena that night, I got a glimpse of why
he probably had come to his decision as easily as he had. With
Rush they were doing 15 to 17,000 seaters. I took my seat in the
upper deck and what I saw out there sitting in the audience
bothered me. When Guy would work with this large a crowd and
they responded to him, he didn't feed off the response—he ran
from it."

"I wondered how many records we weren't selling, and if fans saw
it as I did," continues Loeb. "This was 'negative promotion,' and
the worst thing that could ever happen is playing the large venues
and exposing so many potential fans to it. So now there were two
reasons to get them off the road. Guy was on the verge of quitting,
and their shows were probably hurting them anyway, and so a
story was invented for Rush. We gave them a few weeks notice to
be able to replace us, and a few weeks later pulled them back to
NY. And that was the end of all touring behind *Fire Down Under*."

"I don't remember the final chart position of the single or the LP. I
just remember it was the beginning and the end, at least for many
years until *Thundersteel* brought them some new life. Sure there
were some more records in between, but that moment passed. But
Fire Down Under was the big seller—over 200,000—even if later
the CBS stuff sold well, given that it had all these international
markets, especially Japan, that they sold in; too bad that deal with

CBS Associated was so bad, the royalty in all foreign markets was fractions of fractions."

"Anyway, I had lunch with Guy," continues Loeb, "to see if I could talk him out of it but I was of two minds about it. This sort of band is not Steely Dan and *has* to tour. That was going to be a problem if the band had to do those venues that were over 5,000 seats and up to the massive festivals which they could do. Maybe because Guy never felt intimate with a festival crowd, he just was not happy about the 5,000 and up seaters. So there were limitations if we would continue, but no telling if he would want out of that too. But it was all moot since he wanted out period. He wanted to marry, make a family, and leave this all behind. Later, much to my complete surprise, Mark told me that Guy never really wanted to do it for real. And so there we were, finally cracking through only to be blown back."

"As many would later describe it, Guy really did become an exterminator in NYC and then years later relocated to Florida. And we think the pancreatic cancer that eventually killed him was from the chemicals he had to use in that work. As for whether our paths ever crossed again, he was working one day across the street from the studio at the bar there, exterminating, and stopped in. We talked about him maybe doing something with Mark, with no further obligations, just a last hurrah and he seemed genuinely interested. But decided not to go there again. I respected that. I had no choice in the matter. He had a few kids and remained married to his wife Gina until he died."

Old industry champion Tom Zutaut, instrumental in getting the band its Elektra deal, says, "I rode on their tour bus for a couple of weeks with them when they were opening for Triumph. There's like a pure '80s metal band. And I remember being in Texas and Riot were opening up for Triumph, and it was just insane. Texas went absolutely berserk. But it turned out that Guy Speranza just couldn't handle the pressure of being on a bus and touring and being away from home, and he literally quit the band and got a job as a bank teller at a bank. He couldn't take the instability of the rock 'n' roll touring lifestyle."

"Well, he just freaked out," says Mark. "He just quit the business. He basically got married, and the girl that he married, which oddly enough was the sister of the bass player, Jimmy Iommi, she did not like him being in the business. It was just the standard stupid story. She didn't like him doing the whole thing. In fact I had met with Guy about four years ago for the first time in about 11 years, and we actually started writing together again. He was going through a trial separation and wanted to make a record, possibly record again, so we got together to write some stuff and of course he reconciled with his wife, and I think he's living in Florida now. He became an exterminator. There's been a lot of rumours about that, but it's true. He'd been doing that ever since. So in 1981 or '82 whenever it was, he just got out of the business."

"Guy left out of frustration," adds Rick. "I think he realized, okay, here we are with *Fire Down Under*, he's been in the band for so many years, is the band really going to break? Then there's Billy and Steve having issues with record companies. I think he just had enough of that. He felt it wasn't going to happen. He also wanted to settle down a bit, so it's the combination of both. That was a major change for the band. That was like, oh boy, the sound of the band... nobody sounded like Guy. That's what made the sound of Riot. So that was a big issue."

Lou Kouvaris, guitarist for the band on *Rock City* only, had kept in touch. "After a few years, I had gone down to Brooklyn, and I sat down with Jimmy and with Guy, in Brooklyn. We went with my girlfriend, and we hung out a little bit and exchanged some stories. We talked about old times but I also asked what happened with my dismissal, and they said we really don't know what happened. We don't know. They just wanted you out of the band. It wasn't us. It was the producers and stuff like that. We had sat down and we talked about things that were going on. They were very, very unhappy. Jimmy and Guy were very unhappy."

Indeed they were, because as Pete Bitelli frames it, both of them wound up in Florida essentially to escape the clutches of Riot's management, to remove themselves physically from the orbit of the band, which had established a New York/Texas corridor but not psychological ties straight south.

"This was '82 or so," continues Kouvaris. "I think that Guy was just out of the band. Because he was married to Jimmy's sister, and she didn't really like what was going on. They weren't making

          Martin Popoff

any money. They were making no money. I mean, I got paid for the gigs, but it was nominal; it was crazy. But they were very, very unhappy with the direction. I had a talk with Jimmy, and if you talk to him about Riot, he'll jump out of a friggin' hoop. Like, he goes wild, about how they treated everybody. But him and Pete Bitelli, the ex-drummer, they're great people. They're really nice people. And the other thing, they've had a hard life. I think all of them, musically were really burned by this band. Because again, I don't know how much you know about Steve. He wasn't very, very nice to the band monetarily, and I think he really took advantage of Mark. And I think a lot of Mark's decline physically and mentally really hurt Steve psychologically and stuff. And maybe he internalized it so much that he didn't talk about it with anybody. But there was one time when he got sick of it. He cut ties with Mark, because I talked to Mike Flyntz not too long ago. They invited me to play in Brooklyn with them as a guest guitar player, to come up and play as one of the original guitar players in the legends, so to speak. And they were very gracious."

And so the audition process began to replace the unreplaceable. Guy, with his afro, was like a younger and fitter version of The Dictators' Handsome Dick Manitoba. So his look was odd for heavy metal, but boy, that voice—as Rick opines, Guy was the most distinguishable and distinguished element of the otherwise rather straight-forward Riot sound.

Getting the job was a southern "golden God" type in leather chaps called Rhett Forrester, son of a ballroom dance instructor, who had cut a name for himself playing in bands around Chicago and Georgia, but was now in Manhattan looking to move up, with his last stop before Riot being a band called Rachel.

Rhett had done it all, from lumberjack to gas jockey, from naval academy cadet to promising tennis star—his parents had tried to get him to accept an offered two-year tennis scholarship—but rock was in his blood. Rhett's mother had a dance studio, and although she was pleased that her son was into the arts, she had no idea that he had been instructed in vocal training while at high school, at the Sanford Naval Academy in Sanford, Florida, where he spent his last two years of school. Gravitating to a resort in South Carolina, Rhett eventually moved back to Atlanta, where his career started taking off with local bands.

"My old lady was hitting some tennis, my old man was going for golf and I was going for pussy," Rhett quipped, speaking with Dante Bonutto back in '82 about his first taste of the rock life. "I went to check out a band one night and as I had my harmonica with me, I asked if I could play in the breaks just to show off and stuff. They listened to me, asked me to sit in and offered me a job. That was the killer circuit, man. Five sets a night, seven nights a week, 50 weeks a year, just killing my throat, killing myself—literally. I was beat-up, stabbed, cut, blown-up by my pyrotechnician, electrocuted three or four times to the point of no return and carbon monoxide poisoned after a 36 hour drive in the back of a truck."

Sunday	Monday	Tuesday	Wednesday	Thursday	Friday	Saturday
Monthly Calender of Events			1 EMITS INN	2 MAINE	3 MAINE	4 MAINE
5 SOAP FACTORY	6	7 ORANGEBURG PUB	8	9	10 EMITS INN	11 EMITS INN
12 SOAP FACTORY	13	14 ORANGEBURG PUB	15 EMITS INN	16	17 Call Hotline for Info	18 Call Hotline for Info
19 SOAP FACTORY	20	21 ORANGEBURG PUB	22 EMITS INN	23	24 ORANGEBURG PUB	25 MOTHERS
26 SOAP FACTORY	27	28 ORANGEBURG PUB	29 EMITS INN	30	31 SOAP FACTORY	

Up to Chicago and Detroit with the likes of Human and Blind Man's Bluff, Rhett almost wound up in Joe Perry's solo band. "I was upset at the time, but I'm pleased it didn't come off now," continued Rhett. "All my friends were calling me up saying, 'Don't you be getting into shooting up no junk and that 'cos we hear Joe's a real coconut.' And I said, 'Okay, I'll stick to my regular controlled madness.' I live rock 'n' roll, man; that's my love—I'm a rocker!"

"I took along a tape of two songs and a video I'd done," said Rhett, quoted in the label literature for the record. "It was like one, two, three—the chemistry was right from the start. The next day I came back to their studio and drank beer while they ran through the rest of the auditions. The guys kept winking at me as if to say, 'Don't worry, you've got it!'"

"We were really impressed with Rhett's demo tape because it was so professional," recalled Steve, talking with Todd K. Smith. "He sent it with a photo and bio; everything looked great. And I loved that voice. I mean, he had *the* voice. So we brought him in, and could instantly see the difference he made in the band. He looked great and had such amazing charisma. One of the things that you wonder about as a producer, is how the final product will come across live. One of the first gigs Rhett did with Riot was at the Spectrum in Philadelphia. They were opening for the Scorpions. When the lights went down, Rhett came out like this big monster onto the stage. He just stood there and commanded the audience. I'd never seen that before with this band. He was like a big cloak, protecting the band. The other members felt very comfortable with that. It allowed them to do their own thing."

In the studio, "Rhett was the kind of singer that was very spontaneous," continued Loeb. "He was a one or two take guy. If you didn't get Rhett within the first few takes, you had to give it a rest. There are singers that render or paint with their voice. Rhett on the other hand was the kind of singer you photographed for the moment. As a producer, I didn't have to do much with him. He naturally knew—it was instinctive. We would set up, he'd walk in and, bam, lay it down. Rhett lived for the stage. No matter what

he did or where he was the night before, we knew he would never miss a gig. That was his life force. It was like he'd been out there for a million years. Had I not known he had a mother, I would've thought he was born on the stage."

Drummer Sandy Slavin told *Hit Parader*'s Andy Secher that Guy had left them in, "a rather precarious situation. Just when we thought everything was beginning to turn our way, we found out that we didn't have a lead singer. (Rhett) just blew us away. He sent a videotape of himself that was just incredible. When we saw it, we jumped out of our chairs and said, 'That's the guy we want.' He's fit in amazingly well. He helped write two tracks for the album, and he really gave us a kick in the ass with his energy. He's got a better voice than Guy, so he opens up a whole new direction for us. This is the album that's really gonna break down the door

Swords and Tequila: Riot's Classic First Decade

for us. We've been building up our following over the last couple of years, and we all feel that this is the perfect time for Riot, to break loose. There aren't too many other American bands that are willing, or able, to play heavy metal, and we want the distinction of being recognized as the best American heavy metal band around."

"They found him extremely entertaining in that he lived the part," laughs Steve. "And you know Rhett had been on the way to being a pro tennis player so they really got a kick out of that. So yes, almost a professional tennis player—Rhett was that good apparently. No kids. Gorgeous girlfriend, loved Paul Rodgers, hard drinker, and maybe more stuff that I sort of saw, but not really. He had gorgeous sexy girls around him, and not only could he talk the talk but he was willing to walk the walk. I think it was through Cliff Burnstein who he auditioned for and who passed on him. I became friendly with Cliff and went to see things related to Wall Street and statistics. We both had an interest in demographics and stats. I have tremendous respect for Cliff and I think I asked him if he had any singers I should hear and enter Rhett."

"Rhett was just the product of an audition," explains Mark. "We held a bunch of auditions in New York and we had a bunch of people coming down. We had people flying in from California, a lot of local people, and Rhett, who was originally from Georgia, but was living in New Jersey at the time and was doing a covers band. The initial thing was let's try get somebody who is completely different from Speranza. That was the mind set at the time so that there would be no comparisons. I don't know if that made a lot of sense, but that's what we did. And Rhett walked in and he had amazing charisma. That was the first thing we noticed about him. Unlike Guy, whose image was, you know, Guy had good looks and everything but he was basically like a local guy, pretty much

                    Martin Popoff

down-to-earth, where Rhett personified the swaggering rock star thing. He had done some demos and stuff that he gave us, but I don't think he did any major recordings or anything. But he came down and personified that whole rock thing, and we were quite impressed by his image. He pretty much made a big impression on everybody."

"He was pretty boisterous," chuckles Reale. "He was easy to get along with, but at the same time he was real. The whole image he had on stage wasn't really a put on. He lived that whole thing 24 hours a day. We accepted him how he was, and he worked great within the concept of the band. I think the band's live performances were much stronger, in a visual sense, with him. Partying-wise, he was in control. I mean, Rhett, of course, was a big drinker; he was definitely into drinking. There were drugs at times, that various band members did, but there were never any really bad drug habits or anything like that. And no hard stuff, none at all."

"Basically we said, well, what are we going to do now?" reflects Rick, on the predicament of losing Guy. "We had a second record that we were supposed to do for Elektra. So we auditioned, and basically had videos of various singers. These were singers from a lot of bands playing the club circuit. Most singers were mediocre, just typical club singers. Rhett stood out, just because he had a personality and had stage presence. And he had that bluesy sound, which Mark liked. Both of us were mostly blues- and hard rock- influenced players, and Rhett had a raunch to his sound, and he had the potential to sing the type of songs that Mark would like to write. We saw clips of him, and he had songs he had written. But when you write, you really write around your vocalist. So the style changed. The album we were to make, *Restless Breed*, has songs with bluesier vocal lines, but also Rhett had this raunch to him, which he used on songs like 'Vigilante Killer,' on the second album. So she had the potential to take the band into more of a metal sound, and yet he could do stuff with a bit more soul. Because he was from the South, his influences were a lot different from Guy's."

"And so we jammed with him on some of the older material," explains Rick. "We had to do older material. We had no choice. Plus we had to find a singer who could cover those songs, and yet someone that could take the band into a new direction. It was very similar to how when AC/DC lost Bon Scott, right at their height, but with Brian Johnson, and they just took off to another level. So we were similarly faced with, okay, we're starting to get a fairly good fan base... and then we lost our singer (laughs). So that was a major turning point. Because record companies see that, and they go, okay, now what? And the fans also. But the fans loved the band and they quickly loved Rhett. Rhett was a very flamboyant, colourful singer. And you would think that he was a heavy drinker, but he wasn't over the top. You know, he liked to have a good time, he was a fun person to be with, but I really can't say he was a big drug and drink guy."

As Steve succinctly puts it, the front cover art utilized for *Restless Breed*, issued May 12, 1982, represents the "morphing of band, from Guy to Rhett, trying to keep a foot in the old while stepping into the new." And hence, still slightly obliquely, there's a (backwards) transition featuring half seal and half... Brooklyn Elementary School student, in front of a city at night scene that recalls Thin Lizzy's *Nightlife* sleeve, puffy seal-in-the-moon notwithstanding.

Cracking the cellophane and spinning the vinyl, "Hard Lovin' Man," opens the show, crunching guitars giving way to a slow headbang of a beat, Rhett's leonine roar, and in total, a song that is instantly drinkable for any self-respecting metalhead. Great lyric too, which Steve cites as his favourite on the album, "because it *was* Rhett, or at least the Rhett he wanted everyone to see. I liked the song because it worked so well as a live opener with Rhett. Rhett could immediately grab audiences with that number given his strong visual. On the co-credit there, Doug was Rhett's long-time buddy."

"I co-wrote this one with Douglas Salomone about two days before I joined Riot," explained Rhett. "It was written for possible use in a film called *Vigilante*. I submitted it to the group for the album, and the guys agreed that it was a strong enough song. Riot basically use the arrangement I had, except they beefed it up a little bit."

The gritty metal theme continues with "C.I.A.," although indeed there's a loss of majesty concerning the new Riot sound versus the sum total of *Fire Down Under*. There's an earthiness, a scrappiness to Sandy's drum performance and the knob-job capturing there-of. As well, there's an overtly southern rocking chorus to the thing, a recurring theme throughout the album.

Forrester gets a sole credit on "C.I.A." but Rick Ventura doesn't recall seeing Rhett write using an instrument of any sort. "I don't know, he might have played a bit of piano. Guy definitely played guitar on his own, but Rhett... personally, my songs were presented to Rhett; I basically had all the music worked out as well as the lyrics. It was actually easier for me to write for Rhett, because my writing style and chord structure changes, he basically got it; he got what I wanted. He knew how to phrase. I was totally pleased with the delivery he did on the songs I wrote—he delivered on every track. The chemistry... it was funny, because we'd developed through all the years with the guys in Riot. I mean, I knew Guy from the very early days, even before the band had a record deal, when they were just playing clubs. And as we toured, the band develops a friendship and everybody was really tight. So with Rhett being a very different character, it took time to get comfortable with him."

"The song was composed by me on guitar," confirms Rhett. "I wrote it the day Reagan got shot. It's about the one C.I.A. cat who pulled out his submachine gun during the assassination attempt. It's kind of a spoof of the C.I.A.. Mark took the song and tore it up, turned it into a killer tune. He got so worked up while playing it, he practically slammed his guitar into the studio wall."

Rhett's lyric is in fact a fairly scathing indictment of the "jarhead" mentality he imagines a guy like that must embody. Bloodlust, ego, even a seething disdain for the political class he's sworn to protect... Rhett sees no virtues anywhere within the guy he would have seen on the TV that day.

Title track "Restless Breed" represents the first real musical left turn for Riot since the opening notes of the very first album. Here Rhett is utilizing his southern rock chops to the fullest, on a track that is more roots-rocking than brightly modern of metals.

"I like Rhett's style, particularly on 'Restless Breed'," reflects Mark. "That was the first songs that allowed me to bring out those kind of Paul Rodgers blues influences. So that song is a fond memory, much like 'Gunfighter' from *Born in America*. Rhett's style of singing was similar to Mike DiMeo—they both have that bluesy David Coverdale approach that has always been my preference. With Guy, it was just Guy. We were young, we got together from the same neighborhood, and we just did this original style of hard rock. But to me, Guy was more of a pop vocalist. So naturally when Rhett came into the picture, he had that bluesier style that immediately brought out that side of me, and I began writing songs like 'Restless Breed.' So that song bears Rhett's influence, but it was also Rhett influencing me, Rhett bringing out those inherent influences that I already had anyway."

Quoted in the label bio at the time, Mark had said, "After we finished touring with Rush last December, I went back home to San Antonio, Texas for the holidays. The song was written during that time. It's a follow-up to 'Outlaw,' a similar sort of Texas border story. We polished it up in the studio."

As with "C.I.A." Rhett proves he's capable of painting a more dramatically violent story than Guy had ever attempted, this one celebrating seven who ride into town and burn it to the ground, seeking revenge upon the death of the protagonist's brothers in some sort of bar room altercation.

"After an initial tour he fell in love with it," says Steve, asked about Mark's love of western culture so evident on this song, a passion seeded in a trip to Texas, where as Mark indicated, he eventually took up residence. "Girls, adulation... the band was considered pretty big stuff there because of the incessant radio play Joe Anthony and KISS radio gave them, and Mark liked it all. He had a girlfriend there and kids who would run around and do things for him and I think he just liked the pace more. Mark was never really an urban guy in his head. He always loved Paul Rodgers and Thin Lizzy, and then that expanded into straight-ahead country and blues. He was right there by the Alamo so he loved it. It was everything he wanted. He began slowly living there for longer and longer periods right away after the initial tour the band did which was months after the release of *Rock City* but still before *Narita*. But that was him going for a few weeks at a time, coming back and staying a few weeks and then returning. He continued to do that for at least a year plus, maybe two years, before he started to be in San Antonio the majority of the time."

This desperado vibe to the new record continued through the band's galloping, Lizzy-esque treatment of Eric Burdon & The Animals classic "When I Was Young." Wisely, the band didn't leave the thing limp and mellow, instead bringing it toward heavy proximity with the title track just before it. Says Steve, "'When I Was Young' I think, was a favourite of the A&R guy at Elektra (Tom Zutaut) and there it is." To which Rick adds, "Like 'Born to be Wild,' we'd sit around in the studio and producers would suggest songs. Lots of bands would cover a song and try to update it, make it their own. It might've been Billy or Steve that had suggested the song. And yes, it's got that wild West feel, and Rhett did a good job on it."

Not quite right, according to Rhett. "Eric Burdon & the Animals originally did the song in '67. We had a friend in England send us a list of cover tunes to consider doing, and this one was at the top. I kept pushing for the band to do it, because I love the story line. We sort of heavied out in our version; Mark and Rick play double leads."

"Loanshark" might have bore some influence from Riot's UK buddies Iron Maiden, what with its drum barrage, gallop, prominence of bass guitar and general dark heavy metal feel, with Rhett commenting that, "Kip came up with the basic idea, and we didn't know what the hell to do with it at first. Then Mark started arranging the song while I was writing the lyrics. What I wrote is based on a true story about my getting in trouble with loan sharks about five years ago. I tried to make the lyrics funny,

but the whole thing wasn't so laughable at the time." Maiden is even evoked by the lyric which, like a bunch of Maiden songs, is about an occupation. Again, one can see a definite edge to Rhett's storytelling that was just never there with Guy, and coupled with the trashy all-drums delivery of the thing, this one is a seedy, screechy hot mess of a metal-muncher.

Onto side two, opener "Loved by You" is an admirable party rocker that goes down easy, Rhett screeching to life a lyric that is all Coverdale all through the hot night. Notes Steve, "'Loved by You' was the band trying to find a place in that AC/DC groove and about adding Rhett's blues harp skills, which we wanted to add to the live show but questioned whether it would be accepted or just confuse matters even more."

"Great live tune," agrees Rick, "because he played harp, which added another dimension to the band. So it was a little more bluesy, which I liked. But you could see on the next record, we switch course and go in another direction (laughs)." Adds Mark, "The music was pretty much done live. We did a long jam with Rhett on harmonica we later edited down. The crowd noises, to be honest, were added later. Now, there'll probably be kids who will claim they were there!"

Next is "Over to You," which is a Rick Ventura sole credit and considerably poppy for Riot, in fact, the first of three soft rockers in a row making the middle of side two disconcertingly peaceful. As is usual with Rick, it's hard to figure out what he's trying to say in the song—and to the new girl desperately trying to figure him out—other than that he is a rock 'n' roll vagabond because of this life he's chosen. "This was the first song I sang with Riot," says Rhett. "It was kind of my test. They put me under the pressure cooker to see how I'd do, but the song came easy for me. Later that afternoon, we popped the cork, all had drinks, and I was in the band."

"Without Guy to write with, and Mark pretty much living in Texas, Rick was on his own," reflects Steve. "Rhett didn't hang much with the others. Rhett was from Atlanta and shared little with the guys. But Rick wanted a voice on the record so he still wrote, but now in isolation. He pretty much recorded alone as well, preferring to come in and do everything as an overdub. The challenge was how to keep the old audience and grab some new fans with a singer who had such a different sound and approach. And all the while deliver to the label what they wanted, which no one was really sure of, and what they needed, which was something that could be played at radio. A difficult challenge to say the least."

"Showdown" found Reale writing a bluesy ballad, evoking echoes of Thin Lizzy during that *Nightlife/Fighting* era, along with Mark's newly explored Bad Company vibe. "A song like this is a nice change for us," commented Mark. "We didn't write ballads like this before. Now with Rhett, we don't have to slam audiences in the face with song after song." Adds Rhett, "The chorus needed work at first, but then we got it right. I like singing songs like this one; it gives me a chance to show off my old influences, like Paul Rodgers."

Asked about this left field Reale composition (which struggled to an acceptable #35 on *Billboard*'s Mainstream Rock chart), Loeb says, "The label didn't like change or certainly any changes that were so out front. It was the radio people who were willing to give it a shot. I think they believed if given the right record, they could get the airplay and if the band could get the live dates, perhaps we could salvage it. We gave them 'Showdown' and they did deliver radio—even New York—but the problem was we stopped selling records. 'Showdown' was a 'turntable' hit and that's all. And worse, we began to lose our hardcore base so we had to do a quick pivot to shore up that aspect. We made a live EP quickly and it did stop the bleeding, but by then I think everyone was pretty confused and I think whatever tenuousness that was there at first, turned all negative. We did do a lot of live playing in large venues supporting bands like Scorpions and Kiss and always delivered with a now smaller core audience, but it was over at the label."

                    Martin Popoff

"'Showdown''s a Mark chord progression," recalls Rick. "And Rhett was just perfect for that, because it followed in the vein of 'Outlaw,' I would say. That whole obsession with the West. That's what Mark liked about Rhett, that he could write songs like that and that he could pull off that Paul Rodgers approach. Plus then Rhett would do a song like 'Violent Crimes'—one extreme to the other. I thought there were a lot of good songs on *Restless Breed*."

"Dream Away" is also on the quiet side, but this particular Ventura number is in fact one of the hidden gems on the album, written smartly and yet still in that wistful desperado rock vein. Much more imaginative than "Showdown," "Dream Away" might have been a missed opportunity for single status. Notes Rhett, "Rick wrote this one, but he let me interpret it in my own way. He did all the lead work on the track, with Mark playing rhythm guitar."

"'Dream Away' is one of three songs I wrote just by myself," says Rick. "I would come up with chord structures and lyrics and present them to the band and say, 'Hey, let's try this and see if that works for the band. It's just two different writing styles, a collaboration that made Riot sound the way it did. 'Dream Away' is more of a fantasy-type lyric. But people also write about their girlfriends at times, which I did; a lot of songs are written about experiences with relationships good or bad. I was going through a relationship at that time, so that was reflected in some lyrics on the songs. But the songs Mark and I wrote, we actually had fun, because we got to do songs that we probably could not do with Guy. Guy was quiet and reserved, although you would never think that when he performed. But Rhett was like that on stage and off stage—that was the difference. When he came off stage, he was still the same Rhett, which we had to get used to."

True to form, Rick makes use of imagery like golden rainbows and distant lands and "a thousand different dreams," but at the heart of the song is a search for love, which in the song is just out of reach, a dream away, but worth physically travelling great distances to find.

Restless Breed closes with another welcome heavy metal rocker called "Violent Crimes," a short, combative speed rocker which again betrays this album's shortcomings when the band goes for heavy, arriving at frustratingly punky and small-ish, the new band lacking the expansive sense of ambition and positivity of the band in its "firing on all cylinders down under" Guy Speranza era.

"Kip gave me the riff," notes Rhett, "and I took it from there. I went home that night and wrote the lyrics. It's definitely a street song. We just walked into the studio and did it in one take." And yet again, Rhett paints a depressive picture of those wrapped up in crime, here going so far as to say the tormented tormenter is considering taking his own life, perhaps to stop him from doing his job and killing others.

Just how much of a metalhead was our Rhett? "I don't know if I would consider him a metalhead," laughs Mark, "in the same way that you would call Bruce Dickinson a metalhead. But he was into Halford and Priest, but there was also classic rock, Paul Rodgers. He was pretty much just a rocker."

And what about Kip Leming, who gets a co-write with Rhett on the track. "Kip was into the band Free," says Rick. "And he liked Deep Purple and Led Zeppelin; very similar influences to me, I would say. He basically wrote riffs and generally liked bands with a lot of riffing. So yeah, everybody had good ideas and made them work together as a band."

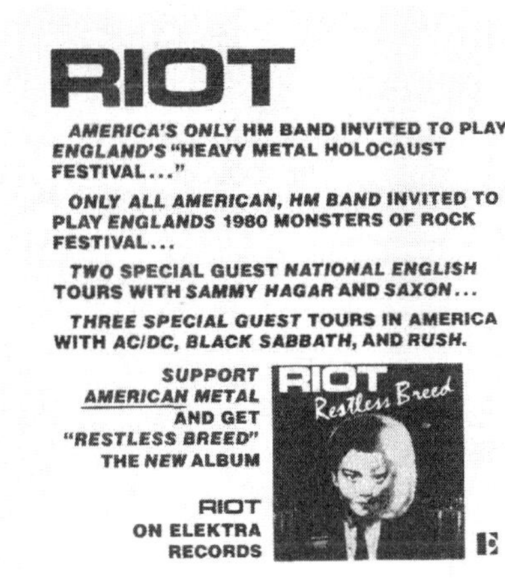

But not exactly, says Steve. "My overall problem with that record is the confusing themes. A western thing with 'Showdown' and 'Restless Breed' and then a very edgy thing with 'C.I.A.,' 'Violent Crime,' 'Loanshark' etc. Of course that actually reflects the dichotomy of Rhett Forrester. He was those two things, but exaggerated versions. I'm afraid Rhett didn't just sing and write about that edge—he lived in some of that world. Listening back now, I realize we were trying to find some place to frame Rhett with the previous Riot incarnation. I also hear now how he was getting to a place that was somewhat similar to Paul Di'anno and a bit of Halford as well, albeit without that very high range. 'Violent Crimes,' 'C.I.A.' and 'Loanshark' were all in that space."

"I guess if anything was a departure, you would have to say it was *Restless Breed*," reflects Mark in summation on this ill-received record, one that maybe should have instigated either a change in direction, a change in singer, but not both at once. "It was a real change from where we were going. So it didn't fare too well with the fans. I like some of this stuff on it, but as far as the whole history of Riot goes, it kind of threw the fans a curve ball."

"There was no time to frame Rhett properly," adds Steve. "*Restless Breed* was thrown together. No time to live with anything long enough to find the best picture. Had I had that, I would have heard his Halford side and tried him there and not just Paul Rodgers and in your face. There were no 'devices' used with Rhett and his voice on *Restless Breed* was in your face—no hiding. But I missed it, I think."

"Billy went out for various dates on most, not me," says Steve, asked about Riot on the road at this juncture. "I went out on some local dates, about as far as Philadelphia's Spectrum where the guys supported Scorpions. Spectrum is a pretty big venue and it was there I could see clearly what a difference Rhett made. When he came out on stage, you never wondered or questioned or needed to ever be anxious. He was a natural out there, feeding off the audience and commanding such a strong presence. Mark could do that too, so between those two, the band was rock-solid live. When the band toured doing smaller headline venues on the West Coast, I went for those, but it was a family affair with a shoestring budget and my wife at the time doing the band's PR. Ellen, a consummate pro PR person with lots of major studio feature movie promotion and PR under her belt, told me from the road that Rhett was absolutely a natural, that he knew exactly what to say and what not to say. She was amazed at what level he was at in regard to that aspect. But the UK didn't like him and I think much of that is because they were so invested in Guy and the huge mistake was Rhett was unable to do any of that material and make it sound decent. So the UK began to turn off."

"With Rhett Forrester, it just wasn't the same," agrees Tom Zutaut, now saddled with a much harder band to market. "Guy had that magic voice, and Rhett Forrester had a mediocre voice that was nothing special. He was sort of like a copycat of a bunch of other people. He sounded a lot like Paul Rodgers from Bad Company as opposed to a guy who had his unique sound. They became less of a metal band and more like Bad Company."

Born in America – "We're almost friends now. Almost."

Peaking early and then stumbling when metal was just getting ready to rule an entire decade, Riot entered 1983 having to break in a new lead vocalist in Rhett Forrester. Their first record with the southerner, *Restless Breed*, found the band pensive and rootsy, and a hastily assembled live EP did little to solidify the situation.

"Riot Live" featured the new lineup doing their new songs, namely "Hard Lovin' Man," "Showdown," "Loved by You," "Loanshark" and "Restless Breed," along with anthem for the ages "Swords and Tequila." And there was some value there: the performances were ferocious and the production powerful and electrifying. "Hard Lovin' Man" was a juggernaut, and "Showdown" was considerably heavied up. "Loved by You" fulfilled its promise as a sleazy party

rocker, underscored by a jam that took it up to 8:02. "Loanshark" was unadulterated early thrash, bonus being a Sandy Slavin drum solo, and "Restless Breed" rocked with authority, slightly faster than the original, Rick and Mark weaving hugely distorted licks and soloing prodigiously. Most interesting for fans, of course, was closer "Swords and Tequila," which, despite its heft, did indeed betray this idea that Guy Speranza songs were a challenge for Rhett, who is slurring, ducking notes, and mercifully placed back in the mix. To the visuals, *"Riot Live"* basically lacked an album cover (essentially designed to look like a budget release, almost a bootleg) and the piece of product went by quick. Before long it was back to the drawing board, Riot eager to get back on the up-ramp built for speed two years back.

"It was definitely a conscious decision to get heavier," says Mark, concerning Riot's fifth album, *Born in America*, issued October 14, 1983, just as metal was about to vault into the stratosphere across the country on the left coast, ignoring New York completely other than Twisted Sister. "We felt that *Restless Breed* was too laid-back, that it was just too much of a departure. The '80s, metal was starting to become a big thing. The neo-classic guitar styles were starting to come into play. So it was definitely a conscious effort to progress."

Hindering any degree of forward momentum, Riot had tumbled out of their major label deal.

"There was no real negotiating on this one," says Steve. "The Canadian dance label Quality offered me distribution in Canada and the US. They had a young marketing guy that loved Riot and convinced the boss to go with the idea of doing a distribution deal as long as we provided the aspects that a dance label was completely unequipped to pull off for a project like this. It was a one-off deal and we had an in-house marketing guy, a radio promo guy, my wife who did publicity, a smaller agency that could book 1500 seaters, and our usual crew and tour manager. It was a slog, and we ended somewhere on the West Coast, and that closed the book for Riot for the next five years until the *Thundersteel* album in 1988/'89. But yeah, in terms of trying to get a better deal, we really had no leverage because we had no alternatives and time was of the essence. Everything had collapsed, Billy and I were over, no label, and if we didn't get out there quickly, there'd be nothing to salvage. But it seemed we could do anything any label could do ourselves based on how little Elektra did for *Restless Breed*."

As for calling the record *Born in America*, "I can only guess now, but it's a good guess," chuckles Steve. "We needed a radio record, we needed a good video clip and a record we could do live that was anthemic. 'You Burn in Me' was certainly a possibility but I think it wouldn't have been as 'rah-rah' as 'Born in America.' *And*, aside from the existing fan base, It was confusing for many fans with respect to just who and what Riot was and where they were from. There was Quiet Riot, there was the NWOBHM association—were they a British band? Canadian, given the Attic Records connection? So we were making a statement that this was Riot from Brooklyn with a new face—that's my best recollection. There were no working titles; I only wish we had the time for that sort of luxury."

Crap album cover as well, the official sleeve featuring nothing more than new ill-conceived logo, an American flag and two chopped-out paste-ins of the seal dude from *Narita*. Cut and paste job? "Yes, sir, exactly right," admits Steve. "No money, so the design of the US and Canada markets had to be my own; other markets did their own cover art. I did what I could and kept it all pretty basic." The alternate cover art wasn't much better, featuring a black and white shot of a girl wearing a Riot shirt.

It's become apparent, through talks with the guys in the band, that they really don't appreciate how little income was around to pay the players.

"They had nothing but their instruments when we began with them," explains Steve, given the floor to plead his case against what we've been hearing from the others. "We bankrolled everything. Back line, tour support for years and even salaried them a bit. Every advance we ever received went back into them. For what? Rehearsal studio, clothes, tour bus or rental cars, crew, tour manager, truck and gas, back line, repairs, food, travel and a hotel room for a shower—figure it out. And what do you get paid for a date at a 1500 seater or as a support band? Maybe $750 or sometimes $1000, which was what we were paid back then. The truck and gas alone ate that up, so who do you suppose covered the shortfall?"

"And then in those periods when there was no label, who covered that? Or the studio. And much has been said about that aspect. I produced eight records or ten, and was I ever paid a production fee for even one? Nope. Some said, well Steve you owned the studio, so wasn't that a conflict and didn't you make money there? My studio was a world class studio. We had lots and lots of huge hits recorded or mixed there. And despite what many preferred to think, the engineers and assistants and tape costs and rentals *all* had to be paid for and were. Did I discount the studio? Yep. And did Mark for example not spend hours and hours recording everything *exactly* as he wanted? Yes he did. And why could he do that? Because it *was* my place. Had it not been, Mark would have had X amount of time and that would have been it. I think the fact we are even discussing the band so many years later is testament to the impact we all made."

"Riot would have ended years and years before it did if not for me," continues Steve, "so clearly I do bristle when I hear any of this stuff. I made it possible for them to stay alive for as long as they did. In later years when I was accused of all sorts of nefarious things, I was really put out by that crap given what sort of a financial hit I took to keep doing the project. In the interim years

                          Martin Popoff

before I began recording the band again, i.e. *Thundersteel* and *Privilege of Power*, what happened for me? A Top 10 record in the UK that I co-wrote, a chart album with a pop artist, three songs that ended up in feature movies and a slew of hits the studio recorded or mixed, and many of them groundbreaking. I surely didn't need to do Riot for money. Why did I do it? I found it to be a labour of love. I looked forward to doing it at least once a year. But I made zero money. Just the opposite."

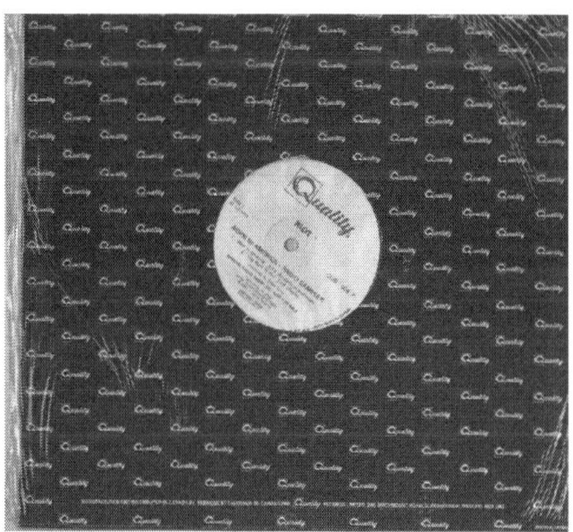

"So here we are on *Born in America*, years later after breaking through all the barriers, being basically back to the beginning. It was all on a wing and a prayer. To clarify something, I gather the story so far has been confusing with respect to the management situation. I mean, we managed them—Billy and me—*but* since we couldn't really do that effectively, we found others to do it so there were a number of people who brought various skills and experiences to the table. Going back, early on, there was a friend, an adult, who managed them for a short while, Arthur Santucci, who did a few Texas and Ohio dates with them. Then there was Fred Heller who had previously managed Lou Reed, Blood Sweat and Tears and Mott the Hoople. He handled the band through the *Narita* and *Fire Down Under* projects. Once we lost the label and we did *Born in America*, we had Bobby Ragona handle them. Bobby had been head of marketing at Millennium Records and so had some road experience. But as I explained, whilst I wanted Q Prime to have it, Billy rejected that idea unless Q Prime agreed to answer to Billy and that was never going to be—and Billy rejected any other deal. So there it is. There was one other guy but that was only for the CBS projects later on."

The drama at this level was alluded to in the credits of the *Born in America* album, which said, "Thanks to Riot and everyone at Greene Street for surviving the nightmare!"

"The nightmare referred to what occurred between me and Billy who seemed intent on destroying everything," says Steve. "It was an ugly break-up to say the least. We had to mix the record twice, separately with two engineers. It was so stressful; it still makes me crazy to even remember how bad it was. Compared to *Restless Breed*, there weren't subtle differences; there were huge differences. We simply had no time for *Born in America*, no time to rehearse, no pre-production, no living with mixes. It was basically recorded and mixed *twice* because of the Billy situation."

Born in America opens with a title track that is the perfect synthesis of metal swagger with southern rock swagger, both wrapped-up in Rhett but underscored by better, boomier production values than were afforded *Restless Breed*. Mark's riff is legion, and even he seems to get the balance right with his transitions. The Riot of *Fire Down Under* is long gone, but the Riot of *Restless Breed* has been emboldened, with Rhett upholding his track record of writing with edge, lacing this celebration of all things American with indictments of the greed that can result from unfettered capitalism and the pursuit of fame.

The ironic jingoistic anthem struggled to a #44 showing on *Billboard*'s Mainstream Rock chart, helping its source album trouble the official album chart at a modest #175. The dual chart placement was aided and abetted by a half-live, half-concept production video for "Born in America," on which Rhett as a commanding front man is ably demonstrated. Noted Sandy at the time, "Rhett reveals his 'true' self in this video, and the Tior figure is prominently in the video. It's not Duran Duran or any crap like that concept-type thing." What Sandy is referring to is that at the end of the video, Rhett tears off his "mask," i.e. his real face, and reveals that he is in fact our seal hero. Interestingly, the school punk depicted in the rote story line around minor delinquency in the classroom suggests a younger version of Rhett, in both look and mischievous demeanor.

"You Burn in Me" strikes a similar balance although the band eased up on the throttle, a little more southern rock, twin leads afire, a chorus that is all Bad Company. But then it's a deep dive into an almost NWOBHM metal with the mechanical gallop of "Wings of Fire," and yet even this one sports transitions comes chorus time that support the union between north and south. Mark's lyric is an intense pastiche of Ronnie James Dio-like imagery, but the story never quite takes off on "wings of fire."

"Now you've got one record under your belt, and it gives you an idea of what you're capable of," figures Rick, surveying the scene. "I see songs like 'Over to You' and 'Violent Crimes' as two totally different songs. And now it's almost like, okay, *Restless Breed* was our first record and now we have to have a follow-up which is supposed to be our fifth album—and with a new singer and a new approach. Energy was key with the original lineup; Guy had a certain delivery and energy to him. And Rhett had a totally different vocal approach and stage presence. Both great in their own way, just different. So we had to zero in now on certain sounds to appeal to fans and really target our audience."

Targeting the audience didn't seem to be a problem, with "Running from the Law" again striking a rich metal vein, its tuneful yet resolute Reale riff sticking to the memory circuits, while Rhett tells yet another tale that could have come right out of the old West and yet one that could be a fugitive lament from any era, given its generalized wording.

Next was the band's third cover in three albums, a lethargic telling of "Devil Woman," made popular by Cliff Richards. Recalls Steve, "I may be mistaken, but I believe we did 'Devil Woman' because Charles Koppleman, who aside from having a son who was a fanatic Riot fan, was also a very influential guy in the music business and I think owned the publishing for 'Devil Woman.' We needed all the help we could get to find a new home quickly, so we did what we had to do. Some of these recordings started out as jokes but weren't half bad so where we could use them, we did."

And then it was back to the band's recurring crime metal theme, with "Vigilante Killer," a rhythmically bashing pure metal tune whose utility was to take the band further away from the sundown rock of *Restless Breed*. Rhett takes us back to the mean streets of New York, celebrating a vigilante who won't put up with being mugged by a 16-year-old punk with a flick knife. Similar of menacing street rock proportions is the band's third road-racing song, "Heavy Metal Machine," which through title alone blared intention. This one had Rhett performing like a thespian wild man while the band pounded out their accompaniment to a no-nonsense Mark Reale riff.

"Where Soldiers Rule" is one of two songs on the album credited to Rick Ventura alone, but even he is toeing the metal line, writing a perfunctory galloping riff that could have come from Maiden, military wind-ups included.

"'Where Soldiers Rule' actually fit in with the record quite well," says Rick. "Lyrically, it's a vision of a future doomed world (laughs). It's funny, my other one on there, 'Promised Land'... they both speak of a different world, a future time and place. And when you look back on it, you see that it marks the very end of my phase with the band."

With Reale's sole-written "Gunfighter," the band keeps its foot pressed hard to the metal pedal, and by this point, for any punter raised on *Fire Down Under* and the NWOBHM and the nascent scene being cooked up in LA... that guy had to be happy that Riot wasn't wimping out. Typical to Mark's preoccupation with western themes, this one tells the tale of a man in tracking pursuit of the villain who shot his daddy dead down by the Rio Grande.

"Promised Land" is an interesting closer, with the band introducing a little party metal in the spirit of *Restless Breed*'s "Loved by You," or indeed, the Van Halen we starting to hear in and about *II*. Which again, has got to hurt, because, again, very much like Y&T, Riot were the bad luck boys when it came to cashing in on a style soon to be celebrated.

"'Promised Land' might have a touch of Aerosmith to it, but not necessarily," reflects Rick. "I used to like Aerosmith quite a bit but I hear more of an Aerosmith vibe on *Fire Down Under* song 'Don't Bring Me Down.' That's pretty apparent, if you check that riff. That is probably more of the influence there. But 'Promised Land' came from more of a Led Zeppelin thing, although I had Ritchie Blackmore influences too, which maybe you can hear on my 'When Soldiers Rule' solo. But these songs, including 'Running From the Law,' yeah, that's when the band started to drift away from the American style of Riot to more of the English influence."

Alluding to what Steve had said about Ventura, Rick says, "Towards *Born in America*, I wasn't in there as much, I'd say because of frustration at the direction Mark wanted to take the band; maybe we had started to see things a bit differently. Mark would see how other bands were doing, and the reaction they were getting. But there was really no need for that, because I always felt Riot had a unique sound. He just wanted image-wise to take it more... because at that time we were touring with Judas Priest, and it was also just on the cusp of the hair metal bands. That's why I always felt the band came out a touch too early (laughs). I mean, when we started, the focus was still punk. We would frequent the clubs in

New York City right when the whole generation of big heavy rock bands—dinosaur bands—was coming to an end. Punk was the new refreshing sound for rock. But it's so funny, metal fans, they are hardcore fans, very much like country music fans. They are your fans from the beginning to the end. Still, when we came out, we were going against the norm. We weren't a punk band. We were just playing the stuff that we liked to play, similar to what we grew up listening to. So we were a little out of place. If we would've come out in the mid '80s, the timing would've been better. Towards the very end, towards the *Born in America* period, Van Halen was out now, Mötley Crüe was starting. There was this string of bands. This was the early spark of the heavy rock that was coming in."

"The code word today is mass confusion, to say the least," quipped Rhett, interviewed backstage in LA by Steven Rosen once the band had transitioned to touring the record. "There have been minor mishaps on the way to playing the gigs. Specifically, we've had everything from literally the trucks being caught in blizzards, and trucks rolled over with all the equipment in it. We've blown up buses. Last year we blew up eight busses. This year we've only blown up two."

"But it's good, any tour," added Kip Leming. "It's always great to play big arenas and things like that; it's always great to play to that many people. But yeah, little handicaps like that. But nothing can stop us. Like we're saying, equipment shit flying out of the truck, blizzards, playing on rented equipment that we've never seen before. But we still do the gigs—we have a passion for it. As far as the business, there's been record companies and stuff that have had different ideas about the band and what we were. They wanted us to have a hit single. Instead we come up with *Fire Down Under*. And we originally did that for Capitol Records. And they said, yeah, that sounds great, but we don't hear the hit single. And we say, wait a minute, this isn't the kind of music where you have hit singles, you know? And these guys, you can't talk to them, because they don't like the music. They're businessmen. They don't hear it; you know, it might as well be Indian classical music. They all just say, 'Hit, I gotta hear a hit!' So we're up against record company stupidity and things like that. But the audience has always been there. That's something that's kept us going. We always go out and play, we're always about energy, and the audience relates to that, I guess. So if business guys could get as hip to it as the audience is, we'd be home-free."

"It's become almost a hip thing now, to like heavy metal," continued Kip. "When we first started out in '76, heavy metal was not like a chic thing at all. Nobody wanted to know about it. It was like, 'Come on, it's over, it's dinosaur rock, it's dead.' We were real. Like, we're not putting hairspray in our hair and makeup, because we happen to think this week we're gonna be heavy metal. Literally, people always tell us about new wave, all this stuff. We just don't do it, you know? We don't feel that music. This is what we do."

Looking at the hair metal that was becoming prevalent in LA in 1984, Rhett called it, "a trendy kind of fashion-y thing that is happening at the moment. But this band definitely stuck to its guns and over the years, it came back in, you know? A lot of these bands have jumped on the heavy metal bandwagon. And that just doesn't get it with us. You can't underestimate the power of airplay, but at the same time, you can't try to contrive things. I mean, if you did, the public would know. Our people would know if we tried to do that. We have a certain amount of tolerance for something like that. Maybe on the last record we had a couple songs that were a bit more different than what was on previous Riot albums as far as depth goes and that type of thing. But we did that, we got it off our chest, and then we carried on with what we do, which is play real fuckin' rock 'n' roll with energy."

Picking up on that, Leming tells Steven, "Yeah, that's what the band has always been about—it's like high energy. The main thing when Rhett joined the band, the other singer could only sing one type of song. We had a lot of material and stuff that he couldn't really sing. So when Rhett got in the band, it was like, wow, so we tried a lot of different things on *Restless Breed*. And this time we came back more to just a live type of thing; we wanted to capture a live sound on the record. And the next one will be even more so after that—it'll really go in that direction."

"Anything that could go wrong has gone wrong as far as management goes," answers Rhett, asked by Steven whether it's now the perfect time for Riot to break. "But yes, timing, man—timing is 75% of this business. We have pretty good timing right now with what's happening with the record, we got new management, we got a new record company, got a new video, got a new tour. We've got a whole new lease on life and we're going to take full advantage of it. That's basically what it needs to take, to get beyond what we've been doing all along, where other bands have sort of slipped by us and stuff. It's all just a matter of timing, and when you're timing is due, it should happen. It's going to happen this year, and in the next few years it will happen for us. We're very confident."

"Oh, those guys," laughs Kip, asked about the huge success that the other Riot—the Quiet one—was experiencing as Rhett and himself talked backstage with Rosen. "To me you're talking about conscious thinking about what we're going to do. That's a band where definitely they thought about, heavy metal's happening, so we're gonna be a heavy metal band. It's a contrived thing. And you know, I think their audience is different than ours, and it hasn't been much of a problem. The kids don't confuse us, but the press sometimes confuses us. We never had a problem with kids coming up to us and saying, 'Well, which one are you, Riot or Quiet Riot?' They don't, ever, because it's a different audience. They get like girls more into them where it's a little more commercial kind of thing. And kids can pick up on it, especially in England. We go to England a lot, where Quiet Riot's not happening because they could see it's a contrived kind of thing. They're very earthy there. They can tell when something's real. I mean, definitely disco has resurged into something, and you know there'll be a disco cut on the next Quiet Riot album."

"I mean, I know some of the behind-the-scenes stuff that happens," adds Rhett, "because. like, the music is marginal. Totally fuckin' contrived. You know, we don't want to stick our fist down anybody's throat that has success. People that make it in this business, they deserve a lot of credit. Because it's very hard to make it in this business. But we don't want to particularly make it in an insincere way, in a dishonest fashion. With them, it's a Top 40 power pop type of situation, but we're obviously with a heavy metal audience who are like loyal to the bone, man. We have fans that are loyal to the bone. They don't jump on whatever wagon is happening this week. They don't have their, you know, Journey album right next to their Riot album. They have like Riot and they have all the heavy metal bands and that's it. It's just not a very generalized audience. Our people like us and they know what we're going to give 'em, and they expect it and we give it to them.

Oh, we wouldn't mind selling three million fucking albums—you kidding? No, I mean, Jesus Christ, we're not cutting down the business end of that deal. Not by any means of the situation at all. But I'm not going to become a fuckin' businessman rocker. I didn't get in this fuckin' business to be a business rocker. I am a rocker, man. And that's the bottom line. If I wanted to be a businessman, I'm quite intelligent—I could've been in business."

Rhett tried to paint a brave face on the band's new deal with Quality Records, telling Steven, "We're taking on a bit more of a controlled madness relationship with the record company right now. As opposed to with a major, where you've really got to compress everything into a six, eight week type of campaign. With this campaign, we'll take the album six, eight months. Were taking it in a process of what we can take, instead of a super high-powered process where they have to move onto the next priority— our record company said we are a top priority. They're not a poor man's/last man's independent label by any means in the game at all. So things are happening as planned as far as strategy goes. We have a strategy this year."

"We got one of the best lawyers in the countries to get us off Elektra," continued Forrester. "Same man that got Linda Ronstadt to Ric Ocasek to some of the guys from The Eagles off the label. He asked those people for six figures, and he asked us to take him out to lunch. So put it like that. We ain't rich men by any means at all, but he did us right and he got us off the label—with a little bit of negotiations. Again, it was like business. Elektra was going in a different direction, and they were having management problems. I don't want to get into it too much, but they were like pirates, and they bought sports channels, and rock 'n' roll was the last thing on their mind. Plus there was so much turmoil. They were firing people that had been working there for 20 years, without any fucking indication. So we figured if that's the way these people are gonna act, like, no, definitely, we didn't wanna be around. Plus the main reason we quit Elektra, they asked me to put on like lipstick and dye my hair and pomp it up, poof my hair and shit like that. And I said forget it, I'm my own man. Put it this way, if I was a little bit light in my motorcycle boots, then I might have done it. Strike that (laughs). That can get me shot. Listen to me, that can get me shot (laughs). But it's so confusing. You have to follow your heart and your instincts, and that's what we do—that's what we do, man."

"It's hard, because you get different people telling you different things," says Kip. "Because you find after a while that you know better than they do. In the beginning you think, these record company guys know something, but ultimately it's like saving their job. It's like job security. So you find... because we're out there doing it all the time—they're not. You know, they're sitting in some office reading something, 'Hey, metal's happening; okay, let's get a metal band.' It's not real, man."

"Mark writes most of the material but Rhett writes some," answers Kip, asked about the construction of *Born in America*. "I try to write some. They don't use it. I write my own lyrics, but nobody uses it. I want to sing; nobody wants me to sing. That's a whole different thing, man. But they don't let me do it. So Mark writes the material, Rhett writes some. Then we go and rehearse a little bit, we go in the studio and we just do it live. Try to get like a live sound. We even do some vocals live, where it makes sense. We go for the feel, we go for the energy, as opposed to, oh, somebody was a little out of time in one place. We want to get that live thing. We don't want it sterile all the time. That's not what this music's about. If you want that kind of stuff, go to the symphony. This ain't the symphony, it's rock 'n roll, it's energy."

"Sometimes there'll be a couple of songs that lend themselves to me actually singing it live," agrees Rhett. "Because they don't get the feel of it unless I'm singing back with it. But we're basically a live type of band anyway. I get a real good feel with the band, and I don't over-extend myself vocally in the studio to where I can't cover it live. But that's the way we work. We use the live vocals as reference and such, but sometimes, yes, we go back to them and we use them, most definitely."

As for his vocal style, Rhett says that, "In the early days I listened to everybody. I grew up with a lot of different things, anyone from James Brown and Paul Rodgers to Ian Gillan, all down the line. I never particularly had a voice that lends itself to sound like anybody else, so I just used all the influences I heard and just put it into my own... what I got here."

"It's not very complicated," concluded Rhett. "Basically, you can get into different aspects of it, but you've got to get it really tight to make it in this business. It's not this, it's not that, it's just recording

                                   Martin Popoff

good albums and going out on the road and playing to the masses. You know, mom gave me permission to come back out on the road. And that's what it takes. And that's what we'll continue to do until... forever. Until I'm dead in my grave, I'll continue to rock."

The guys ended their chat with Rosen hopeful about the future. "Stay on the road, stay on the road, stay on the road," said Kip, asked about the plan from here on out. "Then we're going to go in and do another record real quick, and go back out on the road again for the summer. Touring sells records. Everybody's happy. We're almost friends now. Almost. Yesterday we were friends; today, it's like a little shaky, but we're almost friends."

In an interview with Bob Nalbandian, also on the California swing (and third date in, Concert Factory club, Costa Mesa), Sandy Slavin similarly took the opportunity to distinguish the "Reale" Riot from the Quiet one... "A message you can give the readers is that the real Riot is here! There's been like Quiet Riot, the would-be guys who call themselves heavy metal, but they sound a little Top 40-ish to my ears. It ain't fuckin' metal. We were watching a soap opera the other day, and a guy on it was singing Quiet Riot songs."

Added Rhett, "The message we'd like to say is that there's been a lot of kids who've hung in with us throughout the years when we had to take breaks and with all the bullshit and politics that's gone down, we'd just like to thank all the kids for sticking with us. We don't stick our fist down anyone's throat that makes it in rock 'n' roll if they do it in any type of honest or sincere fashion. But these guys are like parasites to rock 'n' roll and all they've done is exploit Randy Rhoads and deceive the kids, making them think that they're heavy metal with all the money, hype and politics. We are the real Riot! Riot means acting in a wild and unrestrained manner and Quiet Riot is a total contradiction in terms. They're wimps! And I'm gonna stick my fist down all their throats! Print it, don't cut it, it's a take!"

Nalbandian's chat with Forrester and Slavin was prefaced by a sentiment shared among the nascent and burgeoning heavy metal press at the time, that this was a band that was keeping the fires burning for American heavy metal during a latent period.

"Riot is one of the finest heavy metal bands to come out of America," pronounced the legendary west coast scribe. "In fact, this band, as far as I'm concerned, has made a major breakthrough in US metal, for Riot were one of the originators of the new breed of American metal. Since the band's first LP, *Rock City*, released back in '77, they've encountered some rather tough struggles dealing with record companies, yet the band, despite the lack of commercial interest of record companies, etc. and numerous lineup changes, are now rocking harder than ever with the release of their excellent new platter, *Born in America*. Riot seem to be heading straight to the top."

When Rhett tells Bob that the band had signed to Fire Sign in the beginning because, "Back then, it wasn't cool to sign on with major record labels since they weren't acceptive (sic) to heavy metal bands," Sandy offers, "That's why we basically went to Quality also. Because now we've got control over our record, because, like, Elektra wanted us to mellow down. It's like a 'hit single' mentality with the record companies; you've got to have a hit. And we don't really want to tone down for a hit song, so like you're fighting against all these jerks."

Which, of course, was also the story with the band shifting allegiances to Elektra in the first place... "Yeah, again it was that hit single kind of thing," continues Slavin. "You can't convince these jerks. That's why we had the label changes. We did *Fire Down Under* for Capitol originally, and they said, 'We don't hear a hit,' and we said, 'Fuck you! We're not gonna change this record; we really believe in it. But now it's going really good. It's our first time out here. These are like our tune-up gigs, because we've got GT, the new guitarist, in the band, and we've been off the road for a while. So we wanted to get out here and do some smaller gigs. It's good to finally be out here. We're gonna be back to California and keep coming back."

Sandy and Rhett were also looking forward at this time to reliving Riot's glory days in the UK. "The festivals are great," said Sandy, "and we're gonna go back this summer to play some more festivals and we're going to be headlining in England."

Added Rhett, "Mark Reale talked to our friends from Saxon recently in Texas, and they said that the kids in Europe are dying to see me in the band. The kids in Europe are loyal to the band whereas like in America, sometimes the kids will forget you real fast. *Fire Down Under* was one of Riot's most successful records, but we've got the momentum with this new LP now."

But asked about the departure of Guy Speranza, Rhett is not as forthcoming... "This question is starting to God damn bug me! This question should be done and over with. I am the lead singer of Riot and I always will be! It changed the band drastically when I joined, and we all get along quite well. Everybody has a common denominator. They all hate me." To which Sandy quips, "We're still not friends (laughs)."

Born in America, alas, would be the last record for the classic era of Riot, that fine name not emblazoned on an album cover again until Mark built himself a new lineup for 1988's *Thundersteel*.

"The band basically broke up," says Reale. "What had happened was that the last thing we did with Rhett was the *Born in America* tour, which was mainly in conjunction with Kiss and Vandenberg. and we just toured a lot throughout the States and we were just burned-out at the end of that. We were the opening act and we were tired of that, and at the end of that tour I just decided to take a break. Then I moved to

Texas for a couple of years and the band just fell apart. But we did do a reunion tour on the West coast, which must have been 1985 or something, with me and Sandy Slavin, and Don Van Stavern who later became a member of Riot for *Thundersteel*, who I had met in Texas. He was playing bass. So it was kind of a mixture of the original members and new guys. And I think Rhett came down. We had to use a different vocalist for the first two shows, because he was doing a solo record, but then he came out and finished the tour with us. And then the band just kind of fell apart again after that, and I moved back to New York.

I never did join another band. I always wanted to try different projects musically, but nothing ever came up. I was always pretty much focused on Riot."

Other factors surrounding the break-up have Rhett Forrester wanting to go solo, which he did fairly quickly, coming up with an album in 1984. As well, Sandy and Kip were in agreement that things were not progressing, with Sandy getting together with original Riot bassist Phil Fiet in the Adam Bomb solo band situation. For a brief time, Rick, who called it a day about the same time as Rhett, had been replaced in an officially still alive Riot by the 19-year-old Gerald T. Trevino.

"I can certainly tell you all the bad decisions I made, that's for sure," reflects Steve, asked about regrets. "But I did my best to change those things. And I was really powerless because of the way we were structured and if I really pushed things, which I eventually did, it caused more damage—and eventually irreversible damage."

"Frustration with management," is what Rick cites as the main reason for the demise of Riot. "Kip and Sandy and myself were basically fed up with Billy and Steve, and just wanted them out of the picture. We tried to unify the band, all the members, and it just didn't seem like it would happen. Guy was out of the picture by then, but Mark still had these very strong ties to Billy and Steve. I mean, very strong, strong ties. Basically, it was almost like they owned him. And with that record, Mark and Rhett sort of zeroed in on a new sound. Mark wanted to take the band in more of a harder, more progressive—maybe progressive isn't the correct word—but more of a classical heavy rock approach."

Early days drummer Pete Bitelli is exactly of the same opinion, opining that the dynamic was basically Steve and Billy confiding in and collaborating with Mark only, creating a team between the three of them and causing a fissure with the rest of the band. And Pete is of the opinion it was that way because Mark was the least likely from the start—and basically from the core of his personality type—to ask questions about finances or otherwise rock the boat.

"Yeah, and we could never get a clear-cut answer on how any of the records had sold," continues Rick. "The band definitely missed out on its royalties. There were a lot of secrets; a lot of stuff was kept from us, and it was just very frustrating. We were young, and a lot of times, Sandy, Kip and myself may have felt, wow, if we did something or said something we might be out. Because just looking at the history of it, it was very feasible (laughs). The band really didn't get anything. It was just a very sad state, and the three of us, just Sandy and I and Kip, we knew it was coming to an end. And we didn't want anything to do with Billy and Steve anymore. The writing was on the wall."

Pete is pretty adamant that Mark showed no signs of a stomach ailment during his tenure with the band, but Rick, lasting a few more years, says, "Well, we knew there were some issues, but nowhere near to the extent it was in much later years. I really think he kept it to himself. I don't think anybody really knew what was going on. He kept it to himself. Who knows? Maybe it was all the years of aggravation, of him struggling and trying to take the band to a level he always wanted to, and being aggravated by that. Plus the fact, obviously, he did have Crohn's disease. But towards his later years, it just went to a whole different level. But during the period I was with him, I don't think anybody was really aware of any issue."

As for where Rick went next, "I was so disgusted, I'd just had enough of it. Although I almost looked at it as like, wow, we had a good ride and now it's over. But it was very disappointing to watch the various phases of the band, losing Guy right at a critical moment, him leaving the band right after *Fire Down Under*. I thought, well, I don't think we're ever going to get to that level that we were about to receive. And after *Restless Breed*, it became more apparent, because then we were no longer on Elektra. With the new label, everything was very minimal. Basically whatever advances we got from the two prior records, all that went into their studio. And to tell you the truth, drugs. With one of the producers. That's basically what was going on. And I know that first-hand (laughs). And I just formed a band with my buddies and played original material, and just played for ourselves and played clubs. It was just very different from Riot. It was heavy, but I was basically getting to write songs and do songs that I couldn't do in Riot. I probably could've; maybe it was just me. But yeah, you could see the downfall. After *Born in America*, it was like, nobody's going to want to touch this band anymore."

"We were called Silent Partner," continues Rick, who, incredibly, is still to this day a full-time working musician at the club level, 30 years after the end of classic Riot. "Yeah, just a very different band, and I've just been basically doing that. Still writing, still playing, and on a smaller scale, just playing clubs. But it's amazing, Riot fans still say, I think you guys should get some people together and get out there and play. Because this new generation of Riot, that Mark continued for years on, it was very hardcore, bordering almost on thrash metal (laughs). Very different. He just took it in a different direction. But I meet a lot of Riot fans and get Facebook requests. It just never ends. In fact, just recently, the guys, who are now called Riot V—none of the original members—they just continue to play. They did a show, and actually they asked Lou and I to make an appearance and to play on some of their songs. It was very interesting. And the crowd, they remember everything and they were excited to see me. They said they never imagined in all these years I would join the band and make an appearance. It sparks your interest again. There's clips of that, of me with them. I do 'Swords and Tequila' and 'No Lies,' with Riot V in Brooklyn, March 2015. And after the shows, fans were coming up to me with *Fire Down Under* records to autograph—it just never goes away."

Of course, seeing and hearing any appreciable version of a classic Riot lineup is not possible anymore because of the deaths of first singer Guy Speranza, second singer Rhett Forrester and finally leader of the clan (but one wouldn't say patriarch), Mark Reale.

After Riot broke up in mid-1984, Rhett hooked up with Virgin Steele guitarist Jack Starr, singing on his *Out of the Darkness* album, on which the two made use of the The Rods' rhythm section, Gary Bordonaro and Carl Cannedy. Winding up in France, his next

                              Martin Popoff

record was a solo album called *Gone With the Wind*, recorded in September and October of 1984 and issued on French label Bernett before the year was out. In 1988, he'd follow up with a much more professional affair called *Even the Score*, on which Rhett teamed up with axeman Paul Kayen, a.k.a. Paul Kane from Aldo Nova's band.

There wouldn't be much else of substance recorded by Rhett up until his death. He briefly hooked up with Mark to play Riot songs again and worked on the all-star *Thrasher* collaboration metal project. Noted Carl Canedy, overseer of *Thrasher*, "We wanted to give Rhett material that was

completely him. Something with a bluesy, tough edge. He nailed it the first day. Rhett's personality was one that snarled at you. He was always professional, always came in on time and ready to lay it down. And man, what a tremendous voice."

Rhett also tried to get something going with shredder Alex Masi, the demos of which would be released posthumously under the band name Dogbone. Demos followed with bands in Calgary, Alberta (Black Symphony, Dr. Dirty) and LA (Dirty Water), but that would be it. Rhett's very last band would be Mr. Dirty, back in Atlanta where he would meet his demise.

"It's still a mystery to me at this point," reflects Mark, on what caused Forrester's violent demise. "I've heard a couple of different things. I heard one rumour where he was carjacked. You hear everything from he was trying to score drugs, which I don't know that to be true at all. But the last thing I heard was that it was basically this robbery or this carjacking thing. Actually the last thing I heard was that he was with somebody who was trying to score drugs and an argument ensued and he got killed. Rhett and Guy were actually some of the last people I spoke to from the old days. The strangest thing about Rhett dying, is that the night that we were finishing *Brethren of the Long House*, the same night that I got the call from Speranza, first call in 11 years, it was the same night I got a phone call from Don Van Stavern, who had been in Riot for two records. He called me from Texas and told me about Rhett. Because Rhett was also living in Texas for a while, because he had a girlfriend there or something. He had gone back to Atlanta for something or other and that's when it happened."

It is indeed a curious wrinkle in the story there, on February 20, 1995, Steve Loeb explaining to the author by way of a very early example of email communication (!), "What happened was, Guy suddenly reappeared after splitting up with his wife. The same wife who influenced him to leave the stage for the greener pastures of pest extermination. So he reappears, which makes me think that he needed to know that if he wanted to, he could return to the fast life any time he pleased. He and Mark worked on some material and Sony was going to finance the project. Some recording even began, and then… it was déjà vu all over again (as Yogi Berra said). Suddenly he's back together with the wife and she wants him to move to Florida and naturally he agrees. Was I surprised? Nah. And so it goes. So no, Mike DiMeo did the recent tour dates, which went over great. The band will return to tour Japan and support the new record, which is why I've been in the studio with them six days a week since they returned. We're supposed to deliver a finished record to Sony by February 28th. Yeah, like I have some waterfront property for sale in Arizona, if you get my drift. I'd say second week in March, and that would be pushing it."

"Yes, exactly as Steve says, it was just like deja vu all over again," laughs Mark. "It was a shock. Like I said, we were doing the finishing touches on *Brethren of the Long House*, and I got a phone call in the studio, and it was him after 11 years, and it was like yeah, this, that and the other thing. He was basically going through a trial separation and he had two kids, you know? And he wanted to make a record! He was interested in writing some stuff, which was a complete shock. So naturally Steve and I, we're like, 'Yeah!

Let's do it.' But after we had written some tunes, he basically worked out his differences with his wife and decided to blow the whole thing off again, which was a kind of frustrating for us."

The facts as we know them are that Rhett was shot in the back and killed, Saturday, January 22, 1994, in the morning, after leaving his DeKalb County apartment before dawn and driving to (or as far as) the intersection of Lovejoy Street and Merritt Avenue, off the crime-ridden Techwood Homes housing project in Northwest Atlanta, a few blocks north of Centennial Olympic Park. Less factual, the crime has been framed as a dispute over a drug transaction but also an attempted carjacking, although Rhett was in his own car and the two male perpetrators were in their own brown Cadillac.

After what was clearly an argument (as witnessed by a street person) Rhett had managed to drive away from the scene a number of blocks, alert a policeman in his cruiser (which Rhett allegedly collided with), and exclaim "I've been shot!" before collapsing dead, the bullet having pierced his heart.

As mentioned, there were apparently two perpetrators, one who is now also dead, and another who admits to being at the scene but not pulling the trigger. What muddies the waters is that the policeman who last saw Rhett alive had been taking a report from a man who was saying that he had just been robbed by two men in a brown Cadillac, ascribing at least some suggestion of randomness to both crimes.

Rhett was survived by an ex, plus a daughter, as well as his mother La Fortune Forrester and fiancé Lori Plester. Rhett was 37 years of age.

Lori's brother Rick Plester, who had worked with Rhett in the early '90s in Calgary with his band Black Symphony, adds, "I've heard a lot of stuff, me and my sister, and I don't know if she would be willing to talk to anybody about it, because she is still hurting from that even though it was so long ago. But I know that she had mentioned a couple of weeks prior to this happening, that somebody had taken some shots at him. And then another time, somebody had tried to run him over, and he jumped into a garbage bin. And so I don't know if that's related."

But the view, given to the author by another quite authoritative source, that Rhett was in the middle of some sort of drug transaction when he was shot, elicits from Rick the summary comment, "Yeah, that's pretty similar to what I heard too."

I asked Rick for some additional glimpses into the life of Rhett, what he was like fully a decade past his last records with Riot.

"I started that thing, Black Symphony in 1992, I believe," begins Plester. "I put ads out all over, everywhere, trying to find a lead singer, which is almost impossible, especially when you live in Calgary, Canada. Rhett had been in San Antonio at the time and he'd answered the ad, and so I sent him off a cassette tape of the songs, because that's the only way you would do it then, and he really liked them. So when he showed some interest in my songs, and he wanted to come up, I was pretty happy about that. And I had an investor, so we made the plans, and we flew him up there and went in the studio and we recorded three songs. We actually had a drummer, but we decided not to use him and just went with a drum machine on the demos for simplicity. And then we put together a show from there, and we spent about a month rehearsing, and put it together. And so we started to work together, and that's how it started."

Speaking about Rhett's taste in music, Plester figures, "Rhett just liked real rock 'n' roll. Anything that was good. He was quite open, actually, with a lot tastes outside of rock 'n' roll. But he loved the bluesier rock 'n' roll—whiskey rock 'n' roll, as he would call it. He really didn't talk much about Riot, oddly. He'd put it in the past, but seemed quite grateful that he had those experiences. He told me a pretty funny story about touring with Kiss. Gene, I guess, would go on stage, and they're all pissed-off because there was spit and gob all over the stage. Rhett would spit while singing; a lot of singers do that. So one day, apparently, Gene went a bought Rhett a brass spittoon, so when he needs to spit, he could go to the side of the stage and spit in this brass spittoon (laughs)."

"You know, I actually got along well with Rhett," continues Rick, asked for his impressions of the guy. "There was some tensions because of some of the demons he had in his life, through drugs, and in the end, that's why I released him. But during the period that we were together, I still, to this day, even though that band that went on and sold a lot of records with different vocalists, I think Rhett was probably still the best vocalist. I have a lot of respect for his talents. He was a funny guy, fun to be around, and the only thing that got him was the demons, I guess you could call them."

On the subject of Rhett's particular poisons in '92, '93, Plester says, "Rhett didn't really drink all that much, no more than anybody else. He'd have a few beers, a couple drinks and that would pretty much be the end of it. He was never a mess when it came to alcohol, in my days with him. But when he came up to Calgary, he was straight, and he'd been trying to clean himself up. I let him use my apartment for the month, and I went to my girlfriend's. And we found some things there that suggested that he was perhaps doing some heroin or cocaine, or mixing the two. I don't do drugs so I couldn't tell for sure, but there was definitely something going on. And he came to me a couple times and told me that he had a problem and that he was addicted."

"Eventually I moved him into like a resident hotel where you rent by the month, and I think I had him there for probably about three months in that place. And it was during that time was when he suggested to me that he needs to get some help. I didn't even really know what to do. And he started getting angry, and desperate, I guess we'll call it. You know, especially when he wasn't able to get anything. But in any major city, it's not hard to find, and so I guess he ended up finding the stuff. And something went down between him and the drummer, which I didn't like too much, and so I decided to release him from the band because of that. Another time a couple bikers came to my door looking for him. But they didn't give me a problem. In fact, they were very cool to me, actually, once I told them that I had let him go. But you know what? If it wasn't for that, I really was looking forward to working with him musically. We got along great; it was never a music thing."

"I offered to buy him a ticket home," continues Rick, "for his services and everything; I thought I would do that. And 'round about the same time, we got some phone bills that were from the hotel, and he was like calling a lot of 1-888 numbers, or whatever they were at the time (laughs), and there was like a $3000 bill. So I just told him, you know, you're on your own. I hadn't purchased the ticket yet. So he started playing with a local Calgary cover band, worked a couple gigs with them and made enough money and he went... he didn't go back to San Antonio, but he chose to go to Atlanta. Actually, I didn't realize at the time, he took my sister with him (laughs). Yeah, they were an item, and they hid it from me. And the next thing you know, I let him go, and my sister goes with him."

"I remember Rhett Forrester like it was yesterday," recalls Virgin Steele legend Jack Starr, speaking with Andreas Andreou, about his stint with Rhett a few years before Calgary. "First of all we began by talking on the phone and getting to know each other and it was strange because Rhett and I are very different people and we had to learn to trust each other. I remember one day playing a song on the phone to Rhett. The song was called 'Concrete Warrior' and when I finished playing it, Rhett said, 'Jack, you must have wrote that song for me because I am a concrete warrior and when I walk in the streets of New York City I fear nobody.' I though that it was great that Rhett was making the songs come alive. And I even wrote

'Wild in the Streets' for Rhett because it was crazy hanging out with him. It seemed that women and trouble followed him wherever he went. In 1984, I invited Rhett to live in my house on Long Island. It was during the summer and my ex-wife had gone back to France to visit her family and I thought that I could practice a lot and write songs with Rhett. But little did I know that Rhett had other plans, which included a lot of drinking and partying and different beautiful woman coming to the house every night. It was a time that I will never forget. Rhett was like the 'blonde god' in the movie *Almost Famous*. It was hard not to envy him, but at the same time I was so proud that he was in my band."

"When we got to the studio for the first day of the vocals for *Out of the Darkness*," continues Starr, "Rhett showed up late with a bottle of Jack Daniels in his hand and a couple of words that he had written on a napkin. He turned to the engineer and said, 'I am ready, and make sure that you are ready, because I don't like to re-sing the same song twice.' And he was right, because most of the songs were done in one take. And when the church choir came in to sing the backups on the song 'False Messiah,' Rhett looked at me and said, 'This song makes me feel good because it's calling out to God.' Later Rhett told me that he loved Elvis and that some of the best songs of Elvis were his gospel songs because they were the most sincere and spiritual. Rhett, like Elvis, was a southern boy that could be wild and tough, like in his song 'Hard Lovin' Man,' but he could also be sensitive and reflective. It was a great honour working with Rhett Forester—R.I.P.."

Rhett's esteemed predecessor in Riot, Guy Speranza would die nine years later, from pancreatic cancer, on November the 8th, 2003.

"It's just really daunting," said Mark, speaking with the author three days later. "I'm shocked. I knew he was ill for quite some time now. I was speaking with his wife periodically. He was actually diagnosed last April, and I found out shortly after that. And I spoke with him numerous times on the phone. And a lot of old people came out of the woodwork, people I hadn't seen for over 20 years, people who used to hang out with us when we used to play in my basement in Brooklyn. But yeah, the last couple of weeks, the news I was getting was that he was in the hospital and things were looking rough."

"It's rough because, you know, I've done so much since those days," continues Mark. "And to be quite frank, we haven't been close since he left. I saw him briefly in 1994. Believe it or not, he was going through a trial separation with his wife at the time, when they still lived in Brooklyn. Actually Guy had two daughters; one is now 20, graduated college, and one is 17. This was back in '94, when he was in this separation situation. And like I say, he called me out of the blue, and I hadn't seen him at that point through all the years, and he wanted to do some stuff. And I was really excited, and we did some writing sessions together and then he bailed out. They got back together and they moved to Florida and I hadn't seen him since then. But the thing is, when I think of him, I think of him from 1980, when we were young and all that stuff was happening. So aside from the fact that he sang in the band, everything I've done up until now is based on what we did, those records we made. It gave us some kind of cult notoriety, so to speak, and I was able to carry on based on that foundation. So it's a big loss to me in that sense."

"One of the best things about Guy... I mean, first of all, as a singer, he was unique, and I thought he was a great singer. When I first saw him, when we used to play back in the old days, we would have block parties on the weekend in the neighbourhood where we lived, and they would have bands playing. And I saw him playing; he was in a different bands and he was like a local hero at the time. And I saw him singing at one block party and I saw the girls reacting to him, and he had the charisma, the look, the voice. And I turned to my partner, Pete, and said hey, if we can get this guy, we can go places. And we basically approached him. He was actually preparing to leave the music industry at that point. He must've been 18 or 19 years old. He was going to go to college and study to be an architect. So I convinced him to give music another shot. Then we started. So it was that unique sound of his voice. And you know, recording, I think the microphone loved his voice. You know, some guys are really soulful, and then you have some guys that the microphone loves their voice and they record them great. And he had a really slick, tough sounding voice. Combine that with the heavy guitars and stuff, it created that original sound that we had. That was really one of the defining things that helped us get notoriety. And he wasn't pretending. That's one of the odd parts of the music business, is that he was really down-to-earth, there was no ego, there was no pretense about him. He was just a regular guy, basically."

"This news has just spread immediately like wildfire," continues Mark. "Like I say, I knew Guy was sick for some time, but I hadn't told anybody. So nobody knew, other than a few people that were close."

Asked if Guy had still been in the extermination business, Mark says, "I guess. You know, oddly enough, I don't know if I mentioned this to you, but the doctors that diagnosed him strongly believe that it was the result of his occupation. They said that over 20 years of exposures to working with all kinds of chemicals... and I heard from a friend that you're supposed to practice precautions, and somebody said—I don't know if it's true—but I heard through the grapevine that he didn't really practice the proper precautions. Guy's wife told me that the doctors told him that, that they strongly believe. So it's always kind of bad to think that, you know, you leave the band or resign or whatever, and wind up in an occupation that's going to harm you in that way."

"I mean there's definitely a connection. Because they said, it's either like hereditary or it's the result of that. And both of Guy's parents are alive, and they're into their 80s. So it came out of left field. So for someone... it's just so tragic. It hasn't even sunk in to me yet, to be honest. Because I hadn't been close to him for so long, it's more the memory of those days. It's incredible. I haven't seen him much over the years, but I knew he was there. Even in the hopes that we would get together and do something again. Even though you're not seeing him everyday, he's there. Now, all right, I'm not seeing him every day, but he's actually not there."

"Well, I found out he had pancreatic cancer," adds original guitarist Lou Kouvaris, "and that it was a pretty bad. I think he died within eight months or a year of his diagnosis. And a lot of folks were saying that because he got into the pesticide business— not pesticide, but rodent extermination business—that that's what happened. But I went down and spoke in 2011 to Jimmy Iommi and Gina, his wife, and we had a lengthy conversation about Riot and everything, and Guy's death. And Guy never really touched... you know, he was never the one going out there and doing the exterminating and stuff like that. He was in the office. So I don't think it was anything that was chemically induced. I think he just died of a natural occurrence, or a biological occurrence. And that's what happened to him. And he really was a wonderful guy. I had a total respect for Guy and Guy's family."

Pan forward another nine years, and Mark Reale, the musical heart of the band that made Riot real, slips into a coma on January 11, 2012 due to a subarachnoid hemorrhage and finally passes on January 25, after his long battle with Crohn's disease. Mark's beloved mother Frances preceded Mark in death, but his deep relationship with his father Anthony allowed him some joy, and Anthony lives on, keeping alive Mark's memory.

Also keeping Mark's memory alive is Pedro Alonso, an angel of this tragic story, who has created a stirring and loving website dedicated to Mark's memory. Pedro offers pictures of Mark's gravesite (Pete Bitelli says he's been to visit and had a long conversation with Mark), news of his father, a spot of historical press, death notices, funeral news and proceedings, as well as an interview with Mark's best friend and right-hand man, Damon Di Bari, who through his words in that chat with Pedro, also does much to keep Mark's good name eternal.

Again, give the loss of the band's leader and chief music writer and ambitious visionary, and then also the loss of both of the lead singers the band had in that first decade, necessarily spread over the span of these deaths was also the death of the dream that any "classic" lineup of Riot could ever pick up where it left off.

And although it must be said that Guy never recorded again, and Rhett fairly inconsequentially, in fits and starts, one happy dimension of the Riot tale in totality is that Mark indeed was soon to revive the name and create a career for himself as king of a thing called Riot, for almost 30 years after the original band was set to pasture. What this of course allows the fan of Riot in general and Mark in particular, is a considerable body of work to explore once it gets tougher and tougher to pull much extra artistic enjoyment out of the original canon. For this we thank Mark Reale, and it is this next generation of Riot rock we will celebrate, albeit more briefly, in our epilogue, and mostly through the words of Mark himself in conversations held with the author over the years.

Epilogue – "It was the whole Yngwie Malmsteen thing of who could run the fastest and jump the highest."

Once having set himself up more permanently in Texas, after the demise of Riot and an ultimately pointless time in LA, Mark had put together a band called Narita (originally The Mark Reale Project), with members of S.A. Slayer, named so to distinguish themselves from California's ultra-thrash Slayer. A demo was recorded in 1984, but more significant was the collaboration with Don Van Stavern, who would soon become bassist in a new supercharged version of Riot. Other members of Narita included Steve Cooper and Dave McClain, who would go on to drum up a storm for Machine Head.

A couple wheel-spinning years were spent in LA with Van Stavern, during which they tried to get Riot going again with Rhett Forrester and Sandy Slavin. The guys even tried to get legendary Jag Panzer singer Harry Conklin to join the band, but Conklin reportedly blew out his voice after two gigs due to rock 'n' roll boozing.

"Mark would spend his time off from Riot in San Antonio, Texas," confirmed Van Stavern on these points, to Kevin Stewart-Panko. "because he loved the weather; he didn't care much for the New York cold. Mark wanted to keep his chops up, so he asked Ricky (Wahrheit, who introduced Mark to Don) about jamming with local musicians. Ricky mention my band, S.A. Slayer, because we rehearsed at his place. I would help Mark write songs for Riot and for what would end up as a part of Narita. I grew up in San Antonio where Riot was a mainstay on radio down here. I had every Riot record and was definitely a fan. Mark used to tell me all the horror stories about their career. Over the years Riot were the victim of bad management and their decisions, but this really didn't bother me as I was excited to jam with one of my favourite guitar players."

Asked by Kevin about all the rumours of constant relocation in the Riot camp, Don exclaimed, "True! When the members got antsy and decided to regroup, Riot was Rhett Forrester, Sandy Slavin and Mark and they were located in LA. Mark and I travelled to LA, did some rehearsing and writing and started to play out and shop for a new record deal. Rhett was in and out and we had a couple singers come in, including Harry Conklin from Jag Panzer, but nothing was permanent. After no record deal panned out, Mark decided to head back east and rebuild there. Sandy and Rhett didn't want to move and didn't like the 'heavier' music Mark and I were writing at the time, so we went alone to seek out singers and drummers. We ended up with the band's original management and producers from their iconic period."

As Van Stavern relates, licking his wounds, Mark moved back to New York, along with Don, and took up collaboration once again with his old nemesis Steve Loeb. A new deal as equally promising as the old ones, would soon be struck with CBS Records, and on March 24, 1988, Riot would be back in the major race with speedy and technical metal feast for the ears, *Thundersteel*. The title track of the album, would be a carry-over from the Narita demo, which also had included the songs "Liar" and "The Feeling is Gone," neither of which were used for the new record.

Accompanying Mark and Don on *Thundersteel* would be hot 'n' high new vocalist Tony Moore (Christian name: Morabito) and San Antonio percussion master Bobby Jarzombek (ex-Juggernaut), who had replaced Mark Edwards, who would leave for a deal with his band Lion, on Scotti Brothers.

"That was the rebirth of Riot after me living in Texas for two years," reiterates Mark, "and my collaboration with Don Van Stavern, who wielded a much more technical approach. After that Kiss tour, the tour we did for *Born in America*, I had moved to Texas and had pretty much formed a band down there. I met some Texas musicians and formed a band called Narita—we named it after the second Riot record. And we did a few shows here and there. And that's what led back to the *Thundersteel* Riot. Although Don Van Stavern was the bass player, the drummer actually went on to play with Sacred Reich and Machine Head. See, they were a part of a group from San Antonio called Slayer. So it was basically those guys, and I formed this band called Narita. So me and Don started writing tunes together, and when that fell apart, that's what led back to Riot. So Don was from the Texas Slayer, and the vocalist and the drummer weren't. But they were all in Narita. There was this guy by the name of Steve Cooper on vocals, and David McClain on drums. And then when I came back to New York to reform Riot, Don came with me. So he was originally from Slayer, and the vocalist, we found in New York. One of the guys from the studio turned me on to him, Tony Moore. Basically we used a studio drummer for the first few demo tracks, and then we got another Texas musician by the name of Bobby Jarzombek, whose brother Ron was the guitar player in a band called Watchtower. They were a really good progressive metal band, and had a big following in Europe. So Bobby's his big brother, and we got him to join up and that became the *Thundersteel* lineup."

"We pretty much just took the band into the '80s," reflects Mark, asked about the mission for the new Riot. "And I was really getting into the neo-classical sound myself actually. So I was really digging on that, and my collaboration with Don, because Slayer was very technical, progressive metal. So when you took that and you took myself and you put the two of us together, you got this technical approach but still with a very melodic song structure over the top. And that's kind of where we went on *Thundersteel*. I really liked the song 'Flight of the Warrior' from *Thundersteel*; that's probably one of my favourites of the whole catalogue."

Laughs Steve, "The Johnny in 'Johnny's Back,' of course, was all of us and we were ready to rock again... and we did. It was a good career move, *Thundersteel*. It brought the band roaring back, and to my surprise had the band repositioned as one of the top new 'speed metal' bands along with Megadeth—I was pleasantly surprised when I read that in New York's *Village Voice*. And for us to be able to do that was testament to doing the planning for perfect repositioning. I was proud of all of us for pulling that off."

February 28, 1990 brought a second CBS album, and one must mention, a second recorded at the same studio as every other Riot album, Greene Street Recording in New York, and also like all the others, overseen from a production standpoint by Steve Loeb, who was proving adept at keeping up with the times and the dialing in of the new sounds and textures necessary to compete in the late '80s.

"At the time of *The Privilege of Power*, I was still spending a lot of time in Texas," recalls Mark. "And me and Don and our drummer Bobby Jarzombek got to do a lot of jamming together. And at that point I realized I had these great musicians. I think technically that was the best Riot lineup of all time, purely from a technical standpoint. They were far and away the best players. And we went off on this ego trip. *Privilege of Power* was, 'Let's see what we can do, let's spread our wings and see how high we can sing and how fast we can play, and just go crazy here.' And that's what it was. I mean, it's a marketing nightmare. It was very experimental and you wouldn't necessarily know how to categorize it. You had songs like 'Maryanne' that were very, very pop-oriented. Then you had a cover version of Al Di Meola's 'Racing with the Devil on a Spanish Highway,' and then you had a song like 'Dance of Death,' which a speed metal band like Metallica or something would do. It was a really far-flung kind of thing which you couldn't categorize. We utilized brass sections on a couple of the tracks, which had been done before on rock records, but not so much in a heavy metal context. We had a lot of guest appearances, like Joe Lynn Turner on a couple of tracks, a lot of studio guys which you wouldn't associate with us, including T.M. Stevens who's a big, big session player with everybody from The Pretenders to Whitney Houston. We had a guy from the Saturday Night Live band, G. E. Smith. It was just a really strange time."

Steve Loeb considers opening track on the record, "On Your Knees," a highlight of the later years Riot material. "As much

as I did not care for Tony's vocals and never did, I loved the
horn arrangements Randy Brecker did. You know, we had the
greatest NYC section on this track and we had Grandmaster D St
scratching. It was, I thought, a terrific experiment that worked.
Randy and Michael Brecker came to the studio to hear the track I
wanted them to arrange horns for, and when they heard drummer
Bobby Jarzombek, they were both blown away, The guys in that
incarnation of Riot were not your average heavy metal band. They
had gone way, way beyond that."

Resurrecting Riot was a career highlight in Steve's life with the
band. "That we could change personnel and build a new band
around these new guys and have enough of a base to keep it
going... it proved that Riot was, in the end, like a brand that was
more than a band. After a time we knew mega-stardom was not
in the cards, but we could still create, stretch out, experiment and
try to be in front of things. I'm most proud that we had no issue
using a horn section like Tower of Power or the Brecker Brothers or
rapper Grandmaster D St (Herbie Hancock) or outre jazz guitarist
James Blood Ulmer etc., and reach different people. I loved doing
the Al Di Meola cover of 'Racing with the Devil,' signaling we
were interested in a very different musical audience out there—and
pull it off. It was such a risk to do a record like *Privilege* but that's
what it was all about for Riot. At least the Riot I was interested in."

"Sometimes it worked better than other times," continues Loeb,
"but I always wanted to push the envelope. I confess there were
projects that caught me at really bad personal moments and I just
couldn't get my head into things and feel I shortchanged the band.
And if I could do things again, I might have found a better way
to do those projects. What I did was essentially have Mark and
Rod Hui produce while I took an executive production position
so I could over-rule and change and have say about material and
direction if necessary. But that was still shortchanging them and for
that I'll forever feel bad about."

Two years before his death, having constructed a reunion of the
CBS Records-era lineup, Mark looked back and framed this period,
explaining that, "The story with those two records was that
Thundersteel was kind of a natural happening. I had just come off a
low point in my life. I was out in LA for three years, living in my
car. Basically, we did like a little reunion there with Rhett Forrester,

and it went really well, and so I came back to New York and I met Tony Moore, and hence we made *Thundersteel*. *Privilege of Power* was like... I always try to get the best musicians I could play with. That's always been my modus operandi—and then let everybody fly. And so we did *Thundersteel*, it was pretty focused, and then *Privilege of Power* went off the deep end. We had songs on that album that could have been on a Bon Jovi record. We had the Al Di Meola cover, we had songs like 'Dance of Death' which was like death metal. I went crazy because I had musicians playing with me that were incredible. So I tried the idea of let's play faster and sing higher; I tried to push the envelope. So that's the difference between *Thundersteel* and *Privilege of Power*. *Thundersteel* was the entrance, and *Privilege of Power* was, 'Okay, let's just go crazy.' Which is a record company nightmare, because how do you market that?"

In essence, one of the legacies of this period of the band was an early and quite pure crafting of a type of music that was to become big business in seven or eight years, namely what's known as "power metal," a traditional but European-sounding melodic and speedy form, pioneered by Priest, Dio, Maiden and Helloween, to keep the list short. And Mark was doing this in an era known for the cresting, essentially, of both hair metal and thrash.

"Well, I don't want to say it's ego or whatever, but I got involved with musicians that were incredible, so I knew that we could play fast—that's always been the Riot thing from the beginning—but at the same time, I like pop music, man. The melodic aspect... it was the combination of those two things that I think created that whole vibe. Because you've got bands that can play their asses off, and play a hundred miles an hour and it's pretty much all it is, or you have bands that basically do pop-oriented stuff. The thing with Riot was, I combined the two elements of that. And I think that was the appeal to it. I like both aspects of it. I like the testosterone-driven guitar stuff, but at the same time, I'm very emotional, and I like to feel and I like melody—I want to feel melody. So I think it's those two things that pretty much formulated the whole Riot thing during that period."

Yet having provoked metal minds again, and on yet another major deal with considerable reach, soon it was time for Mark to bust things up again and start over.

"Basically what happened was we started to get really huge in Japan," begins Reale. "We did a couple of tours there and it was just incredible. It was 1989 and we had 300, 400 kids at the hotel. It was one of those things—it was doing great. But what happened was Tony Moore left the band, after we did a tour in 1990 for *Privilege of Power*. He left because he was just fed up with the management we had at the time, and he couldn't see us going anywhere. Basically he was right, you know? But he wanted to have separate management which caused a lot of legal hang-ups. So unfortunately he left, and at that point I had to reevaluate what I was going to do."

"And somebody introduced me to Mike DiMeo," continues Mark, "and I started working with Mike in the studio. But at that point I still wasn't sure whether I was going to pursue Riot or pursue something different with him. But we decided to keep Riot going. But sure, that was a little bit of a dead time there. Mike is actually not too dissimilar from Rhett. Mike is R&B-influenced. He loves Stevie Wonder; that's one of his favourite singers. He likes Paul Rodgers; a very R&B rock approach. So that's why when I got together with him we did a lot of experimental things. I was trying to see what his best assets were."

"Before Riot, Mike's biggest claim to fame was... I'm sure you've heard of Howard Stern. He had a sidekick by the name of Stuttering John. And Stuttering John had a band called Josie Slang and Mike was the vocalist. But we did a lot of experimental things. On our first album together, *Nightbreaker*, we did a cover version of 'A Whiter Shade of Pale,' which Mike sounded incredibly good on, which Ritchie Blackmore got his hands on out here in Long Island by some quirk of fate. And Ritchie became very interested in Mike, and Mike almost wound up playing with him. Ritchie still lives up in Connecticut, but he has a house out here on Long Island as well. Mike became very friendly with Ritchie. They have a soccer team here, and Mike plays soccer, and he wound up hanging out with him for a few months. But when I decided that Riot would keep going, Mike pretty much adapted himself to that, and we started writing together. It worked out really cool because to me he has a little bit of that David Coverdale thing happening."

Nightbreaker would be issued on July 22, 1993, but initially only in Japan, followed by Europe in '94 and then in '99 (and '02) on Metal Blade Records—each of the three territories would get unique cover art. Along with old Riot chestnut "Outlaw," there indeed would be the Procol Harum cover, a rendition of Deep Purple's "Burn," and a career favourite of Steve's called "Soldier." "Enter Mike DiMeo on vocals—I loved the way Mike could sing, and 'Soldier' was just a glimpse of what Mike could do. The consummate musician, he's also an incredible talent on keyboards." On board as second guitarist would be Mike Flyntz, who had in fact joined the band for the *Thundersteel* tour dates.

"That was basically the first record with Mike," notes Mark, "and it was quite experimental in that respect. I tried to carry on with the insane fast kind of music as *Thundersteel* and *Privilege of Power*. Although I tried to make it more like *Thundersteel* and not so widespread conceptually as *Privilege of Power*."

Asked about his influences, Mike DiMeo says, "As far as hard rock goes, Paul Rodgers and David Coverdale are definitely up there. They are pretty much everything I wanted to be as far as rock singing goes. I was really more influenced by blues singers like Otis Clay, Sam and Dave, R&B soul singer, Otis Redding. I've definitely seen a change in my style over the last years. On *Nightbreaker*, I made a conscious effort to sing kind of high because they were just coming out of the Tony Moore phase and the guy used to sing into the stratosphere. We were trying to go for that, but I was never and never have been, although I've done a little bit on this record, into really high singing. I think a guy should sound like a guy, you know? (laughs). It's cool to have a high range, to be able to hit high notes, but you've still got to do it with some grit and some power. So I've tried to stay away from doing the really screechy stuff. And I've tried and try to be really conscious about the character I come across with, when I'm singing."

Also in 1993, Metal Blade Records reissued *Rock City* as well as released for the first time *"Riot Live"*, a bare-bones release of a milestone show from the Hammersmith Odeon on London, 1980. Metal Blade would soon reissue the band's rarer recent product as well as become issuer of the band's new records. Confusion reigned concerning *"Riot Live"* however, because not only is the disc named the same as the band's Rhett Forrester-era live EP from 1982, but the cover art featured the same plain red courier text on black background. Further confusing the issue is that in 1992, Sony in Japan had released a Riot live set called *Riot in Japan – Live!!*, celebrating shows in Osaka and Tokyo in 1990. In

1999, Metal Blade would reissue this album as *Live in Japan*. The set marks the debut of Karion's Pete Perez after the departure of Don Van Stavern. An interesting wrinkle to both issues is a studio outtake of the band recording "Smoke on the Water," complete with horn section, during the *Privilege of Power* sessions.

""*Riot Live*" was recorded in England," recalled Mark at the time, with a bit of a struggle. "There are so many. There's a record an Italian company sent me, and that one is a bootleg from a Long Island show at a club. *"Riot Live"* was done either on a Sammy Hagar tour we did in England or with Saxon. I don't know why it was even recorded. The thing is back then, as was quite often in the early years, whenever anything was done, we had very little control over it. It was probably just Steve's doing. That thing was just recorded. I don't think there was ever any mixing of it or anything. Because from what I've heard of it, the guitars are out of tune and all kinds of shit that we likely would have gotten freaked about (laughs)."

In fact, the CD sounds pretty good, demonstrating how tight the band was at blasting through these songs, arguably at the peak of their performance skills, with the guys captured right at their steepest rise of ascendance, a time when Riot was the most exciting thing coming out of America into a buzzing hive of UK metal bands all thinking the same positive thoughts about the future of heavy metal. Besides the expect raft of fine Riot tunes, there's a non-LP selection in "Back on the Non-Stop," which, like much old US rock, mixes boogie with modern riffing. It's understandable this one wouldn't make the grade come time for the third album, as it's the type of old school track that would have sounded behind the times even on *Narita*. A second fun addition is a super-fast version of "Train Kept A Rollin'" which is taken pretty darn near to punk rock extremes.

Next up in the land of new material for the band was *The Brethren of the Long House*, issued by Sony in Japan on November 11, 1995, by Rising Sun Productions in Europe the following year, and then essentially as a reissue by Metal Blade in 1999. Bobby Jarzombek would exit the band for the recording of the record, which was handled by John Macaluso, with Jarzombek back in the fold by the next album.

"One of my favourites," taps Mark, "because that was a concept record that happened by accident. The whole concept was based around the Native Americans in the Northeast. The way that that happened, I mean I've always been into Native American history and culture since I was a little kid, but what happened was is that I saw the motion picture *The Last of the Mohicans*, the newer version with Daniel Day Lewis, and I loved the music in it. I fell in love with the soundtrack, the Irish Celtic kind of sound. I thought, you know, I'd like to do something like that, incorporate that sound into Riot's music somehow. So I got this brainstorming to do an adaptation of the title track. The title track in the movie was so majestic and powerful, I thought this would sound great with a power chords. So I got this idea and I approached this cousin of mine who actually has a music degree and is a great musician, and we scored the track. We got the soundtrack and we basically did our own score and this whole thing. We went into the studio and recorded it and it was pretty wild. We adapted this thing from the movie and pretty much incorporated a heavy metal band into it. And while we were doing that, our vocalist Mike DiMeo, and myself, we thought, hey, this is a pretty interesting subject, very passionate. So we decided to make a concept record out of it and I thought it worked out well. It really helps to have a subject to draw from like that. So that's a kind of special record."

"I like a lot of the stuff that we've done," reflects Mike DiMeo, "but my personal opinion is that some of the mixes on the songs are really hard for me to swallow. Like working with the guys at Greene Street in Manhattan, some of the mixes they came up with, none of the band members were really happy with. And before we even had a chance to complain, it was tracked. So looking back, take *Brethren of the Long House*, the song 'Glory Calling,' when Mark Reale and myself first heard the song, both us looked at each other and like, the vocals on that song are so buried; they are really, really low in the mix. It just stands out; it's like the first thing that hits you, just being a listener. Because I'm a fan of music before anything. You know, a mix can ruin a song if it's not right. And I'm not saying it ruined the song, but when listening back to the catalogue, it's hard to separate yourself from it. Lyrically, on *Brethren*, I actually did do a lot of research. That record was based on the French and Indian war, that whole time, and I did a lot of research and I thought lyrically it was really cool."

Riot's tenth album, *Inishmore*, would mark the first time since *Privilege*, that a Riot album would be issued more or less simultaneously in Japan and the US, with the band now having signed to Metal Blade, who put the record out into 1998, after its November 11, 1997 release date in Japan. The album would be followed in the fall of '98 by a low-key live album called *Shine On*. *Inishmore* would be the first Riot album not lorded over by Steve Loeb, with Mark ending his 19-year relationship with the controversial producer and strategizer.

"*Inishmore* kind of follows in the same vein as *Brethren*," says Mark. "After *Brethren*, I wanted to go back to more of the simpler approach. I think they're all quite similar. Mike DiMeo has matured greatly since *Nightbreaker*. *Inishmore*, of course, really had that Celtic under current. And *Shine On* is the first live album, I have to say, that we had any control

whatsoever over, oddly enough. It's the first album that gets our support in any sense."

"Lyrics are always a last-minute thing," says Mike, "but *Inishmore*... you know, only one time in my life have I ever had what people call writer's block. And I tell you, it was awful, man; it was really hard. It was something that I can't explain how it happened or why it happened. And it came with the *Inishmore* record. I just had so much trouble. I could not put anything down. Lyrically it took me forever. I just could not focus."

Sons of Society, issued September 7, 1999 through Toshiba in Japan and Metal Blade in the US, featured the same lineup as its predecessor, namely Mark Reale and Mike DiMeo, with Mike Flyntz on guitars, Pete Perez on bass and Bobby Jarzombek on drums. With Mark now having broken ties with Steve Loeb, it is the band's second album in a row recorded at Millbrook Studios in New York, production credit going to Mark and Paul Orofino. "*Sons of Society* was a really good record," cites Mike DiMeo. "In my opinion, it was the best we were ever going to do with that lineup. Because when you have guys like Bobby Jarzombek and Pete and Mike Flyntz, who really, when they get together, the

music they write is really progressive, like 'On the Wings of Light.' I mean this stuff is really intricate. And you see, my background is basically blues, more like David Coverdale/Paul Rodgers-type style. And it was always hard for me to settle into a groove with that. So I think *Sons of Society* was pretty much the pinnacle of what we were going to achieve with that lineup."

Three years would pass before Riot came back with their 12th album, *Through the Storm*, issued August 26, 2002, which again finds the brunt of the recording taking place at Millbrook with Paul—at this point, despite their bassist living in Texas, Mark and Mike DiMeo were based in New York, as was their new drummer...

"Musically speaking, I would say that the biggest difference is Bobby, in both respects—Bobby Jarzombek and Bobby Rondinelli," laughs Mike DiMeo. "You know what I'm saying? I mean, if you're familiar with the older records with Bobby Jarzombek on them, Bobby Rondinelli just brings a huge difference in terms of style; it's a big change for us. Bobby Jarzombek, our last drummer, left to play with Rob Halford, and it was kind of a big blow for us because he was an integral part of the Riot sound and losing him changed our sound pretty dramatically. But I think Bobby Rondinelli's playing on this album... you know, a lot of people tell me that it's too simple for Riot. Like I had a couple people last night that were telling me that. But I welcome the change, because Bobby Jarzombek, he's a real busy player, he's fast, a real intricate player, and Bobby Rondinelli is more in the pocket, in the groove, just lays down the groove with less action going on, but I think his rhythm and tempo and feel... he's in a class of his own. He's one of the best hard rock drummers there are."

"I definitely have to say that I love Bobby Jarzombek," says DiMeo, asked about the switch in drummers. "He's one of my best friends and he's a great guy. But I mean, it's really hard for me to find a groove when he's playing those crazy rhythms (laughs). Because I like to sit in the pocket. And when I'm with Bobby Rondinelli, it's really easy for me to do that. He's just very open, he's very sparse, he just lays down the meter and that's it. And I'm free to do what I want to do. So for this record, it was a lot easier for me to express myself. One thing I'm seeing with the interviews I'm doing, people are saying oh, the vocals sound really good on *Through the Storm* and everyone is really happy with them and they're all telling me how much they enjoy them. And I really appreciate it, but at the same time I think that what happened is that I'm just that much more comfortable."

"I mean Bobby... there really was no reason for him not to leave and take that gig with Halford; that was a great gig for him. If you know Bobby Jarzombek, there's no one that can be mad at him (laughs). He's too good of a guy. There's nothing you can say bad about him. He's just a genuinely good person and I mean, I want the best for him. As for the record, we just wanted to be happy with the sound with respect to the overall mix. We tried to stay away from the mistakes made in the past, too much reverb and too much echo. We tried to stay clean, maybe a little bit too clean. Paul Orofino, the guy who produced the record, he tends to be a little bit dry in his mixes. We might have preferred a little more ambience, but I think we achieved overall the good production we were looking for."

Through the Storm featured covers of UFO's "Only You Can Rock Me" and The Beatles' "Here Comes the Sun. "That was Mark's idea. He loves UFO," laughs DiMeo. "We have no other plans for covers right now, but you know, Thin Lizzy, other old twin guitars stuff, these were Mark's influences and it is generally the stuff I was influenced by as well. Mark had some trouble doing the George Harrison cover. I think what happened is that Mark recorded the guitars in upstate New York and he had some sort of problem with the tape and he wanted to add guitars to it, but he wanted to do it on Long Island for some reason. From what I gather, this is what happened. He took the tapes to Mike Flyntz' house and he had to dump it into the computer, and the way it got dumped into the computer, it was playing at another speed. So he had to play the guitars at another speed, and when they re-recorded it, they had to record back at regular speed and dump it back onto tape, some crazy thing like that."

                    Martin Popoff

"If you're familiar with any of the other records I've done, I always have to have some of my political opinions in there somewhere," offers DiMeo, asked about the lyrics on *Through the Storm*. "Basically it's, we should overthrow the government (laughs). I would say I'm a libertarian more than anything. I used to consider myself an anarchist in all senses but I would think a libertarian says it best; I can't help talking about freedom and the importance of freedom, and how people must treasure freedom and people need to value freedom, respect it, defend it. That always comes across in my songs. Otherwise, I think a lot of this record is introspective as well, because the band has gone through a lot of problems in this last year and I think a lot of the lyrics have to do with the stuff I was thinking. But unlike *Inishmore, Sons of Society* and this record, I swear to you, I would sit down and the words just came out faster than I could write them down—one copy, no rewrites."

Journeyman that Bobby Rondinelli is—Sabbath, Rainbow and Blue Öyster Cult have all enjoyed his services)—it wasn't a given he'd be around for the next record. "There's a possibility," hedged Mark at the time. "I'm not really sure right now what's happening. A lot of it is depending on what happens with this record. Of course we hope the record does well, but the better it does, the better chance there is we can get someone like Bobby to join the band permanently. If it does well, we can offer him something, but right now he's busy and he's got a good gig with Blue Öyster Cult." Asked which members of Riot are still most enthusiastic about the brand, Mike says, "I would say it is myself and Mark. We're both trying to do what we can. You know, this music is really in a tough situation right now. It's not really popular enough that we can make a living off of it. And all our judgments have to be weighed by that. Mark called me today and said we had some sort of a tour offer. I don't know if it was legitimate. He was talking about doing 20 shows, and I want to pay the band $200 a show. Now this is in Europe, and that doesn't include buses, you know? We're not little kids anymore. A lot of bands can afford to do that because they live with their parents or something. We're grown men. Most of the people in the band, except for Mark and myself, are married. We just can't afford to go out and play for $25 a night anymore. I mean, I'm a piano player, so I play pretty much every night. I play in blues bands and jazz bands here on Long Island."

"Since I've been in the band, we've never toured the states," continues Mike. "We had an offer from Dio a few years ago to do a tour with him. And at the last minute, well, I'm going to say Mark decided not to do it. And we had a difference of opinion about this. Mark thought that the record company should support us more and I thought that we should do it at any cost. You know, I understand Mark's point of view. We've done a lot of tours where we've made absolutely no money, been out on the road for three months and come home completely broke and in debt! And Mark was fed up at that point. He didn't want to do that anymore, and I agreed with him, but I thought it was important to do that tour. It was the states and what possibly could've gone wrong? I mean, we played in Kosovo, an hour from where there was a war going on and we were in the same predicament, with no money and no one there to help if you got screwed. When you passed the border, going into the former Yugoslavia, they told you, you're pretty much on your own."

"And I just felt, we're in the states here, if anything goes wrong, at least we speak the same language, you know? And we had a big falling out about that. But we put it behind us. But all I know is that every time we went to Europe, we've come home completely broke. And I just can't afford to do it anymore. Unless the label can step up and say yes, you're worth putting on the road; we can do it. The label is in a funny position because I know that these bands, like us, we don't make them a lot. I know we don't make them enough for them to retire on, but I know we make them enough to make it worthwhile for them to continue working with us. And in order for us to start making some money and be prosperous, for us to be doing this, you know, we need to tour! And the label has to be supportive of us. And if they aren't, we're going to stay at the same level. It's a really tough situation, and I know the band has really come to the decision that we cannot spend our own money anymore touring. Because we've gone on the road and just spent all of our publishing money—it's not right anymore."

Ah, business, always lurking in the background of anything Riot was doing, especially up into these complicated years with regular studio and live records issued on disparate labels across the globe.

 Martin Popoff

Asked about the extra wrench thrown in with the Metal Blade reissues, Mark says, "As long as the material's out there, it's good, because the band is still functioning. In one way or another, I think it's going to be helpful. You know, sales-wise in the past, we never knew anything. In those days basically, we never knew what the hell they were going to say. As a matter of fact, even Steve claims not to know accurately because Elektra never really accounted correctly. I've heard all kinds of outlandish things, from 100,000 to a gold record, which I'm sure is ridiculous. That was for *Fire Down Under*, actually. That was allegedly the biggest selling one. I don't believe that, but who the hell knows? These recent ones are pretty modest. We do about 45,000 in Japan, which is funny because gold used to be 50,000 in Japan and they moved it up to 100,000 in 1989 or 1990. So we were just shy of it and then they moved it up. Of course in the states, *Inishmore* was a our first domestic release since *Privilege of Power*."

"Yeah, so far," Mark told me, when I asked how happy he was with Metal Blade. "I get calls all the time for interviews and this and that, so they seem to be on top of it. It's funny, because even when we did *Thundersteel,* and we were shopping labels, I wanted to go with an indie and Steve Loeb wanted to go with a major, and we just waited it out and waited it out. And basically the deal with CBS in the states, is that they got the record for nothing basically. Which was kind of a bad way to make a deal. So in a way I always wanted to be on a label like *Metal Blade,* because I think they know how to deal with this kind of stuff."

And surely European sales can pick up some of the slack—after all, the music Riot was making in this era seemed pumped and primed for European power metal fans to absorb, all the more because this sleek, quick-moving power metal band had distinguished pedigree going for it as well.

"Well in Europe, shoot, to tell you the truth, one of the big fiascos that took place over the last about six years is that—and this is one of the many reasons we separated from Steve—we had to cancel two major tours of Europe. One was in 1993 and one was in 1994, something like that. It was just this ludicrous situation. The band was never set up as corporation the way it is now, and Steve controlled all the purse strings. So any decision that was made, he had to approve it. So there were situations where we desperately needed to go to Europe. We hadn't been there for so long. I was out there with the old band, but the new band hadn't gone. So it was just imperative that we go. And two consecutive tours were canceled because Steve had pretty much pulled the rug out from under them at the last minute. Without getting into the gory details of it, the fans freaked. Because the fans don't know what was going on behind the scenes, and it reflected very badly on us."

"Then all these rumours started flowing around that Riot didn't want to go to Europe, that they didn't want to know their fans, that we wanted too much money. Of course none of this was true. It was just that Steve didn't want to lay out the money to send us over there. Basically what it was is that we were with a small German company at the time called Rising Sun, and they were willing to put up tour support but they wanted it to be recoupable, and I guess Steve had a problem with that. So to make a long story short, the tours were canceled and it reflected incredibly badly on us. Especially two years in a row. So basically what happened was once we got away from Steve, one of the main things is that we made it our business to get over there, which we did. We got over there for *Brethren*. We did a small tour with Skyclad. And then of course we just did this major tour with Virgin Steele spring and summer of '98. So it was building up and we had to live down this whole thing. But when we went out with Skyclad, we had this reputation that we weren't going to show up. So when we went out with Virgin Steele, it was a very slow buildup. And this tour we did with Virgin Steele and the Wacken Festival were of course incredible, unbelievable, great shows for us. It was Virgin Steele, us, and an Austrian progressive metal band called Stigmata. It was a great tour and we finally lived down all this cancellation stuff. And at Wacken, it was unbelievable and we did good. So we're finally living this down now. So we're finally coming back in Europe. I mean, hey, good record sales in Europe can be 50,000 or 100,000, so who knows? Maybe right now we're at about 25,000, 30,000; I'm not sure."

Indeed distribution in Europe was finally picking up again at this point, now that the band was on Metal Blade, who had a strong European presence through their robust German office.

"Well of course, *Nightbreaker* and *Brethren* didn't get any," says Mark. "Until finally, long after the records were released in Japan, Steve managed to make this deal with this small company called Rising Sun, who released them primarily to just Germany. And that's long after the imports have flooded in. So now, long after we've broken with Steve, and we have new management, to my shock, we recorded two or three new songs, if you want to call them demos or whatever, and our new manager went out and secured amazing deals for us. I was very surprised. I mean, after we broke with Steve, Sony actually wanted to re-sign us in Japan. We actually had a bidding war going on in Japan. It was JVC, Sony and Xero Corporation, which is pretty much distributed by EMI. They came along and offered us an amazing deal. I was pretty much in awe. So that's who we're with now, Xero Corporation. These deals were far and away better than our original deal with Sony. And then, of course, Metal Blade signed on, and we've had a few offers in Europe. It was just interesting to me that people were still interested through all the personnel changes and all the craziness."

"To be quite honest with you," sighs Mark, imagining what could have been, "I think the band would have been huge if these guys were like... but they stole my publishing—for years, okay? It's like, I wrote all the songs and never got a dime from them, man. And it's like, what was it, 1997, after my mom passed away, I finally had the wherewithal to get lawyers and to get out of that situation. So from 1997 until now, I'm in control of the band, okay? But basically, prior to that, everything that was written, I don't get a dime from them. And it was to the point where... you know, that's a songwriter's soul, the publishing. Every record that gets sold, there's a publishing royalty paid, which is non-recoupable. It's paid directly to the writer. Steve was taking it for years without even saying, 'I'll give you a quarter of the publishing.' It was like nothing—all the way up through *Thundersteel*, this was going on. So it was frustrating, but the thing that is the saving grace with me

          Swords and Tequila: Riot's Classic First Decade | 159

is the fact that I've got fans. We did Sweden Rock in 2009, and we did a meet and greet and there were like a million fans. That's the saving grace for me."

As for the ensuing and necessary patronage of a studio that isn't Steve Loeb's Greene Street... "Actually, oddly enough, Blue Öyster Cult recorded their last record at the same studio we recorded at, a place called Millbrook, which is in upstate New York, two hours north of New York. They do a lot of rock stuff there. It's a real rock 'n' roll studio, where they did the 

last few Leslie West records, that last Dream Theater side-project thing with Ty Tabor, Platypus. It's a cool environment for that kind of stuff. The thing is, this project I did with Tony Harnell, Westworld, the original rhythms section was supposed to be the Blue Öyster Cult rhythm section, which was Bobby Rondinelli, who used to be in Rainbow as well. He's in Blue Öyster Cult now and has been for quite some time. And he was supposed to do that Westworld thing with me. But by the time we got the whole thing together, Blue Öyster Cult had to go on tour. Bobby is basically a local Long Island guy, and I've of course jammed with him before. As you know, we toured with BÖC in 1980; we did that *Black and Blue* tour. That was when we were still on Capitol and we were touring *Narita*."

Westworld didn't make many waves, but indeed, the AOR-leaning band, featuring Mark and TNT vocalist Tony Harnell, was responsible for three studio albums and one live album, a self-titled in '99, *Skin* the following year, *Cyberdreams* in 2002, and *Live... in the Flesh* from 2001. The project, like Riot, fit well with Mark's old school tastes. "To be honest, I still listen to the old stuff. I'm not much for the newer stuff. I'm not really into the '90s sound, whatever that is. Basically I find it all to be lackluster in terms of the character and roots, and to me there's just no excitement. It doesn't have the electricity that I felt when I was young, like when I used to go to concerts by Rainbow. Ritchie Blackmore would come out on stage and there was just this aura. A lot of stuff today lacks that, and of course to me I think the musicianship is lacking. So I'm a big fan, of course, of Rainbow, Thin Lizzy, UFO, Priest, even, going back, Mountain, Humble Pie, Cream, The Beatles..."

"Westworld and Riot are very different from each other," Mark told Carl Begai. "If you've ever seen Riot live, there's no real comparison in that Riot is all high energy and Westworld is more bluesy and laid-back. I think there are some Riot fans that might be into Westworld, but I think predominantly Riot fans are into Riot."

In the same chat, Reale agreed with Begai's assertion that *Through the Storm* represented a change of philosophy for his band. "It was starting to get preconceived. In the past, we very rarely worked anything out; it was always a go-for-the-moment kind of thing because I always felt that created the most excitement. Working stuff out is fine, but you have to leave room to let stuff happen. And we weren't doing that. I think we became a parody of ourselves on the last record, so on the new one, I stopped worrying about how many fast songs there were and how much double bass there was. All that shit went out the window, and I think we got back to what Riot is all about. With that in mind, people are going to have their favourite albums. I don't mind so much, especially since we've had four singers. The *Thundersteel* period was an oddball era for Riot because it was the whole '80s trip; you had to have big hair, and it was the whole Yngwie Malmsteen thing of who could run the fastest and jump the highest. I've now settled back into my roots, which are more rock-based. It's a more comfortable setting for me."

Four years would pass between Riot projects, and one has got to think that Mark's increasingly painful Crohn's disease was starting to slow the man's activity. As might have been predicted, *Army of One*, issued July 12, 2006, required a new drummer, although otherwise Reale kept steady his work personnel.

As far back as 2003, Mark had told me, "Well, basically, we're going in the studio at the end of this month and laying down basic tracks for the next Riot record. Right now, it's the same people, although we have a local guy here playing drums for us now, Frank Gilchriest, who also does drumming with Virgin Steele. I wanted to get someone local because a lot of the problems that we were having. I mean, I'd love to have Jarzombek back and in fact, I suppose we could've because Rob has gone back to Judas Priest and has put the Halford band aside. But Bob is living out in California now. One of the problems was it was always difficult for us to get organized to do any gigs because we had to fly people around. I wanted to try to make the thing local, so I'm trying to get local people. Pete's living here now, basically, the bass player. And we've got Frank on drums, but otherwise it's the same people. The next record will be heavy. I've been doing a lot of playing and coming up with a lot of riffs. We're just trying to make it real straight-ahead, probably a bit simpler than before, but heavier."

Post-*Army of One*, Mike DiMeo would leave the band to cultivate a career with Randy Pratt's band The Lizards. His replacement for tour dates—in Europe, the US and Japan—would be power metal pro Mike Tirelli, whose debut would be a festival date in Spain.

Shaking things up yet again, Mark would return in the fall of 2011 with *Immortal Soul*, which would find Reale reforming the CBS Records-era lineup, reinstalling on vocals Tony Moore, on bass, Don Van Stavern, on drums, Bobby Jarzombek, with the bonus

The World City Mag
Iron Pages
IR
More Underground
3/94 Heft Nr.28
Juni/Juli '94
7. Jahrgang
A 20785 F
Inkl.
Raritäten-
Börse
RIOT
NIGHTBREAKER
RIOT
rock city
RIOT
REVENGE ON STAGE
(The Unforgettable Years)
RIOT
"RIOT LIVE"
MANOWAR • QUORTHON • OMEN
VICIOUS RUMORS • THE BUSINESS
MESSIAH • CATHEDRAL • LEEWAY
THE OBSESSED • CLOVEN HOOF
SPERMBIRDS

being a second guitarist in the longtime and dependable Mike Flyntz, who was in fact part of the *Thundersteel* touring band.

"Well, a couple years ago we started talking to each other," Mark told me, in September of 2011, in a business-as-usual chat that would turn out to be our last, taking place four months before his death. "Bobby has been playing with Rob Halford and Sebastian Bach, and he's been a side-man and it got to the point where he contacted me and he wanted to be part of something more solid like a band. So we all started talking to one another and I contacted Don, and the whole big linchpin was Tony Moore. Because Tony... we've all been in the industry, playing, doing whatever. I've had different lineups and stuff, but Tony has been out of it for over 25 years, so that was one issue. But he was into it. He said those were the best years of his life, so he was on board. And we're all alive and well and we decided to do it."

"So basically, what we decided to do was... we all live in different parts of the country now. Me and Mike, the other guitar player, live in Long Island. New York, and Bobby and Don live down here in San Antonio where I am now, visiting my girlfriend. And Tony lives in LA—he moved out to LA a couple of years ago, with his wife. So what we did was in 2009, I came down here, and I was down here for three weeks, and worked with Bobby and Don writing new material. Mike Flyntz came down for a few days, and we basically wrote the foundation of what the record is, the music. Tony wrote all the lyrics, okay? But the four of us convened down here and we pretty much put the music together."

"And then what we did was, we did a show down here in San Antonio which was awesome. Because we didn't know what was going to happen, man. Because Tony's been out of it for over 25 years and he was really nervous. He came down here with his wife, and the first rehearsal we did was like magic. It was like no years had passed. I think we did 'Johnny's Back' or something. Tony was completely put at ease at that point. And we did a show down here, and it was a Tuesday night, and it was sold-out and it was packed. The interest in this is a little bit mind-boggling. So we did the show here, and we went to do *Sweden Rock*, and then we came back home, went back over and did a festival in Spain. Then we went to Japan which was sold-out, and it was great, the band was great."

"And so we went forward with the record, and already we're getting all kinds of interest. I mean, we haven't skipped a beat, man. We didn't have a problem getting a record deal, and there is all this interest in this lineup. So we've got this four-week tour that's supposed to start on October 28 in Europe, and then we've got this crazy, friggin' boat cruise going on in January (laughs). We go on a boat from Florida to the Caribbean islands, and it's like all these heavy metal bands. And it's all good, man, and this tour we're doing is with Hammerfall, and I know Hammerfall are fans of my band—they covered one of my tunes, which is way cool. And I'm sure that the Hammerfall singer will get up and do it with us (laughs). As of right now, it's all good."

Addressing the triumphant power metal sound of *Immortal Soul*, the record that would be his last, Mark explains that, "Basically, when we kind of hatched this whole plan of doing this reunion, being a music fan myself, I knew that we had to deliver something that compares to *Thundersteel*. What we tried to do was something like... for instance, if in 1991, Tony never left and we went on from that point, I think this is the next gradual step that we're taking. We know what we have to do. This is like the *Thundersteel* reunion, and for fans of that era, this is what they expect from us—that's the way we approached it."

"And the thing about it is, it's kind of a natural thing, because the way the whole *Thundersteel* thing happened all those years ago, was the fact that me and Don Van Stavern concocted the whole thing, because he's like the metal dude. He writes all the riffs, he's like the speed metal guy and he writes all the riffs, and I'm the Beatles fan, the melodic dude. And that was the formula that worked. Because I like that testosterone, guitar-driven craziness, but at the same time, I've gotta have choruses. I'm really into melodicism, and the only thing that's different on this record is that there's a third guy involved, Mike Flyntz, the other guitar player, who is pretty much akin to me in terms of being melodic. And Don is the metal guy. He comes up with the crazy riffs, and we try to mold a chorus around it, and Tony Moore writes the lyrics. And so it's pretty much a natural move from where we were at that point in time. I think hopefully we achieved what we were trying to achieve in that respect, without disappointing anybody. As a guitar player and a musician, I'm really diverse. But a lot of people probably don't know that, and that's why I had to have the band Westworld. It allowed me to not have to be pigeonholed into a situation. But it's like with Riot, I try to keep Riot true to what people respect from it, and especially this lineup, and know what they expect from us."

Mark never made it onto the *70,000 Tons of Metal* boat cruise of which he spoke. his death on January 25th, 2012 from complications due to his Crohn's disease ensured that *Immortal Soul* would be his last work.

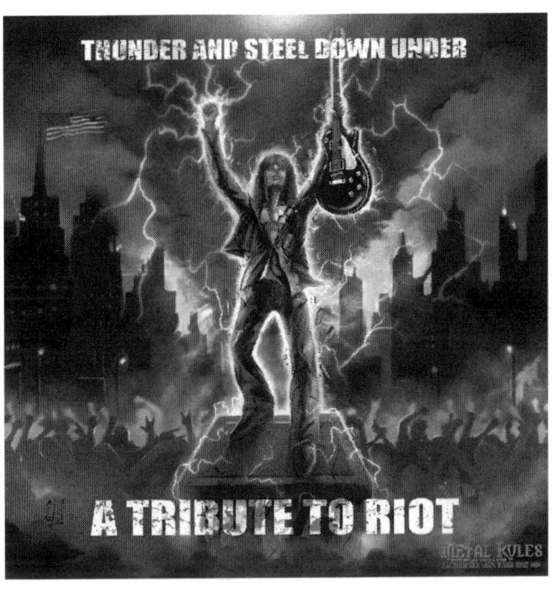

"I had no idea at any time that Mark's life was in danger when recording *Immortal Soul*," explains Mike Flyntz, speaking with Kevin Stewart-Panko. "He wasn't feeling well, but constantly told me to move ahead with the recording of the guitars. He was there for the writing sessions and contributed, but when we started tracking, Mark started to get worse. I would show him my recordings and he would approve them and say, 'Keep going; it sounds great!' He fell into a coma when we went on the *70,000 Tons of Metal* cruise, and we found out that he died while we were at sea. It was one of the toughest days of my life."

"During the pre-production of *Immortal Soul*, Mark was staying with me in Texas and I would take him to the hospital regularly," adds Don. "This was normal as we had been aware of his illness for quite some time. It wasn't out of the ordinary for Mark to have an overnight stay in a hospital and get released in a few days. Mark might have known more than he led us to believe. I think he didn't want to disappoint anyone. That was probably the toughest thing we ever had to do, as band mates, brothers, and human beings. What really made it crazy was that there were five ocean-view state room tickets booked because we had no idea Mark wouldn't make the trip. Of course, we only ended up using four and walking by the empty room was always a reminder of our brother not being there, which he wanted to be so badly. I spoke with him and he and his girl were packed and ready to go. We were to fly to New York on Monday and start rehearsals on Wednesday."

"Bobby and I made the flight, but Mark wasn't at the airport," continues Don. "We contacted him and he said he wasn't feeling well. He said he was going to the hospital and to go ahead and that he would be there by Wednesday. We didn't think that much of it because we have been dealing with his Crohn's outbreaks for years. It was never serious; a couple pills and off ya go. This time he never left the hospital. Mark told us to carry on and that he would meet us back in New York after the cruise."

"On the *70,000 Tons* cruise, we got the worst heartbreaking news you could ever get. There was a knock on my cabin door and I opened it to Mike crying and shaking as he fell into my arms. He didn't have to say a thing. We were later joined by Bobby and Tony and literally had a group hug and cry. The breath was knocked out of us. Passers-by saw four grown men in the hallway of the ship in a state of disbelief and shock. Word spread around the ship of Mark's passing, and every band showed support. Hammerfall, Overkill, Virgin Steele all gave on-stage shout-outs to Mark. Everyone said we had to do the show for Mark. Mike didn't want to do it; he didn't know if he could get through the set. It was really tough, but the crowds were supportive and we gave it our all for Mark. Tony made the announcement and there wasn't a dry eye in the house. I've never played 'Thundersteel' crying like crazy on stage ever before."

Immortal Soul would be the last record under the Riot banner. Indeed, the band, soon to be quite diminished in official personnel beyond losing Reale, had decided to keep working, and under the Riot name. But acceding to the wishes of Mark's father, the band agreed to let the name rest, continuing on as Riot V. Unfortunately the band's fine album, *Unleash the Fire*, had snuck out in Japan under the Riot name, with the subsequent European issue bearing the correction.

"I take care of Mark's father and vowed to him he would never be alone," explains Flyntz. "Mark's mom passed years ago and Mark was an only child. When I take Mr. Reale to doctor's appointments, people mistake me as his son. He corrects them and refers to me as his best friend. That is a huge honour for me. Mark gave me the chance to record and see the world and I will never forget how generous he was. Mr. Reale asked me to continue with Riot so Mark's music will never die. I wouldn't have continued if he didn't want us to."

"We will continue the legacy of Mark and Riot as long as people want it," agrees Van Stavern. "The longevity of a band is through good music and Riot has proven it for years and if the response to *Unleash the Fire* is any indication, it looks like we will continue the legacy for years to come."

Alas, Riot V, as it would comprise for the record and touring duties thus far, consists of firm Riot alumni Van Stavern on bass and Flyntz on guitar, along with drummer Frank Gilchriest, briefly part of Riot, on drums, and then new singer Todd Michael Hall and guitarist Nick Lee, in place of the irreplaceable.

But it's fascinating in the conjecture, that had Riot V continued with both Tony Moore on vocals and Bobby Jarzombek on drums—as was looking like a real possibility—well, then one could see Riot living on in robust and valid form past the demise of Reale. And one could almost envision that that's what Mark would have wanted. Always the fighter and the intrepid music fan, and very much lacking in ego, one can imagine Mark seeing his band—a band used to the revolving door of its members—headbanging on indefinitely, and unselfconsciously, as Riot.

Who knows? Maybe this story isn't fully written. The return of Tony or Mike is always a possibility. Or of a Riot alumnus on the drums. With Steve Loeb and Billy Arnell out of the picture, and

Lou Kouvaris and Rick Ventura and Sandy Slavin still active... again, who knows? And maybe Riot V will thrive. After all, with *Unleash the Fire*, they are whipping up a Riot storm of power metal very much in the vein that Mark had been patronizing for 25 years already. The final piece of the puzzle—the unqualified name—rests with the beloved father, and one must imagine it wouldn't be much hard graft to convince Anthony that Mark would have wanted the esteemed Riot brand to shine, shine on for years to come.

Final word to this tragic tale goes to the beating heart of the band Mark Reale, expressing gratitude, in conversation with the author, for all that he had accomplished.

"In spite of the problems," reflects Mark, "all the music we made and got out there, it got us enough fans that we can go and have this cult fan thing going on, and they stayed loyal. I'm shocked, because I couldn't believe... this whole tour we're going to do in October, November, it's like Hammerfall demanded the promoter to put us on the tour. And to me that's like friggin'… recording our music, that's like so cool, man. To be able to influence other artists. That's why I'm sitting here talking to you (laughs). We can still do this because, whatever music we made and got out there, was strong enough. We established this fan base that—and not only fans, but with other musicians, like Mötley Crüe, Hammerfall, Metallica— that we're able to do this. I look at Lars Ulrich from Metallica and in their tour pamphlet, wearing a Riot shirt. It does it for me. In spite of the mistakes I made, and how naïve I was and whatever went on, that does it for me. The wheels have definitely stayed, man (laughs). But it was great. To be honest with you, man, I can't complain. I've toured the world, I don't know how many times over, I've had great experiences. It is just what it is. Just to be able to affect, not only the fans, but other musicians, it means the world to me."

"Dream Away:" The Fans Speak

Something just felt right about asking the fans to help me celebrate Riot, and so that's what I did. We studiers and students of the band are a small lot, and so there was something comfortable indeed about asking all of you who have bought my books before to sing along with me. Thanks to those who have participated. Reading your kind words for Mark and Guy and the guys made soldiering on with this lonely project more than worth it.

"My favourite Riot album is *Thundersteel*. With a number
of personnel changes affecting the mid-'80s output post-*Fire
Down Under*, Riot found themselves floundering a bit, not hitting
the metal nail directly until '88. Then, out of the black, they
released a scorcher of an album. Culling all the tricks of the more
mainstream '80s metal moves and mashing them into a musket
over-packed with too much gunpowder, Reale and his revamped
colony blew the barrel right off with *Thundersteel*. Although they
still couldn't get away from the cover art curse, inside the grooves
the guys proved and approved their metal acumen. 'Sign of the
Crimson Storm' is all you need to hear to know they were hungry
for the next level. It never came though, thrash really ruling the
day along with little marketing behind the album dooming it
to the discount bin. Too bad, as anyone who snagged this beast
knew the Rioters had come a long way from *Rock City*. Dig it out,
blow off the dust, drop the needle, and start a Riot in your ears!"

"Why should we remember Riot? 1981's *Fire Down Under*
is all you need to hear. At the time, the NWOBHM was exploding
and demoralizing most of what was coming out of the States.
Riot took the best of the Leps, Saxon, and a handful of other
NWOBHM mights and showed what the US could do with meat
and potatoes metal, even laying a couple of pre-thrash speedsters
in the lot. After a couple of wobbly boogie rockers, their third
album really cemented their style. The NWOBHM band of the
US? Yeah, let's not forget those early albums Riot recorded—hard
metal was still few and far between to be found."

Keven Anstett, Belding, MI

"First time I heard of Riot was on the *Monsters of Rock*
album that included songs from Rainbow, Scorps, April Wine and
was a kind of highlight album from the Donington 1980 festival.
'Road Racin'' was the song and it kicked ass. From there I got
Fire Down Under and *Narita*; I liked them because they reminded
me of Van Halen in that it was straight forward rock 'n' roll, and
'Swords and Tequila' was played on the local classic rock station
here in Chicago, WLUP—not many hard rock songs from obscure
bands were played on any radio here in Chicago."

"I saw them live twice, once in 1982 opening for UFO and
Rainbow and once in '83, but I forgot who they opened for. Both
times they rocked with short sets and the fans loved them. Back

in the day, not all opening bands got cheers. Ha ha... once saw The Romantic open for UFO and get booed off stage after four songs. Just recently a buddy of mine saw Riot V and said they were awesome and did the Speranza/Reale versions great justice. Basically, I liked Riot because they were no nonsense, straight hard rock—great riffs, no fillers, no crap, just like Saxon. Thanks again for the great books—keep 'em coming."

Jeff Augustyn, River Grove, USA

"If you were in high school from 1979 to 1983 and into hard rock and metal like me, it was certainly the golden years of discovery. The '70s arena rock bands I loved earlier where losing their edge and a new fresh tougher sound was emerging. Every Friday I scraped together all the money I could and hit every record store in my hometown of Knoxville, TN to ravage the import bins to find as much new flying-under-the-radar hard rock and metal I could. The NWOBHM was in full force and every week I came home with a stack of new vinyl to check out."

"One day that stack included Riot's *Narita*. With that crazy Johnny Seal on the front ready for battle amongst the Japanese graveyard skulls, that record had all the vitality that the '70s bands had lost. There was an urgency in their sound that hooked me immediately. Other than Van Halen having a little fire left in them, Riot was the cream of the crop of American true hard rock and metal at the time. Amongst all of the great NWOBHM bands and other bands from Europe/abroad, Riot was the only American band offering that same quality and freshness."

"*Fire Down Under* would only cement that further. Riot's shining moment and one of my favourite records of all time, I wore the grooves out on that slab of vinyl then and now. Along with Motörhead, Iron Maiden, Saxon, Diamond Head, Angel Witch, Tank and others, Riot was a huge part of the most exciting time for me discovering new metal and creating a bond to an era of music that I would never let go."

Lenny Burnett, Zero Down, Seattle, WA

"At their best, Riot match superior songwriting chops with equally high-level musical chops, and deliver the goods with an infectious energy. My favourite album is *Fire Down Under*, all killer no filler, and it embodies everything they do best."

"I first heard Riot via 'Road Racin',' which was on a mid-price compilation here in the UK, called *Heavy Duty*, which featured the likes of Scorpions, Wild Horses, Whitesnake and Di'anno-era Maiden. It had originally been issued around 1980, and by the time I bought it in 1985, Riot had split. I remember being knocked-out by their track and taking a cassette copy to my guitar teacher and asking him to work out the song and teach me how to play it. Back then, their albums were out of print, so it was a case of pot luck in terms of what I could find second-hand. But I later found *Narita* in my local independent store, X Records, around 1987. They also had a consignment of early '80s patches on sale, and I was delighted to find one of the *Narita* cover art, which was swiftly added to my denim jacket."

"In the summer of '88, I was hanging out in the store, and they put on an album by a band that sounded familiar, but I couldn't place who it was. It opened with a face-melter called 'Swords and Tequila,' and each successive track was great. Halfway through a song I later found out was called 'Outlaw,' I went to the counter and asked my buddy Chris, who I think had put the album on, 'Who's this?' He pointed at the *Narita* patch on the front pocket of my denim jacket, and I bought the album immediately."

"I've never met the guys in person, but interviewed Mike Flyntz this year as the band embarked on a new chapter as Riot V. They're one of those rare bands that has been able to continue in a way that honours the memory of a fallen member without it seeming like a tasteless cash-in. Mike took care of Mark Reale's father when Mark passed away, and was encouraged to carry on by him, and in changing the band name, I feel that he's done that with integrity. I'd like to think Riot'll be remembered for maintaining an amazingly high level of quality throughout their career, despite having to persist in the face of bad breaks that would have derailed less determined bands years before."

Rich Davenport, Rich Davenport's Rock Show, UK

"I'm glad to hear that all is well and that you are continuously writing amazing work. I really appreciate how clear and enthusiastic you are with your writing in all of your books. Your writing is not only entertaining, informative and clear. It is also highly infectious! You are the authority on the heavy metal discourse, and I am honoured that you have asked for my words on a band that I really hold dear to my heart—Riot."

"I remember seeking out *Fire Down Under* after reading the review from your *Riff Kills Man!* book back in the day. I searched high and low for the vinyl and had no luck. One year BW&BK had the song 'Fire Down Under' included on one of the promo CDs. I can remember playing the song for the first time and the hairs on my arms literally stood up. What a killer riff, and that voice… my God! I played that song over and over again. To this day, I still get goose bumps when I hear that opening riff."

"When I finally found *Fire Down Under* (on CD) later that year, I couldn't believe I was actually holding it in my hands! What an amazing record. Not a dog track in the lot. No filler, just killer. So many tracks on that album have been permanently ingrained on my musical psyche. Many faves on that album, especially 'Feel the Same' and 'No Lies.'"

"I dig Riot's early albums because they are honest and raw. That same year I also found *Rock City* on vinyl, and for a debut, wow! A rich palette of solid, catchy, raw and powerful songs that not only rock your socks off, but are also honest and timeless. This is what Riot should be remembered for: their honest, powerful and timeless rock music. Killer guitar tones, a thunderous mix that just smokes the speakers, and that voice— Mr. Guy Speranza."

"It's nice when you find a band that you really connect with that doesn't become too popular. It becomes almost sacred to you. Riot could have had better commercial success over the years; however, the fact that they didn't get too big just adds to their cool factor. Riot sure evolved over the years, eh? I am glad you are focusing on the first five to ten years of the band. *Rock City*, *Narita*, *Fire Down Under*, *Restless Breed* (different vocalist but still amazing album) and *Born in America* are solid and inspiring albums."

"Well Martin, I am stoked about your new upcoming book on Riot! Thanks for asking my opinion on the band! Keep on keeping on, and please *don't stop writing!*"

Colin Drake, Canada

"I'd heard *Born in America* on the radio and went out and bought it at Tower Records in Seattle, plus I remember taking a chance on *Fire Down Under*. Fortunately, I was blown away by *Born* and then said, 'Holy shit!' when I heard *Fire*. Riot is unique. They are too hard to be hard rock and not metal enough to be metal. They stand on the exact midpoint where rock becomes metal or metal becomes rock; call it 'commercial heavy metal' or 'underground hard rock,' in other words, perfect combo of commercial although not commercial, with guitars that are fast but not too fast, and melody that's headbanging. All these points are realized on *Fire Down Under*."

Robert Dumo, Seattle

"Riot were a kick-ass hard rock/metal band that put out several great albums. Mark Reale (rest in peace) was able to adjust the sound of Riot with each different lineup and continue to put out excellent music whether it was *Narita*, *Born in America* or *Thundersteel*. I know many Riot fans consider *Fire Down Under* or *Thundersteel* to be the best Riot albums, but I've always thought that the underrated *Born in America* is a solid slab of kick-ass metal. I love every song on that album and still listen to it every month! My second favourite album would have to be *Narita* because at least half of the songs are 'iPod worthy.'"

"My fondest memory of the band is getting *Born in America* on cassette when I was in the eighth grade. I went to Rocky Mountain Records and Tapes in Fort Collins, CO with the intention of getting Ratt's *Out of the Cellar*. For some reason I ended up with the Riot album and I'm glad I did. The title track has always been one of my favourite songs. I did not know that there was a video for it until just a few years ago. I also recall hearing 'Running from the Law' on an FM radio Top 10 countdown show, probably the only time I ever heard Riot on the radio! I even learned the acoustic intro to 'Wings of Fire' and passed it off as my own composition for my ninth grade music theory class."

"Riot should be remembered as an excellent band that changed with the times but never sold out. They (Mark) continued to put out high quality albums throughout their career. Even though Mark never made it to the level of arena rockers, he never stopped making music."

Chris Fryer, Fort Collins, CO

"Riot were the bare essence of the hard rock garage band always rehearsing for little reward—working class and original. Fidelity not so much; catchy and relentless, yes. *Fire Down Under* is my favourite album... probably ever. It rarely came out of the cassette deck of my buddy's car for two years. Strangely enough, a cover band of young wannabes from my hometown used the name Riot before *the* Riot really came on the scene nationally. Could go on and on about the album, but I think your assessment is right on with what I feel. Riot are probably the only 'unknown' band that if I introduce them to someone in my life that likes hard rock and they say, 'Man, the shit you listen to...' they get an ass-kick escort out of the listening area."

"Mark Reale—R.I.P. I met him in 2004 and he introduced me to a very hot young woman from Miami that I carried on with after my divorce. No names mentioned, but he 'hooked me up' big time and was a very normal guy. I met him via business and asked him to sign what I thought was a copy of *Restless Breed* but ended up being Def Leppard *On Through the Night*. Not sure what happened there; I was in a bit of "a fog" that night. He was cool, a bit shy, humble, and I think hurt about how losing two friends and band mates under trying circumstances had him twisted. Guy had the pipes of a rocker, Forrester of an avenging angel. I really never cared much for anything past *Restless Breed* but then again I'm a big time hard rock snob in some sense."

"Going back, I bought my first Riot album at Hi Ho Records, which was also a swap shop where you could trade your albums with another human on site. I bought Magnum's *Chase the Dragon*, Thin Lizzy's *Black Rose*, and Aerosmith's *Draw the Line* the same day, all on used vinyl. But I never saw Riot live! They were on a bill with Rainbow in early '80s but Ritchie flaked and the show was canned—I hate Blackmore. Bands like Riot, Dio, UFO, Tool, Sabbath, Rage... they changed my life, representing an escape from reality and into fantasy land. Oh how me and a few buddies wanted to be rockers."

Gregg Gemmiti, New Hampshire

"Riot are such a special band for me, and most of my mates don't understand that I praise them as high as, say, Van Halen. But I love their blend of riffing and melodic vocals. Speranza was an unique singer. My fave album is *Fire Down Under*, on which song after song is a classic—at least in my house! But *Narita* is very near. From my point of view, Riot were the first real American metal band. Previous artists were—again, in my view—hard rock. They paved the way for other bands that sold lots of albums later in the '80s."

"My first contact with Riot was the song 'Road Racin'' on the *Monsters of Rock* compilation album, from Donington 1980. I fell in love with the song, but here in Spain, their albums were not released, and I had to ordered them on import; *Fire Down Under* was more or less easy, and then *Rock City*, but not *Narita*. For *years*, it was impossible to find it, until I bought a Japanese copy."

"Right now I own that magic trilogy on CD, *"Riot Live"*, the Rhett Forrester CDs and even *Thundersteel*, but for me, Riot is the Speranza era. I am very happy to have shared my Riot-mania with someone—and to know there's more like me out there!"

Juan Grela, Spain

"I bought *Fire Down Under* in 1981 together with Kix *Kix* and Blackfoot *Tomcattin'*—what a triple. When I heard *Fire Down Under*, I immediately fell in love with this band. Hard, powerful but melodic. Then I bought *Narita* immediately and what can I say? Fantastic album."

"Even the underrated *Restless Breed* album is a joy to listen to. Also in 1981, I bought a ticket for a great concert: Saxon/Ozzy Osbourne/Riot. But it was not to be—Riot cancelled and in the end Ozzy also cancelled. So my chance to see the classic lineup was not to be, although I saw the band later at the *Bang Your Head* and *Keep It True* festivals. And then I met the band this year for the first time, but it was mostly the *Thundersteel* lineup. Mike Flyntz and Donnie Van Stavern try the best to keep the flag high with the new album *Unleash the Fire*, which my label released in Europe, along with *Immortal Soul*, but when I saw ads from the early '80s that Riot played together with Sammy Hagar on a UK tour and I couldn't be there, I got tears in my eyes. Riot will always be remembered for the songs Mark Reale wrote and for the fantastic voice of Guy Speranza."

Olly Hahn, SPV/Steamhammer GmbH, Germany

"Wow, great news on the Riot book. I know this is a labour of love, so tackling an endeavour like this (with such knowledge that it will not be lucrative) makes it even more special to fans like me. I do hope you touch on all of the eras of the band. Someone like me who was too young to witness the first version of the band but counts *Fire Down Under* as a top five metal album and *Thundersteel* as a top ten wants to read about each of the *five* stellar vocalists and their significant contributions. Anyway, thanks again. Keep writing and I promise to keep buying and reading. I wish there were doctorates in metal and that they were accompanied with six figure salaries."

Mike Hein, Cincinnati, OH

"In the late 1970s in the UK, if you were interested in heavy rock and heavy metal, you read *Sounds* weekly rock magazine. If you looked closely at the pages showing the charts of the best-selling records, there was a chart of requested songs for a heavy metal club night held in London and organized by a DJ called Neal Kaye. It was on examining this chart some time in 1979 that I first came across a band with the name "Riot." Over the following few weeks, it became clear that attendees at these heavy metal club nights were requesting more and more songs by Riot. I was intrigued. The albums that these songs came from were *Rock City* and *Narita*."

"On Saturday, August 16th, 1980, I found out what Riot were all about. On this day, in a small village in Leicestershire in the UK, the first *Monsters of Rock* festival was held at Castle Donington. This event was headlined by Rainbow and other acts on the bill were Touch, Riot, Saxon, April Wine, Scorpions, Judas Priest. It was a hot day and the first band on, Touch, received a great welcome, but did not get an encore as allegedly the lead singer had swallowed a bee! (as I found out later from reading the following week's edition of *Sounds*). The compere/host on the day of the festival was none other than Neal Kaye!"

"Riot hit the stage for a short and powerful seven-song set. I remember them being very aggressive with great lead guitar playing from Mark Reale. Guy Speranza sang well and looked at home on the big stage. The crowd loved them! The song of the day for me was 'Road Racin'.' It was all over too soon and the next band up was Saxon who went down really well with the crowd as did the rest of the bands on the day. It was a great day and the Rainbow show marked Cozy Powell's last gig with the band."

"In 1989, Riot released *"Riot Live,"* which I bought a few years later on a trip to Tokyo. On reading the credits, I was pleasantly surprised to see that it contained a great recording of the entire Riot set performed at the Hammersmith Odeon in 1980. Listening to this CD again reminded me what a great band Riot were and that it encouraged me to buy their later releases like *Thundersteel* etc. I have remained a fan of their music throughout the intervening years."

"I never did see Riot play live again. However I did have one brief interaction with Mark Reale in 2002. Mark had formed a new band called Westworld with Tony Harnell from TNT. Westworld released a handful of CDs in the early 2000s and on a trip back to the UK in 2002, I managed to catch them playing at the Z Rock 2002 Music Festival at the Ritz venue in Manchester. There were several bands playing throughout the day, and after a few hours I wandered outside in search of a decent meal. As I was walking down the street, I saw Mark Reale standing by a tour bus, alone. I just nodded and smiled and moved on. Westworld headlined the show and were clearly the best act of the day, doing a ferocious cover of the Black Sabbath classic 'Neon Knights.' Over the years I continued to buy Riot CDs, but for me they never bettered *Narita* and 35 years later 'Road Racin'' is still my favourite Riot track."

David Hughes, Singapore

"The long-gone Island Sound Records in Merrick, New York was the place where I spent all my allowance money. I'd bike up there every Friday night and come home with an armful of records. I was a big Quiet Riot fan at the time and my brain made an automatic association when I saw Riot's *Born in America* up on the wall. It had a cool cover so I gave it a shot. I loved the album, even though it didn't sound a whole lot like Quiet Riot (truth is, we both know who the better band is by a long shot). It was a long time before I got another Riot record (which would have been *Rock City*), and then I began to acquire them... at least the Guy and Rhett years. Truth is, I'm just not as familiar with the post-*Thundersteel* material as I should be, although what I've heard, I really like."

"I love Riot for their diversity yet consistency. There are several different eras of the band to enjoy, but throughout, Reale kept a high level of songwriting and musicianship. The Guy Speranza years are definitely my favourite, and I'd have to go with the majority opinion and say that *Fire Down Under* is my favourite Riot record. The songs are all heavy, yet hooky and the production is excellent, but in an unpolished way that makes you feel like you're sitting in on a rehearsal session."

"The only time I ever got to see Riot was Thursday, August 25, 2005, at the Crazy Donkey in Farmingdale, New York. It was a one-off show that was a warm-up date for a short string of shows they did in Tokyo. Mike DiMeo was the singer at the time, but couldn't do the dates because he had prior commitments with The Lizards, so Mike Tirelli (Messiah's Kiss, Holy Mother, Burning Starr) filled in. I do remember they did a great job in covering their whole career. Your book, I'm sure, will encourage me to complete my Riot collection. Can't wait for this one!"

Jeff Kaplan, New York

"I appreciate Riot for the high energy, no nonsense music of the Speranza/Forester albums—Guy's voice especially. I read in Scott Ian's book that he tried to get Guy to join Anthrax when he was forming the band. I saw them touring for the *Fire Down Under* LP, opening for Rush. This was shortly after *Exit... Stage Left* came out, at the Hartford Civic Center in CT. Rush tried out 'Subdivisions' that night. No doubt Riot should be remembered for being one of the most underrated bands of their time."

Rob Kemp, Connecticut

"Thanks for the opportunity to respond to the questions regarding your Riot book. I have to tell you, the timing of your email was interesting because I have seen the band (such as it is now) just three weeks ago after wanting to see them for decades. So, why do I like Riot? I know your book is centered on the first decade, so what I have to say about the band may not be relevant. I did not listen to them before *Thundersteel*. I was 16 in 1988, and worked at an all-heavy metal record store in Saginaw, Michigan called Heavy Metal Unlimited."

"I loved that store, and loved being 'in the know' with bands that weren't widely known about. A promo copy of *Thundersteel* was sent to the store, and me and the buds latched onto it hard. We listened to it as much as any other album from any other band. I could not believe it was the same Riot band with those hideous album covers! Eventually, I worked my way backwards to the 'old' stuff and fell in love with *Fire Down Under*. However *Thundersteel* was and always will be my sentimental favourite. It was so fast, the licks so hot, and I was totally into those vocalists who sang in the stratosphere. *Privilege of Power* was highly anticipated to say the least, and it did not disappoint. Two of my favourite metal albums to this day."

"Heavy Metal Unlimited was started by a fellow named Joel Sheldon and his friend Rick Hall. Rick had two brothers, Jon and Todd, who were in a local band in the '80s called Harlet. In 2009, I was back in touch with Todd and he was singing and touring with Jack Starr. He also did an album with his band Reverence in 2012, and shortly after was named as the lead singer for Riot. After all these years being a successful businessman and devoted family man, here he was fulfilling a dream. It was surreal to hear him singing all those great Riot songs. He has been very gracious to me as a fan, and has kept me up to speed with the goings-on of the band including the recording of *Unleash the Fire*."

"Last month, Riot had shows booked in Detroit and Chicago. The band flew in a day early and Todd invited all the people from the record store days to a rehearsal concert in Saginaw at his brother Jon's guitar shop. They played a two-hour set for us, and even managed to fit in songs from *Rock City*, *Fire Down Under* and *Restless Breed* which were on the set list for the Japan tour in September. I've been to hundreds of concerts over the years, and was never able to see Riot back in the day because they only played the clubs where I wasn't old enough to get in. So the first time I get to see them is with an old friend singing for them at an invite-only event. Crazy! The band sounded great, the guys were super cool, and of course I made them all sign my vinyl copy of *Unleash the Fire*."

Brad Lewis, Saginaw, MI

"What a coincidence this is, as I just saw Riot V this past Thursday in Osaka, Japan. I got to meet the band and partied with them till 3AM at Bar RockRock. They had with them Lou A. Kouvaris (from the original *Rock City*) and he played on the *Rock City* songs. He's a great guy and the band are great people as well. They played a two-hour set and did songs from every era."

"I like Riot because Mark Reale has always surrounded himself with great talent and always put out such great music. From *Rock City* all the way through to *Immortal Soul* and *Unleash the Fire*, this band has continued to put out great albums. The album I appreciate the most is *Rock City*; this was the first Riot album I heard in 1986 and I love every song on it. The album artwork just hooked me and the songs stood out from a lot of the other '70s groups I listened to at the time."

"A great memory for me was seeing the very first Riot *Thundersteel* reunion show in San Antonio, Texas in 2009. The reason this show is significant was that this was the first time I got to see this lineup live. I tried back in 1990 to go to one of their San Antonio gigs but was denied entry as the show was for ages 21 and up. At the time I was about two months away from my 21st birthday. I would have to wait until 1999 before I would see Riot live and that was with Mike DiMeo on vocals supporting *Sons of Society*. There's some video of this on Youtube and I have seen myself in it. I'm easy to spot as I am the only one wearing a cowboy hat."

"I had the opportunity to see Riot my second time in 2004 in Texas. At the time I had just completed a tour of duty in Iraq as a Marine. I went to the show and brought the current Riot CD *Through the Storm* for them to sign. I saw someone with a laminate on and asked him if he could get Riot to sign this CD as I had taken it with me to Iraq. He then proceeded to get me a backstage pass and I got to meet the band before and after the show. They were very appreciative of my military service and Mike DiMeo even dedicated one of the songs ('Glory Calling') to me from the stage! There's Youtube video of that as well. At this show I met two Japanese girls that flew all the way from Japan for this show. Last Thursday night I met them again in Osaka at the concert!"

"In January 2012 I was all set to see Riot in support of *Immortal Soul* in Virginia, but the promoter cancelled the show. The band still showed up to the venue and signed autographs and hung out with the fans for a couple of hours. I got to meet this version of the band and they were very gracious with the fans. Unfortunately Mark Reale was still hospitalized in San Antonio and passed away several days later."

Scott Mueller, Okinawa, Japan

"I first heard Riot on college radio station WMSC-FM (Gene "The Maniac" Khoury's show) in the very early '80s. I liked it, but it stayed under my radar. I was only about 13-14 then and was just getting exposed to a wide range of heavy music, beyond the Kiss, Aerosmith, Led Zeppelin and Rush that I already loved. I remember Riot playing lots of shows in my area and seeing their shirts around. Later in the '80s when I had my own college radio show, I played some of their songs, mostly from the first three albums."

"But it wasn't until much later, with the *Inishmore* album, that my passion for Riot really ignited. I had read good things about *Inishmore* in magazines so I bought it and was amazed. I then started buying the entire catalogue, delving into every era of the band. As much as I love the classic *Fire Down Under* and others, I would have to say *Inishmore* is my favourite because it really made me a huge Riot fan. During my discovery era I mainly was buying their CDs but I went to a record show — around 2004, before the vinyl resurgence — and I got a pristine copy of *Fire Down Under* for $1! It was fun to have that ridiculous album cover in all of its 12" glory."

"As for live, I saw Riot for the first time at the *March Metal Meltdown* in Asbury Park, NJ in 1999. This was only the second time in my life that while watching a band onstage I actually felt the sensation of my hair being blown back! This was the amazing lineup of Mark Reale, Mike Flyntz, Mike DiMeo, Pete Perez and Bobby Jarzombek. They came bursting out with 'Angel Eyes' and it was unbelievable, and their versions of 'Outlaw' and 'Warrior' had the crowd roaring."

"I did not get to meet Riot in person, but I had the honour of interviewing Mark Reale over the phone. We talked for two hours and he was one of the most sincere and humble people I've ever interviewed. Truly a class act. Oh and I did get to meet Bobby Jarzombek and he signed a couple of my CDs. He was totally cool as well. When I interviewed Mark Reale, he said something to me that I consider one of the top highlights of my career as a music journalist. He said that my review of their set at the *March Metal Meltdown*, which appeared in *Metal Maniacs*, really meant a lot to him and the rest of the band, and encouraged them to keep forging on. It was very rare that an artist ever acknowledged anything I wrote about them or even had a clue of who I was. So that was such a nice connection. I continued to write reviews and support Riot every chance I could."

"Riot should be remembered for perseverance, great musicianship, and the creativity and flexibility to change lineups and reinvent themselves so many times. Mark Reale was a genius and a warrior. R.I.P. Mark – Shine on."

Sue Nolz, *Metal Maniacs* magazine, New Jersey

"When I first heard *Narita* circa 1980, it was one of those 'I'll never forget where I was' moments. The answer? Camping with my metalhead buddies on Mt. Tam north of San Francisco, cranking 'Here We Come Again' on a big-ass boom box and giggling in disbelief during Mark's guitar solo outro. Simply spectacular. But what will Riot be remembered for? Besides their no-frills NWOBHM-style riffage, unfortunately it's the untimely deaths of so many gifted members."

Robert Pardini

"Glad to hear of your Riot project. Like you say, who else would dare to give a damn about such an obscure band?! The early '80s is when I first started getting immersed in hard rock and metal and it was all about the NWOBHM. The only American bands rattling my cage at that time were Van Halen (*Fair Warning*!), Blue Öyster Cult (*Fire of Unknown Origin*!) and an odd shot over the bow by Mötley Crüe. To me, Riot will always be associated with their British counterparts thanks to those incendiary riffs and vocals that went down so smooth and so strong. *Fire Down Under* was a stone-cold '10' (to those who still cared about American rock) when it was released in 1981 and hasn't lost an ounce of its classic power in the years since. I often think that if they were a British band, that album would have nestled right along side the Leppard/Maiden/Motörhead defining statements of the day and made Riot into the legends they deserved to be."

"To this day, when I hear 'Swords and Tequila,' 'Outlaw,' 'Altar of the King' or really any song on this album (not a clunker to be found), the word 'regal' comes to mind for how the deliciously distorted riffs, vocals for miles, and deep rhythm pocket stampede and wash over you in fist-pumping glory. I draw parallels of this album with the Badlands debut at the tail end of the decade (another obscure project for you to tackle) for their distilled purity of everything that makes hard rock everlasting. Both are definitely Top 10ers of all time for those who dare to venture outside the usual suspects."

Jeff Peaper, Chadds Ford, Pennsylvania

"I recall Scorpions, Rainbow and Riot playing Rochester, NY but I was too young to go. Later, I remember cranking 'Don't Hold Back' and 'No Lies' in my friend's Camaro and just loving Riot immediately. I bought *Rock City* at a record store in Toronto; the inner bag had a cartoon cat carrying a handful of records, which became an inner bag I would come across a lot more when picking up used vinyl, and it always reminds me of Toronto. Fast forward, there was a buddy making me a tape of the six-track *"Riot Live"* with me realizing the singer was different—and liking him more than Guy Speranza. *Restless Breed* is a Top 10 album for me, although I was always baffled at the production of *Born in America*. I love it, but it's not mixed as well as the first one with Forrester."

Phil Prestianni, UK

"First, *thank you* for writing about Riot. They are in my opinion one of the best metal bands of all time and also probably one of the most underrated. Their first decade production was the stuff of legend back here in Mexico and records like *Narita* and especially *Fire Down Under* were loved by the underground. I simply love this band and this period."

"Sadly I've never had the chance to see them playing live during the Guy Speranza era. My loss indeed. I will always love *Narita* since it was my gateway to know Riot, but my favourite album is *Fire Down Under*. It is one of my top ten albums of all time; you know, the type of music you will take to be stranded on a deserted island kind of deals."

"I started listening to metal and hard rock around 1983, so I had a long way to walk and since all my friends weren't into it, my only source of all things metal was from magazines like *Kerrang!*, *Circus* and *Hit Parader*. Every week I saved all the money my parents gave me for lunch so I could purchase at least an LP every two weeks. When I finally gathered enough money, I asked my mother to take me to a record store specializing in all things metal and rock."

"My original idea was to buy the Queensrÿche album, *The Warning*, since I read that it was great. But once in the store I was flabbergasted when I saw the most horrible cover ever. The cover in question had some sort of pink sumo warrior with a battle axe standing over thousands of skulls. And to make things even weirder, his head was from a seal… WTF?! I laughed so hard thinking that it was horrible and moved on to find Queensrÿche. But I kept returning to that album and started to think that the band that was crazy enough to use such an ugly image had to be crazy or probably they were so sure that their music was great that they didn't care about the image."

"Such was my ramblings that after awhile I got in my hands the album and couldn't stop looking at it. So when my mom asked me to leave, after 45 minutes watching the album, I decided that I had to own it. So I bought it for 1,500 pesos (around ten US dollars). All the way from the record store I had to endure my sister's whining about how horrible the cover was, but instead of affecting me the wrong way I started to get more and more anxious about listening to it."

"Suffice to say, once I arrived at home, I placed the vinyl in the deck and slowly I placed the needle… first that familiar scratch and then… wham! 'Here We Come Again' started to blast through the speakers and I was hooked for life. I loved the speed of the guitars and the amazing voice of Guy, thinking, wow, it doesn't get any better than this. 'Road Racin',' '49er,' 'Narita,' 'Born to be Wild,' 'Waiting for the Taking,' all of them. I listened at least three time until my mom asked me to change the album."

"Ha, ha, it would only get worse once I got *Fire Down Under* later in the year. I believe that *Fire Down Under* focused the raw passion and power displayed by the band on *Narita* but with better songs. You can't go wrong with 'Swords and Tequila' as an opener, and then you have the title song at an unbelievable speed. But it was 'Outlaw,' with that slow building intro and that riff and those lyrics that had captivated me since—and what's not to like about a song that uses my own country as the main stage for a bank heist? 'He robbed a bank in Mexico, half crazed on tequila'—poetry, man, ha ha."

"The enduring quality of these songs is off the charts. We are talking about an album released in 1981 which still sounds fresh, honest and original. You cannot say the same about many '80s albums. Every time I listen to it, I feel the same adrenaline rush coming from the speakers. For me it is essential on every road trip."

"Riot will be remembered both for those ugly covers (ha ha) and for creating two of the best early US metal albums in history. With *Rock City* they show promised, but it was with *Narita* that they found their style and with *Fire Down Under* they literally put it out of the park. What I liked about Riot was that they didn't sound like anything I'd ever heard at the time, and even today. They sound like Riot and nothing else but pure, unadulterated power. I was learning the ropes of metal and hard rock when I found them—along with how to be a man as a matter of fact—so their music is part of my life and forever will be. Thanks again for helping spread the history of Riot."

Alfonso Said Reyes, Mexico

"I'd seen Riot three times, with Rhett in '83, *Thundersteel* in '88, *Privilege of Power* '90. At The Stone in SF, 1990, I stood in front and leaned over Mark Reale's monitor the whole show. Of the nearly 200 rock shows I've attended, this was the one show that made me deaf; my hearing has never recovered completely. This last March I drove across the USA for the first time (CA to NY) and went nine hours out of my way to San Antonio simply to visit Mark Reale's gravesite. My brother this summer saw Riot V in SF and the band was selling their own merch and were their own roadies for about 200 people in a crappy little club."

"This year I am following my retirement dream of attending every New York Mets game in NY as baseball is my favourite hobby alongside classic heavy metal music and concerts. Just last week I was talking to an usher, Steve, at the stadium and I mentioned that I had a couple guitars. Steve told me he was a drummer and that, "My friend Lou was the guitarist for a band called Riot, not Quiet Riot but Riot.' My jaw dropped as I have to use the same phrase, 'Not Quiet Riot but Riot' all the time discussing favourite bands. Steve proceeded to tell me that before *Rock City* was recorded, Lou (better know to us as L.A. Kouvaris) tried to get him to be their drummer because the guy they had sucked. Steve declined and went into the workforce and never joined. He said, 'Lou is in Japan right now because they are big there and he is their special guest.' This I knew from Riot V Facebook posts."

"Why Riot? I just love fast, aggressive hard rock that has slow passages too (why UFO/Schenker is my favourite). *Fire Down Under* was my first Riot record and my favourite, great songs and it sounds so great *loud!* They have always been a band to share as 'obscure,' but my brother and friends have been fans for years. The band should be remembered for Mark Reale—he is Riot. He was the one constant for every album. Ronnie James Dio, Ronnie Montrose and Mark are three of my biggest losses in hard rock."

"Anyway, thanks for your archiving of the greatest period of music—hard rock until the 1990s. I like to read your thoughts and adventures on Facebook. You are appreciated by us metalheads, headbangers and heavy/hard rock enthusiasts. All the best."

David "Skid" Rowe, California

"Riot—five guys from New York who changed the face of American metal. I walked into my local record store in Chicago with only enough cash to buy two records—'on sale.' It was the winter of 1981 and America was waking up to the sound of a new wave of heavy metal. WLUP was already playing Iron Maiden's 'Wrathchild' so I grabbed *Killers* off the shelf, and then the clerk suggested Riot's *Fire Down Under*."

"These were the days of vinyl, so when I got back to my apartment, it was a religious experience to open the record, set it on the turntable and secure the headphones. Shivers bolted up my spine when the opening riff of 'Swords and Tequila' burst from the album's grooves. It was like a jolt of electricity penetrating my teenage brain. One monster track after another followed—'Fire Down Under,' 'Outlaw,' 'Altar of the King'—all to be etched forever into the soundtrack of my life. When the record ended I played it again and again. Almost 35 years later, I still listen to it regularly."

"Riot came through Chicago both as a club act and an opener for Sammy Hagar, AC/DC, Rush and others. They were a force to be reckoned with on stage. With their twin guitar assault and rhythmic fury they could easily decimate a headline act and often did. Aerosmith, Rainbow and Judas Priest all fell victim to the Brooklyn warriors. The band were five guys, all from various parts of New York City, that bonded over their love of hard rock. For me, the 'classic' lineup was lead guitarist Mark Reale, rhythm guitarist Rick Ventura, singer Guy Speranza with the rhythm section of bassist Kip Leming and drummer Sandy Slavin. Not only were they great players but super nice guys. After their show they took time to talk with their fans, sign autographs and pose for pictures. No pretence, just blue collar rock 'n' rollers!"

"When Guy left the band and vocalist Rhett Forrester joined, I was sceptical. One night, after work, 'Restless Breed' came on the radio and I was hooked again. Rhett brought a southern rock vibe to the band, reminiscent of Bad Company, Lynyrd Skynyrd and Molly Hatchet. Years later, after Rhett passed away, I was fortunate enough to work with his mother in producing a tribute album of his unreleased demos and working song ideas. The disc showcased his incredible talent and proved why Riot, on the verge of international stardom, hired him."

"I consider the first five Riot albums essential listening and believe they are what made them a titanic force. Their fans are some of the most loyal in the world, traveling across continents just to see and support them. Mark Reale led the charge for 37 years before his passing in 2012. His skill and dexterity as a musician sculpted the band's sound and established them as true icons of American metal."

Todd K Smith, Las Vegas, NV

"Fondest Riot memory would have to be dropping the needle on *Fire Down Under*—hearing the opening riff to 'Swords and Tequila' for the first time is something you never forget. I still get goose bumps thinking about it. And the whole album still holds up as a classic. No filler on that one. I've seen the band a couple of times, but the one that stands out was probably 1982, at the Agora Ballroom, Columbus, Ohio, a great, intimate place to see a show and they just tore the place apart. So I'd say, sure, Riot should be remembered for a nice catalogue of quality songs, but also as a great live band."

TS, New York

"I love Riot because they were one of the tragic underdog stories of the heavy metal saga. Their songs were clever and groovy early on, approaching a rare, stadium-mad kind of lightly Southern-inflected, tequila-throated '70s metal until they decided to offer the final statement on American power metal at the time. With a number of singers and while traversing several heavy metal subgenres, Riot excelled creatively even if they never captured the platinum ring they were so very, very worthy of. I mean, name another metal band who could go from jamming like the decadent Aerosmith of old to racing comets with Helloween and Blind Guardian in the midst of a 90-minute set?"

"Riot should be remembered for both their punchy, anthemic mainstream metal that should have made them bigger than the biggest big hair bands, and a sleek, steely take on power/ prog metal that continues to reveal how influential it is. I actually first learned of Riot in the early '90s via a large library reference book (now out of print) I eventually bought directly from the publisher called *Headbangers: The Worldwide Megabook of Heavy Metal Bands*. I was in my early 20s at this time when metal was gravely out of vogue, yet I had found my interest in metal's history and its lesser-known bands renewed somehow."

"I recall going to Eide's Entertainment, a local comics/ music/pop culture institution in my city, and finding *Narita* and *Born in America* in the CD bins. Both were Japanese releases of course, and I must have shelled out $60 for the two of them, all on my meager $8-an-hour salary. The clerk, whose name I cannot recall, was tickled. 'Man, I never thought anyone would buy these on the same day,' he said. 'They've been sittin' around for years!' Later, I'd order *Fire Down Under* as a reissue from one of a number of mail-order import houses. When it arrived on my doorstep, it was like Christmas! These albums held a mystique for me for a number of years since I'd only read about how good they were, and I felt as if I was the only person within 100 miles that cared about Riot. The pre-internet era was a strange and challenging one for Hessians."

Darren Walchesky, Pittsburgh PA

Discography

Given the interesting "inside baseball" of the release history of the Riot catalogue, I've gone fairly deep in terms of this discography, although kept it simple when it came to singles. As well, we've gone for original issues as new releases only, but offered listings for various territories. As with all my books, vinyl-era albums get a Side 1/Side 2 designation, and there's a notes section to point out anything else I figured was important enough to make known, such as changes in band personnel and talk of reissues. The rule of double quotes around songs was excused for neatness' sake, except in the notes section. Track listings are for original US issues, noted for the few cases where other countries came first. Timings are as printed on original vinyl issues. And for consistency with the structure of the book, I've split this section as well into the era for which every album gets a chapter (studio and live together), and then the "epilogue" albums (separating studio and live).

The First Decade (Studio and Live)

Rock City
(Fire Sign FSA87001, November 10, 1977)
Produced by: Steve Loeb, Billy Arnell; except Desperation and Angel: Richard Alexander; Warrior: Steve Loeb, Billy Arnell, Richard Alexander
Side 1: 1. Desperation (2:43) 2. Warrior (3:50) 3. Rock City (3:27) 4. Overdrive (4:10)
Side 2: 1. Angel (3:36) 2. Tokyo Rose (4:19) 3. Heart of Fire (3:00) 4. Gypsy Queen (3:55) 5. This is What I Get (4:12)
Other issues: Canada: Attic LAT 1041; Japan: Victor VIP-4142.
Notes: Guy Speranza – vocals; Mark Reale – guitars; Lou A. Kouvaris – guitars; Jimmy Iommi – bass; Peter Bitelli – drums. Ex-member Phil Fiet plays bass on "Desperation," "Rock City" and "Angel." Reissued by Metal Blade Records. Canadian issue with black border on back versus US which is white. Japanese CD reissue on CBS/Sony (CSCS 5022) includes typical fold-out credits and obi strip; in white jewel case.

Narita
(Capitol ST-12081, October 5, 1979)
Produced by: Steve Loeb, Billy Arnell
Side 1: 1. Waiting for the Taking (5:01) 2. 49er (4:36) 3. Kick Down
the Wall (4:32) 4. Born to Be Wild (2:47) 5. Narita (4:38)
Side 2: 1. Here We Come Again (5:58) 2. Do it Up (3:44) 3. Hot for
Love (5:00) 4. White Rock (2:33) 5. Road Racin' (4:32)
Other issues: Argentina: Capitol 51 1861291; Canada: Attic LAT
1067; Germany: Capitol 1C 064-86 129; Japan: Victor VIP-6623;
Netherlands: Capitol 1A062-86129; UK: Capitol E-ST 12081.
Notes: Rick Ventura replaces Lou A. Kouvaris on guitars. Issued a
second time in Japan in 1981 as well as in Mexico in 1983, Brazil in
1985, and in France in 1989 on CD (Secret Records) and in Japan in
1989 on CD (CBS/Sony). Rock Candy Records' reissue from June
20, 2005 (CANDY001—the company's inaugural release) stands as
the definitive CD version. Japanese CD reissue on CBS/Sony (CSCS
5023) includes typical fold-out credits and obi strip; in white jewel
case.

Fire Down Under
(Elektra 5E-546, February 9, 1981)
Produced by: Steve Loeb, Billy Arnell
Side 1: 1. Swords and Tequila (3:15) 2. Fire Down Under (2:30) 3.
Feel the Same (4:51) 4. Outlaw (4:11) 5. Don't Bring Me Down (3:00)
Side 2: 1. Don't Hold Back (3:12) 2. Altar of the King (4:43) 3. No
Lies (4:18) 4. Run for Your Life (3:15) 5. Flashbacks (4:00)
Other issues: Canada: Elektra X5E-546; France: Elektra ELK K 52
315; Germany: Elektra ELK 52 315; Italy: Elektra ELK 52 315; Japan:
Victor VIP-6773; Netherlands: Elektra ELK 52 315; UK: Elektra K
52315.
Notes: Kip Leming replaces Jimmy Iommi on bass and Sandy
Slavin replaces Peter Bitelli on drums. 1997 German High Vaultage
reissue (HV-1-21) includes bonus tracks "Struck by Lightning"
(3:38), "Misty Morning Rain" (3:07), "You're All I Needed Tonight"
(2:58), "One Step Closer" (2:12) and snippet "Hot Life" (0:23). 1999
Metal Blade Records and Japanese Victor reissues includes bonus
tracks "Misty Morning Rain" and "You're All I Needed Tonight,"
as does the 2010 Metal Blade reissue. Also reissued by Audio
Fidelity in the US on vinyl LP.

Restless Breed

(Elektra E1-60134, May 21, 1982)

Produced by: Steve Loeb, Billy Arnell

Side 1: 1. Hard Lovin' Man (2:48) 2. C.I.A. (3:43) 3. Restless Breed (5:11) 4. When I Was Young (3:25) 5. Loanshark (4:10)

Side 2: 1. Loved by You (5:37) 2. Over to You (3:42) 3. Showdown (3:49) 4. Dream Away (3:43) 5. Violent Crimes (2:30)

Other issues: Canada: Elektra XE1-60134; France: Elektra ELK 52 398; Germany: Elektra ELK K 52 398; Japan: Elektra P-11208.

Notes: Rhett Forrester replaces Guy Speranza on vocals. German High Vaultage reissue from February 20, 2007 includes the *"Riot Live"* EP tracks as bonus tracks, namely live versions of "Hard Lovin' Man," "Showdown," "Loved by You," "Loanshark," "Restless Breed" and "Swords and Tequila." Metal Blade reissues from 1999 (3984-14232-2) and various issues in the 2000s (including a vinyl LP version n 2015) includes no bonus tracks.

"Riot Live"

(Elektra 0-67969, late 1982)

Produced by: Steve Loeb, Billy Arnell

Side 1: 1. Hard Lovin' Man (3:08) 2. Showdown (4:30) 3. Loved by You (8:02)

Side 2: 1. Loanshark (5:27) 2. Restless Breed (5:18) 3. Swords and Tequila (3:57)

Other issues: France: Elektra ELK 967969-0.

Notes: Live EP. French issue features different cover art.

Born in America

(Quality QUS 1008, October 14, 1983)

Produced by: Steve Loeb

Side 1: 1. Born in America (4:33) 2. You Burn in Me (3:38) 3. Wings of Fire (4:40) 4. Running from the Law (4:24) 5. Devil Woman (3:57)

Side 2: 1. Vigilante Killer (3:02) 2. Heavy Metal Machine (3:35) 3. Where Soldiers Rule (3:43) 4. Gunfighter (4:25) 5. Promised Land (3:50)

Other issues: Germany: Zyx 45001; Japan: Fire Sign SP25-5109; Sweden: Jomar Music International JMI 840033.

Notes: Primary issue was on the Quality label from Canada; Quality manufactured the product and distributed it in the US under Quality Records of America Limited. Original Japanese issue features different cover art but Japanese CD issue from 1989 uses the original Canadian/US "flag" cover. US Grand Slamm reissue from 1989 features different cover art. Metal Blade reissues from 1999 (3984-14234-2) and later—there was vinyl as well, in 2015—include no bonus tracks.

Epilogue Years (Studio)

Thundersteel
(CBS Associated Z 44232, March 24, 1988)
Produced by: Steve Loeb, Rod Hui, Mark Reale
Side 1: 1. Thundersteel (3:49) 2. Fight or Fall (4:24) 3. Sign of the Crimson Storm (4:37) 4. Flight of the Warrior (4:17) 5. On Wings of Eagles (5:39)
Side 2: 1. Johnny's Back (5:32) 2. Bloodstreets (4:37) 3. Run for Your Life (4:05) 4. Buried Alive (Tell Tale Heart) 8:56
Other issues: Brazil: Epic 268.012/1-460976; Canada: CBS Associated BFZ 44232; Greece: Epic EPC 460976 1; Japan: Sony 25DP-5080; Netherlands: Epic EPC 460976 1; Spain: Epic EPC 460976 1.
Notes: Only Mark Reale remains from past lineup after break-up of the band. New lineup is Tony Moore – vocals; Mark Reale – guitars; Don Van Stavern – bass; Bobby Jarzombek – drums. Mark Edwards plays drums on "Fight or Fall," "Sign of the Crimson Storm," "On Wings of Eagles" and "Bloodstreets." Canadian copy with credit and photo insert versus US copy which includes credit and photo record sleeve.

The Privilege of Power
(CBS Associated Z 45132, February 28, 1990)
Produced by: Steve Loeb with additional production by Rod Hui, Mark Reale; executive producer: Vince Perozzo
1. On Your Knees (6:37) 2. Metal Soldiers (6:40) 3. Runaway (5:11) 4. Killer (4:53) 5. Dance of Death (7:17) 6. Storming the Gates of Hell (3:43) 7. Maryanne (4:55) 8. Little Miss Death (4:12) 9. Black Leather and Glittering Steel (7:07) 10. Racing with the Devil on a Spanish Highway (7:17)
Other issues: Austria: Epic 466486 2; Japan: Sony CSCS 5053; Netherlands: Epic 466486 1; UK: Epic 466486 1.

Notes: First Riot album of the CD era although issued on LP as well in the US (with sides designated Act One and Act Two. Many guest stars, including the Tower of Power horn section. Reissued in the US by Sony Collectables in 2003 and in Japan in 2009, neither version with bonus tracks.

Nightbreaker
(Sony SRCS 6733, July 22, 1993)
Produced by: Steve Loeb
1. Soldier (4:55) 2. Destiny (4:42) 3. Burn (6:01) 4. In Your Eyes (4:34) 5. Nightbreaker (4:12) 6. Medicine Man (5:36) 7. Silent Scream (5:07) 8. Magic Maker (5:09) 9. A Whiter Shade of Pale (4:56) 10. Babylon (5:05) 11. Outlaw (6:14) 12. Black Mountain Woman (5:07)
Notes: Considerably altered band lineup since *The Privilege of Power* consists of Mike DiMeo – vocals; Mark Reale – guitars; Mike Flyntz – guitar; Pete Perez – bass; Bobby Jarzombek – drums. Initial issue is Japan-only. German issue from '94 is Rising Sun Productions, 084-62222, where "A Whiter Shade of Pale" is replaced with "I'm on the Run." Metal Blade reissue from 1999 (3984-14239-2) features different cover art and lacks "Black Mountain Woman," considered a bonus track on the Japanese issue, replacing it with "Faded Hero" (5:32).

The Brethren of the Long House
(Sony SRCS 7852, November 11, 1995)
Produced by: Steve Loeb
1. Intro/Last of the Mohicans (1:41) 2. Glory Calling (5:11) 3. Rolling Thunder (3:56) 4. Rain (4:58) 5. Wounded Heart (3:56) 6. The Brethren of the Long House (5:24) 7. Out in the Fields (4:03) 8. Santa Maria (3:50) 9. Blood of the English (5:49) 10. Ghost Dance (5:35) 11. Shenandoah (3:57) 12. Holy Land (4:47) 13. The Last of the Mohicans (Reprise) (6:26)
Notes: John Macaluso replaced Bobby Jarzombek on drums. Initial issue is Japan-only. German issue from '96 is Rising Sun Productions (34500-422), with a special edition from the same year (34499-428) including *Riot in Japan – Live!!* on a second CD. Metal Blade reissue from 1999 (3984-14240-2) includes bonus track "Sailor" (6:16).

Inishmore
(Zero Corporation XRCN-2005, November 11, 1997)
Produced by: Mark Reale, Paul Orofino; executive producers: Jeff Allen, Jack Bart
1. Black Water (2:42) 2. Angel Eyes (4:28) 3. Liberty (5:08) 4. Kings are Falling (4:32) 5. The Man (3:54) 6. Watching the Signs (4:34) 7. Should I Run (4:40) 8. Cry for the Dying (4:39) 9. Gypsy (5:20) 10. Inishmore (Forsaken Heart) (1:44) 11. Inishmore (4:32)
Notes: Bobby Jarzombek replaces John Macaluso on drums. Initial issue is Japan-only. US and German Metal Blade issue (3984-14150-2) from 1998 includes "Turning the Hands of Time" not included on the Japanese version, which, in turn adds a rendition of traditional "Danny Boy."

Sons of Society
(Metal Blade 3984-14249-2, September 7, 1999)
Produced by: Mark Reale, Paul Orofino; executive producers: Jeff Allen, Jack Bart
1. Snake Charmer (1:04) 2. On the Wings of Life (4:36) 3. Sons of Society (4:26) 4. Twist of Fate (5:36) 5. Bad Machine (5:06) 6. Cover Me (6:47) 7. Dragonfire (3:38) 8. The Law (3:46) 9. Time to Bleed (4:38) 10. Somewhere (4:16) 11. Promises (4:35)
Other issues: Japan: Z TOCP-65264.
Notes: Japanese issue includes extra track "Queen" (4:28), treated as a standard track at position 10.

Through the Storm
(Metal Blade 3984-14399-2, August 26, 2002)
Produced by: Mark Reale, Paul Orofino; executive producers: Jeff Allen, Jack Bart
1. Turn the Tables (5:22) 2. Lost Inside this World (4:44) 3. Chains (Revolving) (4:43) 4. Through the Storm (6:13) 5. Let it Show (4:37) 6. Burn the Sun (4:26) 7. To My Head (5:59) 8. Essential Enemies (3:49) 9. Only You Can Rock Me (3:56) 10. Isle of Shadows (4:08) 11. Here Comes the Sun (3:21)
Other issues: Japan: Z TOCP-67017.
Notes: Bobby Rondinelli replaces Bobby Jarzombek on drums. Japanese issue includes bonus track "Somebody" (3:42).

Army of One
(Z TOCP-67977, July 12, 2006)
Produced by: Mark Reale, Bruno Ravel; executive producer:
 Jeff Allen
1. Army of One (4:23) 2. Knockin' at My Door (4:19) 3. Blinded
(5:26) 4. One More Alibi (4:55) 5. It All Falls Down (5:36) 6. Helpin'
Hand (5:24) 7. The Mystic (5:43) 8. Still Alive (5:42) 9. Alive in the
City (7:00) 10. Shine (6:33) 11. Stained Mirror (3:46) 12. Darker Side
of Light (6:58) 13. Road Racin' (live) (6:50)
Other issues: Germany: Metal Heaven 00028; US: Longhouse.
Notes: Frank Gilchriest replaces Bobby Rondinelli on drums.
Original Japanese issue includes "Road Racin'" live from Club
Citta, Kawasaki, as a bonus track over and above the German issue.

Immortal Soul
(Steamhammer SPV 309870 CD, November 22, 2011)
Produced by: Riot, Bruno Ravel
1. Riot (5:03) 2. Still Your Man (4:16) 3. Crawling (5:52) 4. Wings
are for Angels (5:11) 5. Fall Before Me (4:55) 6. Sins of the Father
(3:55) 7. Majestica (0:57) 8. Immortal Soul (4:47) 9. Insanity (4:41) 10.
Whiskey Man (4:16) 11. Believe (4:17) 12. Echoes (4:58)
Other issues: Japan: Avalon MICP-11020.
Notes: Considerably altered band lineup since *Army of One*
consists of Tony Moore – vocals; Mark Reale – guitars; Mike Flyntz
– guitars; Don Van Stavern – bass; Bobby Jarzombek – drums.
Steamhammer issue is considered a joint US and German issue.
Also issued by Steamhammer on gatefold double vinyl. German
digipak issue includes live bonus tracks "Johnny's Back" (5:43) and
"Metal Soldiers" (5:00). Japanese issue includes live bonus track
"Fight or Fall."

Unleash the Fire
(Avalon MICP-11177, August 27, 2014)
Produced by: Riot, Joshua Block
Other issues: Germany: Steamhammer SPV 267902
1. Ride Hard Live Free (4:45) 2. Metal Warrior (4:44) 3. Fall from
the Sky (5:10) 4. Bring the Hammer Down (4:32) 5. Unleash the
Fire (4:09) 6. Land of the Rising Sun (4:08) 7. Kill to Survive (5:11)
8. Return of the Outlaw (3:55) 9. Immortal (4:29) 10. Take Me Back
(4:29) 11. Fight Fight Fight (4:36) 12. Until We Meet Again (6:26)

Notes: Considerably altered band lineup—significantly due to the death of founder Mark Reale— since *Immortal Soul* consists of Todd Michael Hall – vocals; Mike Flyntz – guitar; Nick Lee – guitar; Don Van Stavern – bass; Frank Gilchriest – drums. Issued under band name Riot in Japan but then changed to Riot V for subsequent issues. Original Japanese issue includes bonus track "Thundersteel" (live) from *Metal Assault*, Germany, 2014. Issued by Steamhammer as regular CD, digipak and double vinyl with bonus CD of the album and the Japanese bonus track.

Epilogue Years (Live)

"Riot Live"
(Sony Japan CSCS 5024, 1989)
Produced by: Steve Loeb
1. Intro (0:56) 2. Angel (3:42) 3. Do it Up (3:44) 4. Road Racin' (5:06) 5. White Rock (2:54) 6. Warrior (9:08) 7. Narita (3:53) 8. Tokyo Rose (4:49) 9. Overdrive (8:30) 10. Rock City (4:52) 11. Back on the Nonstop (4:17) 12. Kick Down the Wall (4:34) 13. Train Kept A Rollin' (5:43) 14. Road Racin' (7:35)
Notes: Archival Guy Speranza-era live album (from UK shows in April and August of 1980) not to be confused with the Rhett Forrester-era EP of the same name. Remastered by Eddie Shreyer in October 1992 for reissue by Metal Blade in 1993 in the UK, Germany and the US (3984-14011-2).

Riot in Japan – Live!!
(Sony SRCS 5810, April 8, 1992)
Produced by: Steve Loeb
1. Minutes to Showtime (2:02) 2. On Your Knees... in Tokyo! (3:53) 3. Metal Soldiers (4:43) 4. Runaway (5:15) 5. Tokyo Rose... in Osaka! (2:25) 6. Rock City (3:16) 7. Outlaw (4:19) 8. Killer (4:43) 9. Skin & Bones, Part 1 (drum solo) (3:17) 10. Skin & Bones, Part 2 (drum solo) (2:00) 11. Johnny's Back... in Tokyo! (5:24) 12. Flight of the Warrior (4:08) 13. Ladies and Gentlemen... Mark Reale (guitar solo) (3:09) 14. Japan Cakes (guitar solo) (2:22) 15. Narita (2:09) 16. Warrior (5:39) 17. The Dressing Room the Encore Begins... in Tokyo!/The Encore Continues... (3:02) 18. Smoke on the Water... in

                    Martin Popoff

New York (4:04)
Notes: Live album, recorded June 1990 in Osaka and Tokyo. Initial issue is Japan-only. Issued in 1999 by Metal Blade in the US as *Live in Japan* (3984-14241-2), with different album cover.

Shine On
(Metal Blade 3984-14182-2, October 6, 1998)
Produced by: Mark Reale, Paul Orofino
1. Black Water (1:47) 2. Angel Eyes (4:27) 3. Soldier (4:51) 4. The Man (4:04) 5. Kings are Falling (4:34) 6. Bloodstreets (4:19) 7. Swords and Tequila (3:24) 8. Cry for the Dying – Irish Trilogy (tracks 9, 10, 11) 9. Inishmore (Forsaken Heart) (1:40) 10. Inishmore (4:30) 11. Danny Boy (2:49) 12. Liberty (5:18) 13. Gypsy (5:12) 14. The Last of the Mohicans (intro) – Glory Calling (7:00) 15. Thundersteel (4:00) 16. Outlaw (4:00) 17. Warrior (5:44)
Other issues: Japan: Zero Corporation XRCN-2025.
Notes: Live album, recorded on the Japanese tour 1998. Japanese issue features different cover art from US and German Metal Blade issue.

Singles and Miscellaneous

Warrior/Tokyo Rose, Japan: Victor VIP-2593, 1977, picture sleeve 7"
Rock City/Gypsy Queen, Japan: Victor VIP-2629, 1977, picture sleeve 7"
Born to Be Wild/White Rock, Netherlands: Capitol 1A 006-86173, 1979, picture sleeve 7"
Born to Be Wild/Narita, Canada: Attic AT 209, 1979, non-picture sleeve 7"
Outlaw/Rock City (live), UK: Elektra K 12565, 1981, picture sleeve 7"
Outlaw/Rock City (live), UK: Elektra K 12565 T, 1981, picture sleeve 12"
Outlaw/Rock City (live), US: Elektra E-47218, 1981, picture sleeve 7"
Outlaw/Outlaw (mono), US: Elektra E-47218, 1981, picture sleeve 7" promo
Road Racin'/The Big Beat (Billy Squier), US: Capitol SPRO-9425/6, 1982, split white label 12" promo
Born in America – Radio Sampler, Canada: Quality QUS 1008 P, 1983, white label promo 12" in die-cut generic brown Quality sleeve, featuring "Born in America," "You Burn in Me," "Running from the Law" and "Devil Woman."

Warrior (live)/Born in America, Germany: Zyx Zyx 5146, 1984, picture sleeve 12"

Thundersteel, Flight of the Warrior, six more tracks by Fifth Angel, Sanctuary and Slammin' Watusis, US: Epic 5E 44254, 1987, eight track 12" sample for commercial sale

Thundersteel/Flight of the Warrior, US: CBS Associated ZAS 01083, 1988, 12" promo, blue label in black die-cut generic cover with sticker

Privilege of Power Sampler, US: CBS Associated, January 12, 1990, four tracks

Riot, Japan: Sony SRCS-6902, November 21, 1993, 16 track Star Box series compilation CD with 36-page booklet

Greatest Hits '78-'90, Japan: Sony 755625, 1994, 16 track CD compilation with same track listing as the Star Box series CD

Angel Eyes/15 Rivers/Red Reign/Turning the Hands of Time, US: Zero Corporation XRCN-2018, 1997, CD EP consisting of four tracks from the *Inishmore* sessions

Thundersteel/The Privilege of Power, UK: IronBird IBIRD2 0005, 2009, 2CD issue of two albums

Thundersteel/The Privilege of Power, Germany: Steamhammer SPV 265081, 2013, 2CD issue of two albums

Source Credits

Besides interviews with various Riot members, managers and other characters in this old school metal movie conducted over the past 20 years, the following press sources have been quoted. A sincere thanks to all of these folks who gave Riot a bit of love—believe me, there weren't many of you. We are a small group who did our part to keep Mark and the band hopeful when ultimately, that hope was unfulfilled, and in some respects unfounded.

Billboard. There's a Riot Coming On And Fire Sign's Delighted by Adam White August 19, 1978.
Brave Words & Bloody Knuckles. Riot: Storm Warning by Carl Begai. #64. November 2002.
Creem. Heavy Metal's New Wave by Rick Johnson. October 1980.
Crystal-Logic.blogspot.ca. Interview with Jack Starr by Andreas Andreou. 2012.
CuttingEdgeRocks.com. The Sky is Crying: A Tribute to Rhett Forrester by Todd K. Smith.
Elektra/Asylum Records. Riot label bio. 1982.
Forrester, Rhett – *Hell or Highwater*. TCE Production. 1996.
Good Times. *Rock City* record review by David Fricke. June 6-19, 1978.
Headbanger, The. Riot: An Interview with Rhett & Sandy by Bob Nalbandian. No. 8, Spring 1984.
Hit Parader. Riot by Andy Secher. Number 217. October 1982.
Iron Fist. Shine On by Kevin Stewart-Panko. Issue #13. Feb/Mar. 2015.
It's Only Rock 'n' Roll. Riot burns San Antonio by Cliff Dunn. Vol. 2, No. 7. 1981.
Kerrang! I'm a Rocker by Dante Bonutto. 1982.
Music Express. *Fire Down Under* record review by Chris Churchill. Issue #51. 1981.
New Heavy Metal Revue, The. *Fire Down Under* record review by Brian Slagel. Issue #2. August - September, 1981.
Powerline. Mark Reale has a lot of pride in new Riot album by Patrick Prince. November 8, 2011.
Riot - *Fire Down Under*: Flashbacks - About the Album and its Recording by Steve Loeb. July 1997. High Vaultage Records.
Rosen, Steve. Interview with Riot. 1984.
Sounds. Ruck City by Geoff Barton. April 19, 1980.
Sounds. Sammy Hagar/Riot, Newcastle concert review by Ian Ravendale. April 19, 1980.
Sounds. Slight Riot by Geoff Barton. April 26, 1980.
Sounds. *Fire Down Under* record review by Phillip Bell. 1981.

Photo Credits

Every effort has been made to obtain the necessary permissions with reference to illustrative material. We apologize for any omissions in this respect and will be pleased to make the necessary acknowledgement of credit in any future editions. Most photography and scans are from the author, with additional images kindly provided by Rich Galbraith, Bill Baran and Riot's European record label legend Olly Hahn—these modern-era shots, shown in the Epilogue, are by Riot's own Don Van Stavern! Don can be experienced hot-rocking Riot V at a fine venue near you. Additional images courtesy of Todd K. Smith, Virgin Steele axemaster Jack Starr, and Rhett's mom, La Fortune Forrester.

Design Credit

This book was skillfully and artfully designed by Eduardo Rodriguez, who can be reached at eduardobwbk@gmail.com. The photography used to create the front cover comes courtesy of photographer legend Rich Galbraith, who can be reached at rtgenid@suddenlink.net, and the back cover, Bill Baran, who can be reached for sales at wbaran3204@rogers.com.

Acknowledgements

A big, big thanks to Steve Loeb, who with both frankness and intelligence offered his insights into both the band's and his own triumphs and failures.

Thanks also to John Chronis, American Dog legend Michael Hannon and pioneering California metal guru Bob Nalbandian for conducting searches through their press archives.

As well, thanks to Don Van Stavern and Mike Flyntz for all they do for the band's memory and help with Mark's dad. I'm sure we'll be doing some brainstorming soon on how to handle a second Riot book that gives the modern-era band as much detailed examination that this book did for the early years.

Finally, a very special thanks to Todd K. Smith, who not only did much to keep Rhett's memory alive after his death, through his writings and reissues, but also helped commandeer Rhett's distraught mother, La Fortune, through the funeral and grieving process.

About The Author

At approximately 7900 (with over 7000 appearing in his books), Martin has unofficially written more record reviews than anybody in the history of music writing across all genres. Additionally, Martin has penned 50 books on hard rock, heavy metal, classic rock and record collecting. He was Editor In Chief of the now retired *Brave Words & Bloody Knuckles*, Canada's foremost metal publication for 14 years, and has also contributed to *Revolver, Guitar World, Goldmine, Record Collector, bravewords.com, lollipop.com* and *hardradio.com*, with many record label band bios and liner notes to his credit as well. Additionally, Martin has been a regular contractor to Banger Films, having worked for two years as researcher on the award-wining documentary *Rush: Beyond The Lighted Stage*, on the writing and research team for the 11-episode *Metal Evolution* and on the 10-episode *Rock Icons*, both for VH1 Classic. Additionally, Martin is the writer of the original metal genre chart used in *Metal: A Headbanger's Journey* and throughout the *Metal Evolution* episodes. Martin currently resides in Toronto and can be reached through martinp@inforamp.net or www.martinpopoff.com.

Martin Popoff – A Complete Bibliography

Swords And Tequila: Riot's Classic First Decade (2015)
Who Invented Heavy Metal? (2015)
Sail Away: Whitesnake's Fantastic Voyage (2015)
Live Magnetic Air: The Unlikely Saga Of The Superlative Max Webster (2014)
Steal Away The Night: An Ozzy Osbourne Day-By-Day (2014)
The Big Book Of Hair Metal (2014)
Sweating Bullets: The Deth And Rebirth Of Megadeth (2014)
Smokin' Valves: A Headbanger's Guiide to 900 NWOBHM Records (2014)
The Art Of Metal (co-edit with Malcolm Dome; 2013)
2 Minutes To Midnight: An Iron Maiden Day-By-Day (2013)
Metallica: The Complete Illustrated History (2013)

Rush: The Illustrated History (2013)

Ye Olde Metal: 1979 (2013)

Scorpions: Top Of The Bill (2013)

Epic Ted Nugent (2012)

Fade To Black: Hard Rock Cover Art Of The Vinyl Age (2012)

It's Getting Dangerous: Thin Lizzy 81-12 (2012)

We Will Be Strong: Thin Lizzy 76-81 (2012)

Fighting My Way Back: Thin Lizzy 69-76 (2011)

The Deep Purple Royal Family: Chain Of Events '80 – '11 (2011)

The Deep Purple Royal Family: Chain Of Events Through '79 (2011)

Black Sabbath FAQ (2011)

The Collector's Guide To Heavy Metal: Volume 4: The '00s (2011; co-authored with David Perri)

Goldmine Standard Catalog Of American Records 1948 – 1991, 7th Edition (2010)

Goldmine Record Album Price Guide, 6th Edition (2009)

Goldmine 45 RPM Price Guide, 7th Edition (2009)

A Castle Full Of Rascals: Deep Purple '83 – '09 (2009)

Worlds Away: Voivod And The Art Of Michel Langevin (2009)

Ye Olde Metal: 1978 (2009)

Gettin' Tighter: Deep Purple '68 – '76 (2008)

All Access: The Art Of The Backstage Pass (2008)

Ye Olde Metal: 1977 (2008)

Ye Olde Metal: 1976 (2008)

Judas Priest: Heavy Metal Painkillers (2007)

Ye Olde Metal: 1973 To 1975 (2007)

The Collector's Guide To Heavy Metal: Volume 3: The Nineties (2007)

Ye Olde Metal: 1968 To 1972 (2007)

Run For Cover: The Art Of Derek Riggs (2006)

Black Sabbath: Doom Let Loose (2006)

Dio: Light Beyond The Black (2006)

The Collector's Guide To Heavy Metal: Volume 2: The Eighties (2005)

Rainbow: English Castle Magic (2005)

UFO: Shoot Out The Lights (2005)

The New Wave Of British Heavy Metal Singles (2005)

Blue Öyster Cult: Secrets Revealed! (2004)

Contents Under Pressure: 30 Years Of Rush At Home

& Away (2004)
The Top 500 Heavy Metal Albums Of All Time (2004)
The Collector's Guide To Heavy Metal: Volume 1: The
Seventies (2003)
The Top 500 Heavy Metal Songs Of All Time (2003)
Southern Rock Review (2001)
Heavy Metal: 20th Century Rock And Roll (2000)
The Goldmine Price Guide To Heavy Metal Records (2000)
The Collector's Guide To Heavy Metal (1997)
Riff Kills Man! 25 Years Of Recorded Hard Rock & Heavy Metal
(1993)

See martinpopoff.com for complete details and ordering
information.

Ye Olde Metal "Discography"

- detailed examination of early hard rock and heavy metal albums
- each from brand new interviews with the artists, plus some archived material
- critical analysis and trivia as well
- 6" x 9" format
- most with rare, previously unpublished photos
- limited to 1000 individually hand-numbered copies
- personalized and signed by the author
- photography by Rich Galbraith
- more on the way, each examining a year at a time!

Ye Olde Metal: 1968 To 1972

Blue Cheer – Vincebus Eruptum, MC5
– Kick Out The Jams, Sir Lord Baltimore –
Kingdom Come, Bloodrock – Bloodrock,
Warpig – Warpig, Cactus – One Way… Or
Another, Mountain – Nantucket Sleighride,
Uriah Heep – Look At Yourself, Nitzinger –
Nitzinger, Dust - Hard Attack, Humble Pie –
Smokin', Buffalo – Dead Forever…, Captain
Beyond – Captain Beyond, Trapeze – You
Are The Music… We're Just The Band

Ye Olde Metal: 1973 To 1975

Status Quo – Piledriver, Alice Cooper –
Billion Dollar Babies, New York Dolls
– New York Dolls, Uriah Heep – Sweet
Freedom, Nazareth – Loud 'N' Proud,
Montrose – Montrose, Bachman Turner
Overdrive – II, Deep Purple – Burn, Robin
Trower – Bridge Of Sighs, Buffalo – Only
Want You For Your Body, Bachman Turner
Overdrive – Not Fragile, Alice Cooper
– Welcome To My Nightmare, Nazareth
– Hair Of The Dog, The Dictators – Go
Girl Crazy!, ZZ Top – Fandango, Budgie –
Bandolier, Foghat – Fool For The City, Deep
Purple – Come Taste The Band

Ye Olde Metal: 1976

Max Webster – Max Webster, Scorpions – Virgin Killer, Point Blank – Point Blank, Angel – Helluva Band, Rex – Rex, Moxy – II, Teaze – Teaze, Lone Star – Lone Star, Starz – Starz, Ted Nugent – Free For All, Boston – Boston, Foghat – Nightshift, Kansas – Leftoverture

Ye Olde Metal: 1977

Derringer – Sweet Evil, Angel – On Earth As It Is In Heaven, Sweet – Off The Record, Moxy – Ridin' High, The Dictators – Manifest Destiny, Starz – Violation, Triumph – Rock & Roll Machine, Styx – Grand Illusion, Motörhead – Motörhead, Lone Star – Firing On All Six, Dirty Tricks – Hit & Run, Piper – Can't Wait, Goddo – Goddo, Ram Jam – Ram Jam, Rex – Where Do We Go From Here?, Point Blank – Second Season, Hydra – Rock The World, Legs Diamond – A Diamond Is A Hard Rock

Ye Olde Metal: 1978

The Hounds – Unleashed, Frank Marino & Mahogany Rush – Live, Starz – Attention Shoppers!, Yesterday And Today – Struck Down, Teaze – On The Loose, Ram Jam – Portrait Of The Artist As A Young Ram, The Dictators – Bloodbrothers, The Boyzz – Too Wild To Tame, Starz – Coliseum Rock, The Godz – The Godz, DMZ – DMZ, Styx – Pieces Of Eight, Pat Travers – Heat In The Street, Dead Boys – We Have Come For Your Children, Streetheart, Meanwhile Back In Paris…, Uriah Heep – Fallen Angel

Ye Olde Metal: 1979

New England – New England,
Nazareth – No Mean City, Bad Company –
Desolation Angels, Motörhead – Overkill,
TKO – Let It Roll, Triumph – Just A Game,
Legs Diamond – Fire Power, City Boy –
The Day The Earth Caught Fire, Blackfoot
– Strikes, Streetheart – Under Heaven Over
Hell, Hounds – Puttin' On The Dog,
Foreigner – Head Games, Riot – Narita,
Whitesnake – Lovehunter, April Wine –
Harder... Faster, Teaze – One Night Stands

Price breaks available on multiple orders. Just email <u>martinp@inforamp.net</u> and tell me what you want and where I'm shipping to and I'll quote ya! See <u>www.martinpopoff.com</u> for ordering details on the first five of the Ye Olde Metal series plus approximately 25 other titles.